Bottle, Draught and Keg

An Irish Drinking Anthology

compiled by

Laurence Flanagan

Gill & Macmillan

Gill & Macmillan Ltd
Goldenbridge
Dublin 8
with associated companies throughout the world

© Laurence Flanagan 1995

0 7171 2334 0

Print origination by Typeform Repro Ltd, Dublin
Printed by Colourbooks Ltd, Dublin

A catalogue record is available for this book from the British Library.

1 3 5 4 2

This book is dedicated to the memory of T. J. McGurran, who died on 21 February 1995. As proprietor of the Errigle Inn, Belfast, he was the proprietor of the first pub in which I drank (legally) as a schoolboy. He was a fine man and a great publican.

Contents

Hangovers

Inept or Excessive Drinking

Peculiar Parties

Poitín

Pub Conversations

Pubs and Publicans

Refined Drinking and Parties

Social Drinking

Weddings

Whiskey

Introduction

'Is amlaid domel Conchobar a flaith: trían ind laí oc déscin na macraide, a trían n-aill oc imbirt fidchille, a trían n-aill oc ól chorma conid gaib cotlad de.' (This is how Conchobar spends his time of sovereignty: one third of the day spent watching the youths, another third playing fidchell, another third drinking ale till he falls asleep therefrom.) This was said by Fergus of his estranged king, in Táin Bó Cúailnge, in totally complimentary vein, implying that this sort of life-style was eminently suitable for a king. This attitude to drinking as in some ways an heroic pastime has persisted in Ireland over the intervening two thousand years, between the conventional dating of the Táin and the present day. Even the Cavan proverb 'Dólfadh sé an Bhóinn is an tSionnain in a cuideacht' (He would drink the Boyne and the Shannon along with it) implies that this constitutes a memorable achievement.

Of course this 'heroic' attitude to drinking caused, and still causes, problems: the man who sought to drink the Boyne and the Shannon dry would realise he could never quite succeed—but might continue in his efforts and become an acknowledged alcoholic. In the 1980s it was estimated that in the Republic of Ireland, out of a total population of 3.5 million, there were at least 70,000 alcoholics—in addition to a considerable number who would admit to being simply 'heavy drinkers'. The misery and social destruction caused by heavy drinking in its turn led to the total abstinence movements of the nineteenth century, with such legendary figures as Father Mathew, and to a situation where, compared with the 70,000 alcoholics, there were some 150,000 sworn total abstainers—mostly in the 'Pioneer' movement. No doubt each of these opposed groups feeds on the other—the more alcoholics there are, the greater the efforts to turn them into abstainers. Conversely, who in Ireland, however moderate a drinker, has not suffered from the 'Pioneer hand', where at a wake, for example, he is poured by a zealously generous Pioneer a glass (not in the technical sense) of whiskey that would flatten an ox.

Sometimes, rather cynically, one is tempted to believe that this is done so that when the recipient drains it to the dregs and instantly falls prostrate on the floor the donor can triumphantly say: 'See! I told you so!'

In Ireland, however, it is not mandatory to belong to either extreme—although, possibly, there is in the Irish character an innate tendency to occupy a precarious position on one horn of any dilemma—often, indeed, a position so precarious that a sudden change of chosen horns can almost pass unnoticed and the horns miraculously change into two stools. For those who do not adopt the 'heroic' attitude to drinking, and do not feel so threatened that they must totally abstain, there are many choices.

The choice, in fact, is endless—and has been so for many a century: you can 'carouse and make merry' like the nine lovely women described in the *Colloquy of the Ancients*; you can act out a ritual, supping port fastidiously with a long-known adversary; you can even—if you are small enough and innocent enough—curl up in a wardrobe with a bottle of brandy. You can, of course, if you are a mere apprentice drinker, convert your first taste of porter into buff-coloured puke, and, as you gradually grow more expert and controlled, having dutifully served your time, advance to the stage where you find no difficulty in confining yourself to converting your stout into water.

Above all, you can enjoy the pleasures of the Irish pub—hopefully one that has neither been 'modernised' (which is the same as being vandalised) nor 're-antiquated' (which is often the stage after 'modernisation' but shares with it the same synonym). They're becoming fewer and farther between, though fortunately some do still exist, as do those who serve in them. Here it seems appropriate to remind readers that the fact that *you* address the bar staff by their Christian names is not the gauge of your being well known in the establishment; that comes when *they* address you by yours, even if you've never seen them before. Above all you can, if you're lucky and in the right company, share in the pub conversations that still are such a feature of Irish pubs—where, sensibly, neither darts, draughts nor dominoes disturbs the ambience and where television is not merely unheard but unheard of.

There are, of course, many social occasions where drink, of one sort or another (preferably one sort and several others), flows—sometimes, indeed, it would seem, with the same volume as our old friends the Boyne and the Shannon. These include wakes (where the generous Pioneer is most likely to be encountered), where it is considered the done thing to drink to the memory, rather than the health, of the dear departed, and weddings, where a little lubricant is an essential factor in lowering the friction between yourself and a roomful of people you've never met before and, if you can so organise it, are never likely to meet again. In addition, of course, there are countless parties, feasts, balls and the like, ranging from those, like Bricriu's, where the advance arrangements cover such things as building a special 'ornamented mansion' as well as devising some rather special party-games, to the simple kind of diversion arranged to take the revellers' minds off the fact that a gunboat is pouring shells into a nearby building. While engaging in any of these social occasions there is a wealth of fine drinking songs available—in Irish or English, and, like hymns, ancient or modern—to indulge in.

The most appropriate conclusion seems to be the old toast:

> Sláinte agus saol agat,
> Bean ar do mhlan agat,
> Talamh gan chíos agat,
> Gob fliuch agus bás in Éirinn.

Abstinence and Sobriety

A Drunken Man's Praise of Sobriety

This poem from Last Poems, *by W. B. Yeats, is unusual in its use of the word 'punk'. The word is employed not in its contemporary American sense but in its original Elizabethan sense: a punk was a prostitute.*

Come swish around, my pretty punk,
And keep me dancing still
That I may stay a sober man
Although I drink my fill.
Sobriety is a jewel
That I do much adore;
And therefore keep me dancing
Though drunkards lie and snore.
O mind your feet, O mind your feet,
Keep dancing like a wave,
And under every dancer
A dead man in his grave.
No ups and downs, my pretty,
A mermaid, not a punk;
A drunkard is a dead man,
And all dead men are drunk.

Total Abstinence

This excerpt from Temperance Papers *by Rev. I. N. Harkness, published in 1869, is typical of temperance papers of the period.*

We now come to what we believe is the true remedy for our intemperance. We advocate total abstinence from all intoxicating drinks as beverages. Let them be removed from common use. Let them, if you will, appear on the shelves of the apothecary, but let them disappear from our side-boards, dining-tables, etc. Let men drink tea, coffee, milk, water, but let whiskey, ale, porter, and the so-called wines, be utterly given up; then shall the British people live soberly at all events, and a way will be opened to teach them to live righteously and godly in this present world.

Some say, it is sinful to use these drinks. This is a question that at present is not settled. Some eminent men are on the one side, many equally eminent on the other. Truth, on which ever side it lies, will ultimately gain the victory. For the present, therefore, as it is a debateable position, we do not take this ground. But we present an argument that must recommend itself to every fair and impartial mind. We say—(1) that we as Christians should do all the good we can in our day and generation, and (2) that we can do more good by totally abstaining from these intoxicating drinks, than by any use of them we might make, however moderate that use may be.

I. As to the first, that we *should do all the good in our power*. Is there any necessity either to prove it or enlarge on it? To a mind brought out of darkness into light it is almost a self-evident proposition. Is not Titus instructed, and along with him every other Christian minister, to put the people in mind 'to be ready to every good work?' Are we not commanded to 'prove all things, and hold fast that which is good?' Have we not been called, and saved with the very design, that we should be lights in the world and the salt of the earth, and that we should so let our light shine before men, that they may see our good works and glorify our Father who is in heaven? Is it therefore legitimate for us Christians to adopt any other position towards a good cause than that of hearty union and co-operation? Is sympathy enough? Are good wishes sufficient? Is it open to us to stand idly by while others are bearing the burden and heat of the day? Can we, in consistency with our Christian profession, take any other course in regard to this or any other question, than that which will on the whole be best calculated to do the most good to ourselves and others with whom we come into contact? These questions admit of only one answer.

II. *We hold that more good can be done in our present circumstances by Total Abstinence than by any use, however moderate.*
We say, in present circumstances. The force of our argument lies in this. We can understand circumstances different when to use them might be demanded—when it would be proper to come 'eating and drinking'. But we speak solely of our present surroundings. These are all we have to do with. Not what we should do had we lived with Methuselah or Noah, or with our Lord in Palestine, but what, on the whole, is best in this year of grace, 1867, and in this empire of Britain, surrounded as we are, on every side, by gross drunkenness; thousands yearly going down to drunkards' graves, and thousands more coming on with a steady flow to fill their places. Now, we hold it is incontrovertible that total abstinence is best. Who will deny this? Who will soberly and calmly oppose it.

The two candidates for our acceptance are moderate drinking and total abstinence. Now, let us take a sheet of paper and rule on it two columns. Put one of these candidates at the head of one column, and the second at the head of the other. Then enter first all the benefits and blessings that are conferred on the community by moderate drinking, and after that enter all the benefits and blessings conferred by total abstinence, strike the balance, and carry on the account to the next page.

Here also have two columns, head them the same way, and then enter in the first the evils of moderate drinking, and second, the evils of total abstinence, tot up the account, and tell how the final balance stands.

3

We can well understand what amazement this arithmetical calculation will bring to some people. Studying the first page, there may be something said for moderation. Is it not generally considered that these drinks do some good to our health? Do they not promote digestion? Do they not pleasantly exhilarate the spirit and revive the exhausted frame? Are they not calculated to promote sociality? This is about all that can be said for them. But then how this is overwhelmed by the entries on behalf of total abstinence. See the wonderful advantages conferred by it if it were universally adopted. Saving of money so great that with it we could feed all the poor of the empire. Cessation of crime to such an extent, that we might close at least half our prisons, and disband half our police. Increased health both of body and mind, so that we might do away with a large number of our hospitals and lunatic asylums. Enlarged prosperity among our people, so that workhouses would be little called for. Freedom from temptation and the snare of the devil, in which thousands are caught. And above all, the delivery of multitudes from a drunkard's death and a drunkard's doom. These, and many others, that are not specified, are the blessings that would accompany and flow from total abstinence. Who then can doubt, even in the first page, to which side the balance belongs?

But it is when we turn to the second page that any wavering doubts are at once and for ever removed. This is the 'evil' page. Here we are to tell the evils done by these two candidates for our acceptance. And alas! moderate drinking, your column is like the prophet's roll, filled with mourning, lamentation, and woe. Is it not, in the first place, an enormous waste of money that might be better spent? Does it not, admittedly, in the long run injure the health? Is it not *the way of temptation?* Is not this the very ground where the young are trained to be future drunkards, and, therefore, future criminals, paupers, and lunatics? Is not this the door by which thousands, we might say millions, have entered on the way to hell? These are some of the evils of this practice. Does it follow from this that it is a practice that God approves of and Christ delights in? Demons, we are sure, rejoice to see it so, but a God of goodness must look on it with a frown. But now as to total abstinence, what are the evils connected with it? Please to produce these evils. Can you do so? Is *it* a way of temptation? Does *it* lead men headlong to the devil? Bring to the light and let us see any young man it has ruined. Show us the family into which it has brought destitution and misery. Show us the paupers, criminals, lunatics it has made. Who can say we became poor or wicked, or mad because we would not drink? Enter into the realms of the lost, and out of its myriads of lost souls, bring one who shall say, 'My first step on the doomed path was when I became a total abstainer.' You are amazed to discover that the 'evil' column of total abstinence must remain blank, while the 'good' column is filled to overflowing with benefits both for time and eternity.

These are undeniable facts, and in their presence you will pardon us saying that it is inconceivable how in these lands, and at such a time as this, THE CONSCIENCE OF ANY CHRISTIAN CAN BE AT REST WHO IS NOT A TOTAL ABSTAINER.

Alcoholism

Drink and Time in Dublin

This amusing piece by Flann O'Brien, or Myles na gCopaleen, appeared in Irish Writing *in 1946.*

—Did you go to that picture 'The Lost Weekend'?
—*I did.*
—I never seen such tripe.
—*What was wrong with it?*
—O it was all right, of course—bits of it was good. Your man in the jigs inside in the bed and the bat flying in to kill the mouse, that was *damn* good. I'll tell you another good bit. Hiding the bottles in the jax. And there was no monkey business about that because I tried it since meself. It works but you have to use the half pint bottles. Up the chimbley is another place I thought of and do you know the ledge affair above windows?
—*I do.*
—That's another place but you could get a hell of a fall reaching up there on a ladder or standing on chairs with big books on them. And of course you can always tie the small bottles to the underneath of your mattress.
—*I suppose you can.*
—But what are you to do with the empties if you stop in bed drinking? There's a snag there. I often thought they should have malt in lemonade syphons.
—*Why didn't you like the rest of 'The Lost Weekend'?*
—Sure haven't I been through far worse weekends meself—you know that as well as I do. Sure Lord save us I could tell you yarns. I'd be a rich man if I had a shilling for every morning I was down in the markets at seven o'clock in the slippers with the trousers pulled on

6

over the pyjamas and the overcoat buttoned up to the neck in the middle of the summer. Sure don't be talking man.

—*I suppose the markets are very congested in the mornings?*

—With drunks? I don't know. I never looked round any time I was there.

—*When were you last there?*

—The time the wife went down to Cork last November. I won't forget that business in a hurry. That was a scatter and a half. Did I never tell you about that? O be God, don't get me on to *that* affair.

—*Was it the worst ever?*

—It was and it wasn't but I got the fright of me life. I'll tell you a damn good one. You won't believe this but it's a true bill. This is one of the best you ever heard.

—*I'll believe anything you say.*

—In the morning I brought the wife down to Kingsbridge in a taxi. I wasn't thinking of drink at all, hadn't touched it for four months, but when I paid the taxi off at the station instead of going back in it, the wife gave me a look. Said nothing, of course—after the last row I was for keeping off the beer for a year. But somehow she put the thing into me head. This was about nine o'clock, I suppose. I'll give you three guesses where I found meself at ten past nine *in another taxi*?

—*Where?*

—Above in the markets. And there wasn't a more surprised man than meself. Of course in a way it's a good thing to start at it early in the morning because with no food and all the rest of it you're finished at four o'clock and you're home again and stuffed in bed. It's the late nights that's the killer, two and three in the morning, getting poisoned in shebeens and all classes of hooky stuff, wrong change, and a taxi man on the touch. After nights like that it's a strong man that'll be up at the markets in time next morning.

—*What happened after the day you got back at four?*

—Up at the markets next morning *before* they were open. There was another chap there but I didn't look at him. I couldn't tell you what age he was or how bad he was. There was no four o'clock stuff that day. I was around the markets till twelve or so. Then off up town and I have meself shaved be a barber. Then up to a certain hotel and straight into the bar. There's a whole crowd there that I know. What are you going to have and so on. No no, have a large one. So-and-so's getting married on Tuesday. Me other man's wife has had a baby. You know the stuff? Well Lord save us I had a terrible tank of malt in me that day! I had a feed in the middle of it because I remember scalding myself with hot coffee and I never touch the coffee at all only after a feed. Of course I don't remember what happened me but I was in the flat the next morning with the clothes half off. I was supposed to be staying with the brother-in-law, of course, when the wife was away. But sure it's the old dog for the hard road. Drunk or sober I went back to me own place. As a matter of fact I never went near the brother-in-law at all. Be this time I was well into the malt. Out with me again feeling like death on wires and I'm inside in the local curing meself for hours, spilling stuff all over the place with the shake in the hand. Then into the barber's and after that off up again to the hotel for more malt. I'll give you a tip. Always drink in hotels. If you're in there you're in for a feed, or you've just had a feed or you've an appointment there to see a fellow, and you're having a small one to pass the time. It looks very bad being in bars during the daytime. It's a thing to watch, that.

—*What happened then?*

—What do you think happened? What could happen? I get meself into a quiet corner and I start lowering them good-o. I don't know what happened me, of course. I met a few pals and there is some business about a greyhound out in Cloghran. It was either being bought or being sold and I go along in the taxi and where we were and where we weren't I couldn't tell you. I fall asleep on a chair in some house in town and next thing I wake up perished with the cold and as sick as I ever was in me life. Next thing I know I'm above in the markets. Taxis everywhere of course, no food only the plate of soup in the hotel, and be this time the cheque-book is in and out of the pocket *three or four times a day*, standing drinks all round, kicking up a barney in the lavatory with other drunks, looking for me 'rights' when I was refused drink—O, blotto, there's no other word for it. I seen some of the cheques since. *The writing!* A pal carts me home in a taxi. How long this goes on I don't know. I'm all right in the middle of the day but in the mornings I'm nearly too weak to walk and the shakes getting worse every day. Be this time I'm getting frightened of meself.

Lookat here, mister-me-man, I say to meself, this'll have to stop. I was afraid the heart might give out, that was the only thing I was afraid of. Then I meet a pal of mine that's a doctor. This is inside in the hotel. There's only one man for you, he says, and that's sleep. Will you go home and go to bed if I get you something that'll make you sleep? Certainly, I said. I suppose this was about four or half four. Very well, says he, I'll write you out a prescription. He writes one out on hotel notepaper. I send for a porter. Go across with this, says I, to the nearest chemist shop and get this stuff for me and here's two bob for yourself. Of course I'm at the whiskey all the time. Your man comes back with a box of long-shaped green pills. You'll want to be careful with that stuff, the doctor says, that stuff's very dangerous. If you take one now and take another when you get home, you'll get a very good sleep but don't take any more till tomorrow night because that stuff's very dangerous. So I take one. But I know the doctor doesn't know how bad I am. I didn't tell him the whole story, no damn fear. So out with me to the jax where I take another one. Then back for a drink, still as wide-awake as a lark. You'll have to go home now, the doctor says, we can't have you passing out here, that stuff acts very quickly. Well, I have one more drink and off with me, *in a bus*, mind you, to the flat. I'm very surprised on the bus to find meself so wide-awake, looking out at people and reading the signs on shops. Then I begin to get afraid that the stuff is too weak and that I'll be lying awake for the rest of the evening and all night. To hell with it, I say to meself, we'll chance two more and let that be the end of it. Down went two more in the bus. I get there and into the flat. I'm still wide-awake and nothing will do me only one more pill for luck. I get into bed. I don't remember putting the head on the pillow. I wouldn't go out quicker if you hit me over the head with a crow-bar.

—*You probably took a dangerous over-dose.*

—Next thing I know I'm awake. It's dark. I sit up. There's matches there and I strike one. I look at the watch. The watch is stopped. I get up and look at the clock. Of course the clock is stopped, hasn't been wound for days. I don't know what time it is. I'm a bit upset about this. I turn on the wireless. It takes about a year to heat up and would you believe me I try a dozen stations all over the place and not one of them is telling what the time is. Of course I knew there was no point in trying American stations. I'm very disappointed because I sort of expected a voice to say 'It is now seven thirty p.m.' or whatever the time was. I turn off the wireless and begin to wonder. I don't know what time it is. *Then*, bedamnit, another thing strikes me. *What day is it?* How long have I been asleep with that dose? Well lookat, I got a hell of a fright when I found I didn't know what day it was. I got one hell of a fright.

—*Was there not an accumulation of milk-bottles or newspapers?*

—There wasn't—all that was stopped because I was supposed to be staying with the brother-in-law. What do I do? On with all the clothes and out to find what time it is and what day it is. The funny thing is that I'm not feeling too bad. Off with me down the street. There's lights showing in the houses. That means it's night-time and not early in the morning. Then I see a bus. That means it's not yet half-nine, because they stopped at half-nine that time. Then I see a clock. It's twenty past nine! But I still don't know what day it is and it's too late to buy an evening paper. There's only one thing—into a pub and get a look at one. So I march into the nearest, very quiet and correct and say a bottle of stout please. All the other customers look very sober and I think they are all talking very low. When the man brings me the bottle I say to him I beg your pardon but I had a few bob on a horse today, could you give me a look at an evening paper? The man looks at me and says what horse was it? It was like a blow in the face to me, that question! I can't answer at all at first and then I stutter something about Hartigan's horses. None of them horses won a race today, the man says, and there was a paper here but it's gone. So I drink up the bottle and march out. It's funny, finding out about the day. You can't stop a man in the street and say have you got the right day please? God knows what would happen if you done that. I know be now that it's no use telling lies about horses, so in with me to another pub, order a bottle and ask the man has he got an evening paper. The missus has it upstairs, he says, there's nothing on it anyway. I now begin to think the best thing is to dial 0 on the phone, ask for Inquiries and find out that way. I'm on me way to a call-box when I begin to think that's a very bad idea. The girl might say hold on and I'll find out, I hang on there like a mug and next thing the box is surrounded by Guards and ambulances and attendants with ropes. No fear, says I to meself, there's going to be no work on the phone for me! Into another pub. I have the wind up now and no mistake. How long was I knocked out be the drugs? A day? Two days? Was I in the bed *for a week*? Suddenly I see a sight that gladdens me heart. Away down at the end of the pub there's an oul' fellow reading an evening paper with a magnifying glass. I take a mouthful of stout, steady meself, and march down to him. Me mind is made up: if he doesn't hand over the paper, I'll kill him. Down I go. Excuse me, says I, snatching the paper away from him and he still keeps looking through the glass with no paper there, I think he was deaf as well as half blind. Then I read the date— I suppose it was the first time the date was the big news on a paper. It says 'Thursday, 22nd November, 1945.' I never enjoyed a bit of news so much. I hand back the paper and say thanks very much, sir, for the loan of your paper. Then I go back to finish me stout, very happy and pleased with me own cuteness. Another man, I say to meself, would ask people, make a show of himself and maybe get locked up. But not me. I'm smart. Then begob I nearly choked.

—*What was the cause of that?*

—To-day is Thursday, I say to meself. Fair enough. But...*what day did I go to bed?* What's the use of knowing to-day's Thursday if I don't know when I went to bed? I still don't know whether I've been asleep for a day or a week! I nearly fell down on the floor. I am back where I started. Only I am feeling weaker and be now I have the wind up in gales. The heart begins to knock so loud that I'm afraid the man behind the counter will hear it and order me out.

—*What did you do?*

—Lookat here, me friend, I say to meself, take it easy. Go back now to the flat and take it easy for a while. This'll all end up all right, everything comes right in the latter end. Worse than this happened many's a man. And back to the flat I go. I collapse down into a chair with the hat still on me head, I sink the face down in me hands, and try to think. I'm like that for maybe five minutes. Then, *suddenly*, I know the answer! Without help from papers or clocks or people, I know how long I am there sleeping under the green pills! How did I know? Think that one out! How would *you* know if you were in the same boat? (Before continuing, readers may wish to accept the sufferer's challenge.)

—*I am thinking.*

—Don't talk to me about calendars or hunger or anything like that. It's no use—you won't guess. You wouldn't think of it in a million years. Look. My face is in my hands—like this. Suddenly I notice the face is smooth. I'm not badly in need of a shave. That means it *must* be the same day I went to bed on! Maybe the stomach or something woke me up for a second or so. If I'd stopped in bed, I was off asleep again in a minute. But I got up to find the time and that's what ruined me! Now do you get it? Because when I went back to bed that night, I didn't waken till the middle of the next day.

—*You asked me how I would have found out how long I had been there after finding that the day was Thursday. I have no guarantee that a person in your condition would not get up and shave in his sleep. There was a better way.*

—There was no other way.

—*There was. If I were in your place I would have looked at the date on the prescription!*

Counterparts

Taken from one of the stories in James Joyce's Dubliners *of 1914, this excerpt illustrates not only the pressing need for alcohol but also the self-pity so often associated with it.*

He felt his great body again aching for the comfort of the public-house. The fog had begun to chill him and he wondered could he touch Pat in O'Neill's. He could not touch him for more than a bob— and a bob was no use. Yet he must get money somewhere or other: he had spent his last penny for the g.p. and soon it would be too late for getting money anywhere. Suddenly, as he was fingering his watch chain, he thought of Terry Kelly's pawn-office in Fleet Street. That was the dart! Why didn't he think of it sooner?

He went through the narrow alley of Temple Bar quickly,

muttering to himself that they could all go to hell, because he was going to have a good night of it. The clerk in Terry Kelly's said *A crown!* but the consignor held out for six shillings; and in the end the six shillings was allowed him literally. He came out of the pawn-office joyfully, making a little cylinder of the coins between his thumb and fingers. In Westmoreland Street the footpaths were crowded with young men and women returning from business, and ragged urchins ran here and there yelling out the names of the evening editions. The man passed through the crowd, looking on the spectacle generally with proud satisfaction and staring masterfully at the office-girls. His head was full of the noises of tram-gongs and swishing trolleys and his nose already sniffed the curling fumes of punch. As he walked on he preconsidered the terms in which he would narrate the incident to the boys:

'So, I just looked at him—coolly, you know, and looked at her. Then I looked back at him again—taking my time you know. "I don't think that that's a fair question to put to me," says I.'

Nosey Flynn was sitting up in his usual corner of Davy Byrne's and, when he heard the story, he stood Farrington a half-one, saying it was as smart a thing as ever he heard. Farrington stood a drink in his turn. After a while O'Halloran and Paddy Leonard came in and the story was repeated to them. O'Halloran stood tailors of malt, hot, all round and told the story of the retort he had made to the chief clerk when he was in Callan's of Fownes's Street; but, as the retort was after the manner of the liberal shepherds in the eclogues, he had to admit that it was not as clever as Farrington's retort. At this Farrington told the boys to polish off that and have another.

Just as they were naming their poisons who should come in but Higgins! Of course he had to join in with the others. The men asked him to give his version of it, and he did so with great vivacity, for the sight of five small hot whiskies was very exhilarating. Every one roared laughing when he showed the way in which Mr Alleyne shook his fist in Farrington's face. Then he imitated Farrington, saying, '*And here was my nabs, as cool as you please,*' while Farrington looked at the company out of his heavy dirty eyes, smiling and at times drawing forth stray drops of liquor from his moustache with the aid of his lower lip.

When that round was over there was a pause. O'Halloran had money, but neither of the other two seemed to have any; so the whole party left the shop somewhat regretfully. At the corner of Duke Street Higgins and Nosey Flynn bevelled off to the left, while the other three turned back towards the city. Rain was drizzling down on the cold streets and, when they reached the Ballast Office, Farrington suggested the Scotch House. The bar was full of men and loud with the noise of tongues and glasses. The three men pushed past the whining match-sellers at the door and formed a little party at the corner of the counter. They began to exchange stories. Leonard introduced them to a young fellow named Weathers who was performing at the Tivoli as an acrobat and knockabout *artiste*. Farrington stood a drink all round. Weathers said he would take a small Irish and Apollinaris. Farrington, who had definite notions of what was what, asked the boys would they have an Apollinaris too; but the boys told Tim to make theirs hot. The talk became theatrical. O'Halloran stood a round and then Farrington stood another round, Weathers protesting that the hospitality was too Irish. He promised to get them in behind the scenes and introduce them to some nice girls. O'Halloran said that he and Leonard would go, but that Farrington wouldn't go because he was a married man; and Farrington's heavy dirty eyes leered at the company in token that he understood he was being chaffed. Weathers made them all have just one little tincture at his expense and promised to meet them later on at Mulligan's in Poolbeg Street.

When the Scotch House closed they went round to Mulligan's. They went into the parlour at the back and O'Halloran ordered small hot specials all round. They were all beginning to feel mellow. Farrington was just standing another round when Weathers came back. Much to Farrington's relief he drank a glass of bitter this time. Funds were getting low, but they had enough to keep them going. Presently two young women with big hats and a young man in a check suit came in and sat at a table close by. Weathers saluted them and told the company that they were out of the Tivoli. Farrington's eyes wandered at every moment in the direction of one of the young women. There was something striking in her appearance. An immense scarf of peacock-blue muslin was wound round her hat and knotted in a great bow under her chin; and she wore bright yellow gloves, reaching to the elbow. Farrington gazed admiringly at the plump arm which she moved very often and with much grace; and when, after a little time, she answered his gaze he admired still more her large dark brown eyes. The oblique staring expression in them fascinated him. She glanced at him once or twice and, when the party was leaving the room, she brushed against his chair and said '*O, pardon!*' in a London accent. He watched her leave the room in the hope that she would look back at him, but he was disappointed. He cursed his want of money and cursed all the rounds he had stood, particularly all the whiskies and Apollinaris which he had stood to Weathers. If there was one thing that he hated it was a sponge. He was so angry that he lost count of the conversation of his friends.

When Paddy Leonard called him he found that they were talking about feats of strength. Weathers was showing his biceps muscle to the company and boasting so much that the other two had called on Farrington to uphold the national honour. Farrington pulled up his sleeve accordingly and showed his biceps muscle to the company. The two arms were examined and compared and finally it was agreed to have a trial of strength. The table was cleared and the two men rested their elbows on it, clasping hands. When Paddy Leonard said '*Go!*' each was to try to bring down the other's hand on to the table. Farrington looked very serious and determined.

The trial began. After about thirty seconds Weathers brought his opponent's hand slowly down on to the table. Farrington's dark wine-coloured face flushed darker still with anger and humiliation at having been defeated by such a stripling.

'You're not to put the weight of your body behind it. Play fair,' he said.

'Who's not playing fair?' said the other.

'Come on again. The two best out of three.'

The trial began again. The veins stood out on Farrington's forehead, and the pallor of Weathers' complexion changed to peony. Their hands and arms trembled under the stress. After a long struggle Weathers again brought his opponent's hand slowly on to the table. There was a murmur of applause from the spectators. The curate, who was standing beside the table, nodded his red head toward the victor and said with stupid familiarity:

'Ah! that's the knack!'

'What the hell do you know about it?' said Farrington fiercely, turning on the man. 'What do you put in your gab for?'

'Sh, sh!' said O'Halloran, observing the violent expression of Farrington's face. 'Pony up, boys. We'll have just one little smahan more and then we'll be off.'

A very sullen-faced man stood at the corner of O'Connell Bridge waiting for the little Sandymount tram to take him home. He was full of smouldering anger and revengefulness. He felt humiliated and discontented; he did not even feel drunk; and he had only twopence in his pocket. He cursed everything. He had done for himself in the office, pawned his watch, spent all his money; and he had not even got drunk. He began to feel thirsty again and he longed to be back again in the hot, reeking public-house. He had lost his reputation as a strong man, having been defeated twice by a mere boy. His heart swelled with fury and, when he thought of the woman in the big hat who had brushed against him and said *Pardon*! his fury nearly choked him.

His tram let him down at Shelbourne Road and he steered his great body along in the shadow of the wall of the barracks. He loathed returning to his home. When he went in by the side-door he found the kitchen empty and the kitchen fire nearly out. He bawled upstairs:

'Ada! Ada!'

His wife was a little sharp-faced woman who bullied her husband when he was sober and was bullied by him when he was drunk. They had five children. A little boy came running down the stairs.

'Who is that?' said the man, peering through the darkness.

'Me, pa.'

'Who are you? Charlie?'

'No, pa. Tom.'

'Where's your mother?'

'She's out at the chapel.'

'That's right...Did she think of leaving any dinner for me?'

'Yes, pa. I—'

'Light the lamp. What do you mean by having the place in darkness? Are the other children in bed?'

The man sat down heavily on one of the chairs while the little boy lit the lamp. He began to mimic his son's flat accent, saying half to himself: '*At the chapel. At the chapel, if you please!*' When the lamp was lit he banged his fist on the table and shouted:

'What's for my dinner?'

'I'm going...to cook it, pa,' said the little boy.

The man jumped up furiously and pointed to the fire.

'On that fire! You let the fire out! By God, I'll teach you to do that again!'

He took a step to the door and seized the walking-stick which was standing behind it.

'I'll teach you to let the fire out!' he said, rolling up his sleeve in order to give his arm free play.

The little boy cried '*O, pa!*' and ran whimpering round the table, but the man followed him and caught him by the coat. The little boy looked about him wildly but, seeing no way of escape, fell upon his knees.

'Now, you'll let the fire out the next time!' said the man, striking at him viciously with the stick. 'Take that, you little whelp!'

The boy uttered a squeal of pain as the stick cut his thigh. He clasped his hands together in the air and his voice shook with fright.

'O, pa!' he cried. 'Don't beat me, pa! And I'll...I'll say a *Hail Mary* for you...I'll say a *Hail Mary* for you, pa, if you don't beat me...I'll say a *Hail Mary...*'

The 200 Year Old Alcoholic

This song by Liam Clancy was recorded at the Gaiety Theatre, Dublin, as part of the album 'Makem and Clancy in Concert'.

When I was eighty I started smokin'
Took to drinkin' at eighty-five
At ninety I started courtin'
Thank God that I was alive

At ninety-five I took to the gamblin'
Determined to rake in a pile
At a hundred I made my first million
And I started livin' in style.

Chorus:
O it's never too late to start livin'
To get out and have some fun
The sun will be just as shiny in the mornin'
As the first day the world begun.

Well I moved to an uptown penthouse
Used fifties to light my cigars
Developed a taste for fine champagne
And drove fast Italian cars
But the doctor, he give me a warnin'
And a lecture on right and wrong
If I didn't give up my sinful ways
I couldn't live very long.

Chorus

Now I'm a two hundred year old alcoholic
And the nicotine's caught up on me
But worst of all, in this mornin's mail
I got a suit for paternity!!
But I'm not really unhappy
'Cause maybe I'll have me a son
And his mornings will be just as shiny
As the first day the world begun.

Chorus twice

The Erris Hotel

Dermot Healy's A Goat's Song *of 1994 is one of the most frightening descriptions imaginable of alcoholism and its effects. This extract is an example.*

He walked the few miles through the falling dark to Belmullet and stood at the bridge. He ordered a coffee and sat in the sun lounge of the Erris Hotel. It looked out on the street where Catherine would arrive. A country couple and a brightly dressed, middle-aged American in check trousers entered. The countryman, who was wearing a baseball cap, disengaged himself from the others and sat down by Jack.

'You have any Yanks in your family?' he asked.

'No,' replied Jack.

'That's a brother of mine gone in.' He nodded towards the bar.

'I see.'

'Are you staying here?'

'No.'

'You must have a girl,' he said after a while.

'I do,' Jack smiled.

'Well, then, she must be very beautiful,' the man nodded sagely. 'I live up the pass with my sister. That's her gone in with him. He's just in for the Christmas holidays, God bless us. We're going out for a bite tonight, but I'll sit here with you.'

Jack turned to look at him, the schoolboy face, the simple hands, the brown eyes high in the sockets and the sockets high in the head, the marvelling forehead. Jack pointed at the baseball cap. 'Have you been across the water?'

'Not at all.' He leaned closer and looked into Jack's eyes.

'Where are you from?' he asked.

'Leitrim.'

'Holy God,' he said, 'they have their problems there, too. Would you like a drink?'

'No thanks,' said Jack.

'You're better off. They don't tell you everything when you're drunk,' and he tapped his skull.

Now, both men looked at the street through the lace curtains waiting for Catherine. Soon the man's sister loomed in the lounge. She gestured over her shoulder sharply with her thumb in that condescending, familiar manner used with someone you consider touched. Her brother looked at her a long time. There was a mild rebellion in his failure to recognise her. Behind her, the American brother hovered uncertainly.

'I'll have to go now,' he said, looking at his sister.

'Goodbye,' said Jack.

'Good luck, Leitrim,' he replied.

He saw her on the road to the west, foot to the ground in the Lada, African freedom songs playing on the car stereo. Or with her head firmly slanted as she held the car in first at some lights.

He did not want to think of the past; she had given herself to him— perhaps there was a note of hesitation, maybe it was not complete commitment, maybe some part of her was holding back—but there was hope.

What words he could conjure seemed trite and inconsequential. How extraordinary it was that he could describe what he saw—the contents of a sun lounge or what's afoot on a village street—and yet not be able to articulate the chaotic events that had thrown their lives into turmoil. These, too, had a sequence. But where do you step into a life to say: *Here it begins!*?

Some part of him had stopped on the hour. A part of him was refusing to go forward till something terrible happened. He saw the gardener at the bar.

'I met your lady friend as she was leaving town last Sunday,' sneered the gardener.

'Oh yeah?'

'Yes. She was asking if you were drinking.'

'What did you say?'

'What could I say?' replied the gardener.

Everyone at the bar stopped talking. Just when everything seemed possible, the nightmare had started again.

'Well I'm sober now,' declared Jack.

'Is that so?' said the gardener, and he laughed.

'I think I'll go a bit further,' said Jack. At that moment his sobriety seemed a small price to pay for happiness. He always thought that the price would be more ephemeral, exotic, metaphysical. He felt humiliated and debased that her love demanded something as mundane as sobriety. A few weeks had passed and he'd been sober. She, too, wherever she was, was sober. *Let us grow old and sober together.* Yes, why not. She was coming to see him. But what did it all mean? Why did it feel so trivial? How do you build from within as your identity falters? He left the hotel.

Something was wrong.

Someone had been living through all of this on his behalf—a stranger. Now he had to create something from nothing. A man. He didn't know what expression he should wear. What politics he had. Or the architecture that surrounded him. Yet once, out of habit, he walked in his shoes.

For her he must remake himself. But she had all the materials which he needed to begin.

As he sat waiting in the darkened sun lounge in the early evening, a bus disgorged a gaggle of youths and six priests onto Main Street. It had begun raining and they were drenched in the downpour. 'That's a shocking evening,' a priest said to Jack. The youngsters were sent into the eating house beyond the lounge for chips and sausages. Immediately they created an uproar. The sorry-looking priests, with brandies and gins, came into the lounge. A buxom woman brought them salmon sandwiches.

'Where are you from?' Jack asked the priest nearest to him.

'Castlebar,' he replied. 'We are giving the altar boys of the diocese a day out.'

'You didn't, by any chance, pass a Lada on the road?'

'I'm sure we passed plenty,' the priest laughed.

Jack looked into his eyes. 'A blue Lada. Maybe it was broken down. And a woman. She'd be wearing a black scarf.'

'Not that I can remember,' said the priest.

The priests hunched over their drinks in a single-minded way.

Some wore old childish ganseys, others black, loosely knit vests. Here the back of a neck bulged, there it was graceful and white and reeked of a fleshly morbid sensuality. They chewed the white bread and lettuce with relish. One man, back from the missions, tanned and feral, talked of Chile, the Shining Path and Christopher Columbus while he sipped a Baileys Irish Cream. Then their conversation dropped to whispers. Jack gagged a little, and stabbed a finger into his thigh to control his stomach. His eyes watered.

'Don't look so sad, me buck,' the missioner called across, 'it might never happen.'

The nausea made Jack swoon. He gagged again and pressed his finger deep into his thigh till the nail punctured the skin. The smell of old drink seemed to erupt from the pores of his body.

He was standing in the rain down on the Shore Road looking out at the violent sea which made no sound. Turning, he saw two dogs watching him, also silently, through a blue galvanise gate. One stood, his snout resting on his forepaws in the hole behind which the bolt is shot home. The other was stretched flat out on the cobbles so he could see under the corner of the gate. They were brown-and-white sheepdogs. Daisy lay in the middle of the road with his snout cushioned on a handful of grass and watched them. The three dogs and the man regarded each other silently.

The hotel gardener, shaking his disconsolate head and fingers, as if he were feeding birds, foundered down the road.

'How are you?' shouted Jack.

The gardener did not answer, but stopped, looked and moved on with an ironic smile.

'Don't worry about it,' mumbled Jack.

Dusk was falling. The surf rose silently. Outside a pub two tractors sat with their engines running. Local girls, high-cheeked, with jet-black Spanish hair, and dressed in virgin white, spilled out of a house speaking Irish. Dusk was falling quicker. The beach, when he reached it, was possessed of a low light. The sand was a quiet phosphorescent carpet. Suds lay the landward side of the wrack.

It was Saturday night, and all the Catholics were headed for evening

Mass. The old sabbath was being rejuvenated. The roads on the peninsula were lit by a convoy of trundling cars. The town was deserted, except for the hotel where the priests sat drinking, and the eating house, where the altar boys were shooting pool. An old gambling machine blinked on and off. In the distance, on the mainland, limestone glittered as if the sun were shining.

He walked a street of ruined houses, then took a short cut across the lawns of the small industrial estate. The names were floodlit— Warners (Éire) Teo, Ionad Cloch Iorrais, Ruibéar Chomhlacht Atlantach Teo, Fás. He went along a road where old shopfronts stared back with blank faces. The light from Eagle Island lighthouse swept across the sky three times. Count eight. Three times again. He stood on the new bridge. A light came on in the golf club. Nurses stepped into cars at the hospital. Standing there he listened to the alarming silence. The black sky blinked again.

'Isn't it getting late terribly early,' Mrs Moloney, the receptionist, said to him when he re-entered the hotel.

'Were there any calls for me?'

'No,' she said. 'There was none since you last asked.'

'Are you sure?'

'Yes, Jack.'

'Fair enough.'

He stood by the desk wondering what to do.

He went into the bar.

'Hugh.'

'Jack.'

'Aye.'

'No sign yet?' asked Hugh.

'No,' answered Jack, 'that's about it.'

The wind thrashed against the glass windows in the roof.

'I think I'll have a brandy.'

'Why wouldn't you?'

'A brandy and crème de menthe I think.'

Hugh filled a double measure.

'Good luck,' Hugh said.

It was only as he entered the sun lounge that Jack became aware of the glass in his hand. He stopped on the threshold and looked at the glass and thought, how did that happen? It was as if he had been transformed into someone else, someone he had once been. Someone he disliked entirely. In his sleep on the boat he'd often dream of drinking and wake with immense relief to find that it had not happened. The glass of whiskey he'd been swallowing in some unlit room of his consciousness he'd find did not exist. Now it did. It sat whole in his hand. After his two weeks of sobriety he'd ordered a drink without thinking. If she comes now what will I do? *I'll not drink it!* He found the carpet under his feet. *I have not drunk it yet!* Holding the drink away from him he made his way to a deserted corner of the room and put the glass down at a safe distance from himself.

'There's the buck back,' said one of the priests. 'Call me Peter,' he added. 'We hear you do a bit of writing.'

'I'm afraid you have the wrong man,' said Jack.

If she'd been coming today, she'd have been down by now.

'Sit down with us,' said Father Peter, 'and give us some of your crack.'

He sat down with the priests. They all sat round waiting for Catherine.

While he slept his body had ballooned out. A calf-hide receptacle of warm blood, he lay on his side. The panic that was his first reaction, could not be smoothed away. Everything was charged with static.

He got up and dressed. His clothes stank of damp heat. Fungus had bloomed overnight on the walls. As he entered the middle room Gay Byrne's voice suddenly boomed forth speaking to a woman of some distant sexual problem. 'Jesus Christ,' said Jack, and switched the radio off. He threw half a mackerel from a Donegal Catch packet to the wild cat who was screaming at the door. When Daisy ran under his feet, full of earnest early-morning enthusiasm, Jack roared at him. The dog, his tail curled up under his rump, backed away into a corner of the room. 'And stay there!' shouted Jack. He saw the misshapen image of his own face in the dog's black eye as the animal circled the table.

'Stop looking at me,' he said to the dog. Daisy immediately turned away.

Jack spat out a globule of sick. The white fluid turned dry as if he had spat on a hot pan.

Something had happened to his mind. His consciousness had always been protected by a sieve, but while he'd slept the holes had grown larger. Now the holes were as big as cherrystones. And they were growing bigger by the minute.

He put one hand on the mantelpiece and stayed that way a few minutes. Where did Sunday go? I must have slept through it all. Then, sitting by the radio, he saw a bottle of sherry standing, the cork still half in. And tenderly he thought with a smile: I saved that for myself.

The priests left that.

A Taxi in New York

The total confusion and loss of touch with reality that comes with obsessional drunkenness is well captured in this extract from Dermot Healy's A Goat's Song *of 1994.*

When he was wet and cold enough he went into the nearest pub. But he didn't drink there. Nor in the pub after that. No, he was looking for someone. In the third pub he was looking for no one, but found instinctively that he was. This is what I'm doing here, he reminded himself—looking for someone. The men drinking there watched him for a second as if they, too, understood—that you keep searching till you find the right place to begin the day's drinking.

He sat down, thinking he had reached the place. He put his hand in his pocket to search for money. When he looked up each face had grown pale and ignorant and hostile. Then indifferent. Each was cocooned, not a human soul stirred among them. It was as if there was nobody there.

'I was looking for someone,' he said to the barman and left, taking care as he did not to walk into anything.

He moved on with the drinker's ploy for fending off the first drink. The first drink that must be taken when all the signs are right. But none of the pubs was right. Loud TVs, piped music, strange glances. Eventually, in the fourth pub, he found that someone he was searching for. That someone who was no one. The person who didn't exist was an excuse to move on. But here, in the low light, that non-person was.

He stayed in the fourth pub because he recognised the girl who had been covered in soot and tied to the pole. Now she was sitting with three other women at the bar drinking hot whiskey.

Jack was glad to see her again.

'I'm in mourning,' he said.

'Are you all right?' she asked.

'I've been pissing balls,' he replied, 'and I keep them back in my room. I keep them in little bags.'

'We had a brother went like you,' she said.

He ordered his first drink. 'I like a Harvey's Bristol Cream for breakfast.'

'Is that so?'

'I like the taste in the nose.'

'Do you want to join us?'

'Nah,' he said, 'I'm getting the train to Dublin.'

They drank. The old feeling of being a camera returned. He panned the bar. He focused on the women with their hair piled and blow-dried who sat around him. Cuff links gleamed. Men lifted drinks to their lips. It's a B-movie, that's what my subconscious is, and he laughed.

'Tell us the joke,' said the bride-to-be. 'You remind me of my da.'

'He'd be a Mullarkey,' said Jack, 'from Muinguingane.'

The camera closed in on her face. Unabashed, she stared back.

'How do you know?' she asked.

'That would be telling,' he said.

'Go on,' she said.

Little pods of soot stood like flecks of rain on her lashes and brows and in the corners of her eyes. The corners were inordinately exposed. What holds the eye in tension so that it can see? Her eyes closed as she waited for his reply. The darkness seemed to last a long time.

He sat into a taxi in New York. He was quite happy to find the warm upholstery against his back.

'How long have you been driving taxis?' he asked the figure behind the wheel.

'This is not a taxi,' the man replied.

'I've always wanted to go in a taxi through New York,' said Jack, looking at the city.

The man replied with words Jack could not understand. They passed beneath high buildings, and arcades lit up, and small ponds that were behind dark trees. A brilliant sign for GINGS, UNDERTAKERS, sped by. Jack continued to talk away about America. Kafka never went, you know, he said. Is that so? asked the chauffeur. No, said Jack. It just goes to show you, said the chauffeur. Yes, said Jack, but he got there still the same. For you see, explained Jack, time is not linear. It does not go in straight lines. Indeed it does not, agreed the driver as he flicked a light on his wide and shining instrument panel. That's not to say it's cyclical either, continued Jack. No, the man nodded. It goes, said Jack, leaning forward, in stops and starts. That's right, said the chauffeur.

Eventually the taxi pulled in. The man came round, still wearing his light blue chauffeur's outfit, and opened the door. Thank you, said Jack grandly. He got out awkwardly. He was very tired. And must have slept a little. Because now he saw that the chauffeur was not a chauffeur at all. The policeman led him into the barracks.

'I found him sleeping out on the side of the road,' said the guard to an orderly who was standing in a wide blue shirt.

'I wasn't sleeping,' said Jack, 'I was hitching home.'

'He was lying stretched out on the side of the road and could have been run over,' said the guard.

'I was hitching,' said Jack. Then he added, 'I might have sat down.' He thought again. 'No one was stopping.'

'Where were you going?' asked the orderly.

'I was going to Belfast.'

'Were you now.'

'Yes I was.'

'Well, son,' said the guard, 'if you were going to Belfast, you were on the wrong road.'

Jack reconsidered, then he remembered. 'I'm sorry,' he said, 'I was actually going to Dublin.'

'That's a horse of a different colour.'

'I must have missed the train.'

'I'd say you did. It's three in the morning.'

'I'm charging him with being drunk in a public place,' said the guard.

'Right.' The orderly was taking out a clean sheet and about to write down the details of what happened when the sergeant appeared.

'That's Jack Ferris,' declared the sergeant. 'From Kilty.'

'That's right,' said Jack, gratefully.

'That's the playwright,' he said.

'That's right,' said Jack.

'You live only two doors up from me. We're neighbours at home.'

'That's right,' said Jack, 'Can I make a phone call?'

'Fire away.'

'You see,' explained Jack, 'the woman might be worried.'

So while the guard explained where Jack had been found, Jack dialled the theatre. In the far distance he heard a recorded voice repeating the times of various shows. 'Catherine,' he said, 'can you pick me up?'—he swung round to look at the group of policemen—'I'm in the Garda station in Ballina.'

He listened a moment over the phone. 'That's a pity.'

'I'm afraid she can't come,' he said, replacing the receiver.

'Never mind,' said the sergeant. 'We'll drive you home.'

The guard who had wanted to arrest him sheepishly led him out to the squad car and Jack sat into the back. The sergeant got in behind the wheel. The guard sat silently in the passenger seat. Then the orderly closed the barracks and sat in beside Jack.

'I'll be glad of the spin,' he said. 'We're not expecting trouble tonight anyway.'

'It's all for the sake of art,' said the Leitrim man. 'Where do you live?'

'Mullet.'

'Fuck me,' said the sergeant.

Dawn was breaking on the Atlantic when the squad car pulled in at the gate that opened onto the path that led to his bare back wall.

'You live here?' asked the sergeant.

'I do.'

'Fuck me,' said the sergeant.

Anti-social Drinking

I Know You're Going
to Miss Me

This brief episode is from Frank O'Connor's An Only Child.

Father didn't drink for two years. He had drunk himself penniless, as he frequently did, and some old friend had refused him a loan. The slight had cut him so deep that he stopped drinking at once. The friend was wrong if he assumed that Father would not have repaid that or any other loan, but, still, it was a great pity that he hadn't a few more friends of the sort.

It was no joke to go with Father on one of his Sunday outings with the band, and I often kicked up hell about it, but Mother liked me to go, because she had some strange notion that I could restrain him from drinking too much. Not that I didn't love music, nor that I wasn't proud of Father as, with the drum slung high about his neck, he glanced left and right of it, waiting to give the three taps that brought the bandsmen in. He was a drummer of the classical type: he hated to see a man carry his drum on his belly instead of his chest, and he had nothing but scorn for the showy drummers who swung or crossed their sticks. He was almost disappointingly unpretentious.

But when he was on the drink, I was so uncertain that I always had the feeling that one day he would lose me and forget I had been with him at all. Usually, the band would end its piece in front of a pub at the corner of Coburg Street. The pubs were always shut on Sunday until after last Mass, and when they opened, it was only for an hour or two. The last notes of 'Brian Boru's March' would hardly have been played before Father unslung the drum, thrust it on the young fellows whose job it was to carry it, and dashed across the road to the pub, accompanied by John P., his great buddy. John P.—I never knew what his surname was—was a long string of misery, with an air of unutterable gravity, emphasised by the way he sucked in his cheeks. He was one of the people vaguely known as 'followers of the band'— a group of lonely souls who gave some significance to their simple lives by attaching themselves to the band. They discussed its policies and personalities, looked after the instruments, and knew every pub in Cork that would risk receiving its members after hours. John P., with a look of intense concentration, would give a secret knock on the side door of the pub and utter what seemed to be whispered endearments through the keyhole, and more and more bandsmen would join the group peppering outside, while messengers rushed up to them shouting: 'Come on, can't ye, come on! The bloomin' train will be gone!'

That would be the first of the boring and humiliating waits outside public houses that went on all day and were broken only when I made a scene and Father gave me a penny to keep me quiet. Afterwards it would be the seaside at Aghada—which wasn't so bad because my maternal grandmother's people, the Kellys, still lived there and they would give me a cup of tea—or Crosshaven, or the grounds of Blarney Castle, and in the intervals of playing, the band would sit in various public houses with the doors barred, and if I was inside I couldn't get out, and—what was worse for a shy small boy—if I was out I couldn't get in. It was all very boring and alarming, and I remember once at Blarney, in my discouragement, staking my last penny on a dice game called the Harp, Crown, and Feather in the hope of retrieving a wasted day. Being a patriotic child, with something of Father's high principle, I put my money on the national emblem and lost. This was prophetic, because since then I have lost a great many pennies on the national emblem, but at least it cured me of the more obvious forms of gambling for the rest of my days.

On another occasion, after what had seemed an endless day in Crosshaven, I found myself late at night outside a locked public house in Cork opposite the North Cathedral, waiting for some drunk to emerge, so that I could stick my head in the door and wail: 'Daddy, won't you come home now?' At last, in despair, I decided to make my own way home through the dark streets, though I had never been out alone at night before this. In terror, I crept down the sinister length of

Shandon Street, and crossed the street so that I might escape seeing what I might see by the old graveyard, and then, at the foot of Blarney Lane, I saw a tiny shop still open. There were steps up to the hall door, and railings round the area, and the window was small and high and barely lighted by one oil lamp inside, but I could plainly see a toy dog in it, looking out at me. Praying that it wouldn't be beyond my means, I climbed up the steps. Inside, a door on the right led from the hall to the shop, where the counter was higher than my head. A woman came out of the little back room and asked me what I wanted. I told her I wanted to know the price of the dog, and she said it was sixpence. I had earned a lot of pennies by standing outside public houses that day, and sixpence was exactly what I had, so I threw it all on the counter and staggered out, clutching my protector. The rest of the way up Blarney Lane I walked without fear, setting my woolly dog at every dark laneway to right and left of me with a fierce 'At 'em, boy!' Fortunately for myself, I was fast asleep when Father arrived home, distracted over losing me.

As for keeping him off the drink, I never did it but once, when I drank his pint, became very drunk, smashed my head against a wall, and had to be steered home by himself and John P., both of them mad with frustration and panic, and be put to bed.

Resurrection Man

This description of the notorious 'romper rooms' associated with loyalist paramilitaries is from Resurrection Man *by Eoin McNamee.*

Victor was in Maxies the night they got John McGinn. They had picked him up earlier on the Crumlin Road. Maxies was to be the Romper Room. The name was taken from a children's television programme where the presenter looked through a magic mirror and saw children sitting at home. You sent in your name and address if you wanted to be seen through the mirror. The magic mirror had no glass. It was thought to contain secrets of longevity. It gave you access to the afterlife.

'What's your name?'

'John.'

'John fucking who?'

'John McGinn.'

'Through the magic mirror today we can see John McGinn. Hello John. We'll call you Johnnie. Do your friends call you Johnnie? We're your friends.'

We share your sense of bewilderment. Your intense loneliness. You were in a hurry walking down the Crumlin Road. You were going to work, to a night class, to meet a woman in a bar. We can hear her crying because you didn't turn up. We share her sadness. We will be a comfort to her.

'Over to you Victor.'

'Fucking butterfingers.'

'Hey, he near broke my foot. He's got something hard in there.'

'It's his fucking skull.'

'He levitated. I swear to God he levitated over the bar. He's a magician or something.'

'Here's a message for the fucking Pope.'

Billy McClure was the first to use the Romper Room. He was familiar with forms of initiation. He had convictions for paedophilia and knew that complicity was everything. It was a question of maintaining a ceremonial pace with pauses and intervals for reflection. There had to be a big group of participants. Twenty or thirty was good, particularly if they were close-knit. That way you could involve whole communities. You implicated wives and children, unborn generations. The reluctant were pressed forward and congratulated afterwards.

'Good man, Billy.'

'I seen teeth coming out. I definitely seen teeth. There's them on the floor over there.'

'You can come around our place give the wife one of them digs any time, Billy.'

There were long pauses for drinking. Men crowded round the bar eager to buy rounds for the whole company. The victim was ignored.

He lay on the ground between the poker machine and the pool table. There was blood on the ground, bits of scalp. Victor would wander over with a drink in his hand, stir McGinn with his boot and stare blankly at him as if he were a specimen of extinction.

Later Victor would see that these events had formal structure. The men settled down after the first round of drinks. They took their jackets off and precision became important. A whole range of sounds could be extracted from the victim. The third stage came around 3 a.m. No one spoke. The men's breathing was laboured. It was 3 a.m., hour of mile-deep disappointments. Futility and exhaustion began to set in.

At 4 a.m. Victor took McGinn into the toilets where he cut his throat.

Balls, Feasts and Banquets

Bricriu's Feast

*Bricriu was a trouble-maker and so one could hardly expect his feast
to be trouble-free—indeed, he went to great lengths to ensure that it
was not! However, a feast an entire year in the preparation is
difficult to ignore; it must have been the biggest party ever given in
Ulster at least. We, tactfully, will leave the feast before the trouble
begins, although the ground has been laid for it. This text is believed
to have been written down about AD 875. The translation is by
George Henderson.*

Bói fled mór la Bricrind Nemthenga do Chonchobur mac Nessa ocus
do Ultaib huile. Bliadain lan dó oc tinól na flede. Dorónad iarom
tegdas chumtachta lais fri frithailem tomalta na flede.

Bricriu of the Evil Tongue held a great feast for Conchobar mac Nessa
and for all the Ultonians. The preparation of the feast took a whole
year. For the entertainment of the guests a spacious house was built by
him. He erected it in Dun Rudraige after the likeness [of the palace] of
the Red Branch in Emain. Yet it surpassed the buildings of that period
entirely for material and for artistic design, for beauty of
architecture—its pillars and frontings splendid and costly, its carving
and lintel-work famed for magnificence.

The House was made on this wise: on the plan of Tara's Mead-
Hall, having nine compartments from fire to wall, each fronting of
bronze thirty feet high, overlaid with gold. In the fore part of the
palace a royal couch was erected for Conchobar high above those of
the whole house. It was set with carbuncles and other precious stones
which shone with a lustre of gold and of silver, radiant with every hue,
making night like unto day. Around it were placed the twelve couches
of the twelve heroes of Ulster. The nature of the workmanship was on

a par with the material of the edifice. It took a waggon team to carry each beam, and the strength of seven Ulster men to fix each pole, while thirty of the chief artificers of Erin were employed on its erection and arrangement.

Then a balcony was made by Bricriu on a level with the couch of Conchobar [and as high as those] of the heroes of valour. The decorations of its fittings were magnificent. Windows of glass were placed on each side of it, and one of these was above Bricriu's couch, so that he could view the hall from his seat, as he knew the Ulster men would not suffer him within.

When Bricriu had finished building the hall and balcony, supplying it both with quilts and blankets, beds and pillows, providing meat and drink, so that nothing was lacking, neither furnishings nor food, he straightway went to Emain to meet Conchobar and the nobles of Ulster.

If fell upon a day there was in Emain a gathering of the Ulster men. He was anon made welcome, and was seated by the shoulder of Conchobar. Bricriu addressed himself to him as well as to the body of the Ulster men. 'Come with me,' quoth Bricriu, 'to partake of a banquet with me.' 'Gladly,' rejoined Conchobar, 'if that please the men of Ulster.' Fergus mac Róig and the nobles of Ulster also made answer: 'No; for if we go our dead will outnumber our living, when Bricriu has incensed us against each other.'

'If ye come not, worse shall ye fare,' quoth Bricriu. 'What then,' asked Conchobar, 'if the Ulster men go not with thee?' 'I will stir up strife,' quoth Bricriu, 'between the kings, the leaders, the heroes of valour, and the yeomen, till they slay one another, man for man, if they do not come with me to share my feast.' 'That we shall not do to please thee,' quoth Conchobar. 'I will stir up enmity between father and son so that it will come to mutual slaughter. If I do not succeed in doing so, I will make a quarrel between mother and daughter. If that does not succeed, I will set each of the Ulster women at variance, so that they come to deadly blows till their breasts become loathsome and putrid.' 'Sure 'tis better to come,' quoth Fergus. 'Do ye straightway take counsel with the chief Ultonians,' said Sencha, son of Ailill. 'Unless we take counsel against this Bricriu, mischief will be the consequence,' quoth Conchobar.

Thereupon all the Ulster nobles assembled in council. In discussing the matter Sencha counselled them thus: 'Take hostages from Bricriu, since ye have to go with him, and set eight swordsmen about him so as to compel him to retire from the house as soon as he has laid out the feast.' Furbaide Ferbenn, son of Conchobar, brought Bricriu reply, and showed him the whole matter. 'It is happily arranged,' quoth Bricriu. The men of Ulster straightway set out from Emain, host, battalion and company, under king, chieftain and leader. Excellent and admirable the march of the brave and valiant heroes to the palace.

The hostages of the braves had gone security on his behalf, and Bricriu accordingly bethought him how he should manage to set the Ulster men at variance. His deliberation and self-scrutiny being ended, he betook himself to the company of Loigaire the Triumphant, son of Connad mac Ilíach. 'Hail now, Loigaire the Triumphant, thou mighty mallet of Bregia, thou hot hammer of Meath, flame-red thunderbolt, thou victorious warrior of Ulster, what hinders the championship of Emain being thine always?' 'If I so choose, it shall be mine,' quoth Loigaire. 'Be thine the sovranty of the braves of Erin,' quoth Bricriu, 'if only thou act as I advise.' 'I will indeed,' quoth Loigaire.

'Sooth, if the champion's portion of my house be thine, the championship of Emain is thine for ever. The champion's portion of my house is worth contesting, for it is not the portion of a fool's house,' quoth Bricriu. 'Belonging to it is a caldron full of generous wine, with room enough for three of the valiant braves of Ulster; furthermore, a seven-year-old boar; nought has entered its lips since it was little save fresh milk and fine meal in springtime, curds and sweet milk in summer, the kernel of nuts and wheat in autumn, beef and broth in winter; a cow-lord full seven-year-old; since it was a little calf neither heather nor twig-tops have entered its lips, nought but sweet milk and herbs, meadow hay and corn. [Add to this] fivescore cakes of wheat, cooked in honey withal. Five-and-twenty bushels, that is what was supplied for these fivescore cakes—four cakes from each bushel. Such is the champion's portion of my house. And since thou art the best hero among the men of Ulster, it is but just to give it thee, and I so wish it. By the end of the day, when the feast is spread out, let thy charioteer get up, and it is to him the champion's portion will be given.' 'Among them shall be dead men if it is not done so,' quoth Loigaire. Bricriu laughed at that, for it liked him well.

When he had done inciting Loigaire the Triumphant to enmity, Bricriu betook himself into the company of Conall the Victorious. 'Hail to thee, Conall the Victorious, thou art the hero of victories and of combats; great are the victories thou hast already scored over the heroes of Ulster. By the time the Ulster men go into foreign bounds thou art a distance of three days and three nights in advance over many a ford; thou protectest their rear when returning, so that [an assailant] may not spring past thee, nor through thee nor over thee; what then should hinder the champion's portion of Emain being thine always?' Though great his treachery with regard to Loigaire, he showed twice as much in the case of Conall the Victorious.

When he had satisfied himself with inciting Conall the Victorious to quarrel, he hied to the presence of Cuchulainn. 'Hail to thee, Cuchulainn, thou victor of Bregia (*i.e.* Bray), thou bright banner of the Liffey, darling of Emain, belov'd of wives and of maidens, for thee to-day Cuchulainn is no nick-name, for thou art the champion of the Ulster men, thou wardest off their great feuds and frays, thou seekest justice for each man of them; thou attainest alone to what all the Ulster men fail in; all the men of Ulster acknowledge thy bravery, thy valour and thine achievements surpassing theirs. What meaneth therefore thy leaving of the champion's portion for some one else of the men of Ulster, since no one of the men of Erin is capable of contesting it against thee?' 'By the god of my tribe,' quoth Cuchulainn, 'his head shall he lose whoso comes to contest it with me.' Thereafter Bricriu severed himself from them and followed the host as if no contention had been made among the heroes.

* * *

While the feast was being spread for them, the musicians and players performed. The moment Bricriu spread the feast with its savouries, he was ordered by the hostages to leave the hall. They straightway got up with drawn swords in their hands to expel him. Whereupon Bricriu and his followers went out to the balcony. Arrived at the threshold of the palace, he called out, 'That Champion's Portion, such as it is, is not the portion of a fool's house; do ye give it to the Ulster hero ye prefer for valour.' He thereupon left them.

Anon the spencers rose up to serve the food. The charioteer of Loigaire the Triumphant, to wit, Sedlang mac Riangabra, then rose up and said to the distributors: 'Do ye assign to Loigaire the Triumphant the Champion's Portion which is by you, for he alone is entitled to it before the other young braves of Ulster.' Then Id mac Riangabra, charioteer to Conall the Victorious, got up and spake to the like effect. And Loig mac Riangabra spake thus: 'Do ye bring that to Cuchulainn; it is no disgrace for all the Ulster men to give it to him; it is he who is most valiant among you.' 'That's not true,' quoth Conall the Victorious and Loigaire the Triumphant.

They then got up upon the floor and donned their shields and seized their swords. At one another they hewed till the half of the palace was an atmosphere of fire with the [clash of] sword- and spear-edge, the other half one white sheet from the enamel of the shields. Great alarm gat hold upon the palace; the valiant heroes shook; Conchobar himself and Fergus mac Róig got furious on seeing the injury and the injustice of two men surrounding one, namely, Conall the Victorious and Loigaire the Triumphant attacking Cuchulainn. There was no one among the Ultonians who dared separate them till Sencha spake to Conchobar: 'Part the men,' quoth he. [For at that period, among the Ultonians, Conchobar was a god upon earth.]

Thereupon, Conchobar and Fergus intervened, [the combatants] immediately let drop their hands to their sides. 'Execute my wish,' quoth Sencha. 'Your will shall be obeyed,' they responded. 'My wish, then,' quoth Sencha, 'is to-night to divide the Champion's Portion there among all the host, and after that to decide with reference to it according to the will of Ailill mac Mágach, for it is accounted unlucky among the men of Ulster to close this assembly unless the matter be adjudged in Cruachan.' The feasting was then resumed; they made a circle round the fire and got 'jovial' and made merry.

Bricrui, however, and his queen were in their soller. From his couch the condition of the palace was observable to him, and how things were going on withal. He exercised his mind as to how he should contrive to get the women to quarrel as he had likewise incited the men.

The Little Brawl at Almhain

This short description of a banquet is from Standish O'Grady's
translation; we leave before the brawl begins.

It was a pleasantly sonorous banquet on the greatest scale that by Finn son of Cumall son of Trenmor was convoked in Leinster's spacious Almhain: which feast being now prepared and all ready for the eating, the good men and great gentles of the Fianna came to enjoy it. Now they that apart from Finn were the noblest of these, and the most honourable, were: the mighty Goll mac Morna; Ossian son of Finn, Oscar son of Ossian; mac Lugach of the terrible hand, Dermot of the lightsome face, and Caeilte son of Ronan; the vigorous children of *Dubhdíorma*, the children of *Smól*, and *Dubhdáboirenn's* people; *Goll gulban*, the swift-footed Corr and his sons: Conn, Donn, Aedh and Anacan; Ivor son of the valorous and victorious Crimthann, and two that were sons to the king of Leinster (they both also standing to Finn in the relation of alumni), with Coirell grandson of Conbran. To the feast came likewise two that were sons to the king of Scotland, and along with them divers bold impetuous scions from among the sons of the whole world's kings and chiefest nobles.

Thither came moreover the Fianna of all Ireland; then Finn sat in the chief captain's seat at the fort's one mid-side, the mirthful Goll mac Morna at the other, and under either of them the chieftains of his own folk; after which every man of the company, according to his degree and patrimony, sat in his own appointed and befitting place, even as everywhere and at all times previous had been their use and wont.

Altogether marvellously then the servitors rose to serve and to supply the hall: they laid hold on jewelled drinking horns, studded (every flashing and elaborate goblet of them) with fair crystalline gems and wrought with cunning workmanship in shining patterns, and to those good warriors all were poured strong fermented draughts of smooth luscious liquors: then merriment waxed fast in their youths, audacity and spirit in their heroes; in their women, kindness and gentleness; in their poets, knowledge and the gift of prophecy.

Straight and promptly now a crier stood up and, for the inhibition of serfs and pilferers, rattled a coarse iron chain; a long one of antique silver he shook to check the gentles and chief nobles of the Fianna, likewise their erudite by profession, and all listened hushed in silence. Fergus Truelips, Finn's poet and the Fianna's, rose and before Finn son of Cumall sang the songs and lays and sweet poems of his ancestors and forbears. With the rarest of all rich and costly things Finn and Ossian, Oscar and mac Lughach, rewarded the bard wondrously; whereat he went on to Goll mac Morna and in front of him recited the *bruidhne* or 'Forts', the *toghla* or 'Destructions', the *tána* or 'Cattle-liftings', the *'tochmarca'* or 'Wooings', of his elders and progenitors: by operation of which artistic efforts the sons of Morna grew jovial and of good cheer.

The Description of an Irish Feast

This poem, credited as having been 'translated almost literally out of the native Irish', is by Jonathan Swift (1667–1745).

O'Rourk's noble fare
    Will ne'er be forgot,
By those who were there,
    And those who were not.
His revels to keep,
    We sup and we dine,
On seven score sheep,
    Fat bullock and swine.
Usquebaugh to our feast
    In pails was brought up,
An hundred at least,
    And a madder our cup.
O there is the sport,
    We rise with the light,

In disorderly sort,
  From snoring all night.
O how was I tricked,
  My pipe it was broke,
My pocket was picked,
  I lost my new cloak.
I'm rifled, quoth Nell,
  Of mantle and kercher,
Why then fare them well,
  The de'il take the searcher.
Come, harper, strike up,
  But first by your favour,
Boy, give us a cup;
  Ay, this has some savour:
O'Rourk's jolly boys
  Ne'er dreamt of the matter,
Till roused by the noise,
  And musical clatter,
They bounce from their nest,
  No longer will tarry,
They rise ready dressed,
  Without one *Ave Mary*.
They dance in a round,
  Cutting capers and ramping,
A mercy the ground
  Did not burst with their stamping,
The floor is all wet
  With leaps and with jumps,
While the water and sweat,
  Splishsplash in their pumps.
Bless you late and early,
  Laughlin O'Enagin,
By my hand you dance rarely,
  Margery Grinagin.
Bring straw for our bed,
  Shake it down to the feet,

Then over us spread,
    The winnowing sheet.
To show, I don't flinch,
    Fill the bowl up again,
Then give us a pinch
    Of your sneezing, a Yean.
Good Lord, what a sight,
    After all their good cheer,
For people to fight
    In the midst of their beer:
They rise from their feast,
    And hot are their brains,
A cubit at least
    The length of their skenes.
What stabs and what cuts,
    What clattering of sticks,
What strokes on the guts,
    What bastings and kicks!
With cudgels of oak,
    Well hardened in flame,
An hundred heads broke,
    An hundred struck lame.
You churl, I'll maintain
    My father built Lusk,
The castle of Slane,
    And Carrickdrumrusk:
The Earl of Kildare,
    And Moynalta, his brother,
As great as they are,
    I was nursed by their mother.
Ask that of old Madam,
    She'll tell you who's who,
As far up as Adam,
    She knows it is true,
Come down with that beam,
    If cudgels are scarce,
A blow on the wame,
    Or a kick on the arse.

O'Rourke's Feast

*This is the first verse of the poem 'literally' translated by Jonathan
Swift, and originally written by Hugh MacGauran; this is supposed
to be the only poem by another author for which Carolan composed
a tune. In fairness to Swift, his translation can be sung to that tune.*

Pléaráca na Ruarcach i gcuimhne gach uile dhuine
    Dhá dtiocfaidh is dá dtáinic is dá maireann go fóill.
Seacht bhfichid muc, mart agus caora
    Dhá gcasgairt don ghasraidh gach aon ló.
Céad páil uisge bheatha is na meadra dhá líonadh,
    Ag éirghe ar maidin is againn do bhí an spóirt.
Briseadh do phíopa-sa, sladadh mo phóca-sa,
Goideadh do bhríste-sa, loisgeadh mo chlóca-sa,
Chaill mé mo bhairéad, m'fhallaing agus m'fhiléad,
    Ó d'imthigh na gairéid ár seacht mbeannacht leó.
Cuir spraic ar a' gcláirsigh sin, seinn suas a' pléaráca sin,
    An bucsa sin, 'Áine, agus greadóg le n-ól!

Lanigan's Ball

*A celebration of the timeless mixture of dancing, drinking and
ructions.*

In the town of Athy one Jeremy Lanigan
Battered away till he hadn't a pound,
His father he died and made him a man again,
Left him a farm and ten acres of ground,
He gave a grand party to friends and relations,
Who did not forget him when come to the wall,
And if you but listen, I'll make your eyes glisten,
At the rows and the ructions of Lanigan's ball.

Myself to be sure got free invitations,
For all the nice girls and boys I might ask.
And just in a minute both friends and relations,
Were dancing as merry as bees round a cask.
Miss Judy O'Daly that nice little milliner,
Tipped me the wink for to give her a call
And soon I arrived with Peggy McGilligan,
Just in time for Lanigan's ball.

There was lashings of punch and wine for the ladies
Potatoes and cakes there was bacon and tea,
There were the Nolans, Dolans, O'Gradys
Courting the girls and dancing away
The songs they went round as plenty as water,
From the Harp that once sounded in Tara's old Hall,
To sweet Nelly Gray and the Rat-catcher's daughter,
All singing together at Lanigan's ball.

They were doing all kinds of nonsensical polkas
All round the room in a whirligig,
But Julia and I soon banished their nonsense.
And tipped them a twist of a real Irish jig.
Och mavrone, how the girls they got mad on me
And danced till you'd think the ceilings would fall,
For I spent three weeks at Brooks's Academy,
Learning steps for Lanigan's ball.

The boys were as merry the girls all hearty.
Dancing away in couples and groups
Till an accident happened young Terence Macarthy,
He put his right leg through Miss Finerty's hoops.
The creature she fainted and cried 'Meelia murther'
Called for her brothers and gathered them all
Carmody swore that he'd go no further
Till he'd have satisfaction at Lanigan's ball.

In the midst of the row Miss Kerrigan fainted
Her cheeks at the same time as red as the rose,

Some of the lads decreed she was painted,
She took a small drop too much I suppose,
Her sweetheart Ned Morgan so powerful and able
When he saw his fair colleen stretched by the wall,
He tore the left leg from under the table,
And smashed all the chaneys at Lanigan's ball.

Boys, oh boys, 'tis then there was ructions,
Myself got a lick from big Phelim McHugh,
But soon I replied to his kind introduction,
And kicked up a terrible hullabaloo.
Ould Casey the piper was near being strangled,
They squeezed up his pipes, bellows, chanters and all,
The girls in their ribbons they all got entangled,
And that put an end to Lanigan's ball.

Mick the Dalty's Ball

This was a song popular in Counties Wicklow and Wexford. 'Cash the Piper' was in fact John Cash—born in Co. Wexford in 1832—and for some fifty years he played the pipes in the south-eastern counties of Ireland.

My name is 'Cash the Piper',
    And I'm seen at race and fair;
I'm known to all the jolly souls
    From Wicklow to Kildare;
I've played at dance and wedding
    From Bray to Clonegal,
But the cream of entertainment
    Was at 'Mick the Dalty's' ball.

I received a special order
    To attend at eight o'clock;
I took the train to Rathdrum,
    Then walked to Glendalough.
The boys around the neighbourhood
    Assembled one and all,
Saying, 'You're welcome, "Cash the Piper",
    To "Mick the Dalty's" ball.'

And when I entered I beheld
    A table brimming o'er
With beef and bread and bacon,
    And stout and punch galore;
We all sat down and ate our fill,
    Like cattle in a stall,
For 'eat and drink'—it was the word
    At 'Mick the Dalty's' ball.

The feast being o'er, the cloth removed,
    I played a dashing reel,
When one young lady on the floor
    Displayed a toe and heel,
With 'Will the Dalty', 'Will the *gaum*',
    For such I must him call;
He slapped his flat foot on the floor
    At 'Mick the Dalty's' ball.

The family names were 'Jim' and 'Will',
    With 'Andy' and old 'Mick';
The guests were 'Tom' and 'Paddy', too,
    And Martin, Hugh, and 'Dick';
There was Mary, Kate, and Nancy,
    With one they did not call—
All danced before me on the floor,
    At 'Mick the Dalty's' ball.

And when the dance was over,
  The dancers all sat down;
In tumblers, tins and teacups,
  The punch went steaming round,
While rough and ready Hugh struck up,
  And sang the 'Ould Plaid Shawl',
Which brought three cheers with laughter loud
  At 'Mick the Dalty's' ball.

The longest night must have its dawn,
  The sweetest pleasures end,
The jolliest crowd must part at last,
  And home their footsteps bend,
So when loud upon our revels rang
  The cock's loud morning call,
We all shook hands and took our leave
  Of 'Mick the Dalty's' ball.

Beer and Other Drinks

The Thirsty Poet

This Irish poem by an anonymous poet is translated by David Green and Frank O'Connor. After that input of mead it is difficult to see how thirst can remain!

> Bendacht úaimm for Eithni n-ollguirm,
>   ingen Domnaill dáiles bir,
> oca n-esbius íar cúairt chathrach
>   for neim nathrach
> eire ochtair chethrar bachlach
>   sítchenn srathrach, srúaimm di mid.

* * *

A blessing from me on glorious Eithne, daughter of Domnall who casts a spear, with whom, after searching through a poisonous town, I have drunk a stream of mead that was load enough for thirty-two wry-necked haltered hauliers.

The Twin-Rivals

This excerpt from Farquhar's The Twin-Rivals *of 1702 shows a dedication to the merits of brandy.*

Enter JACK *with the brandy bottle.*
Here, boy, this glass is too big; carry it away, I'll take a sup out of the bottle.
  [*Exit* JACK.]

Ben. Would. Right, madam. And my business being very urgent—
in three words, 'tis this—

Mrs Man. Hold, sir, till I take advice of my counsel.—[*Drinks.*]
There is nothing more comfortable to a poor creature, and fitter to
revive wasting spirits, than a little plain brandy. I an't for your hot
spirits, your rosa solis, your ratafias, your orange-waters, and the like:
a moderate glass of cool Nantes is the thing.

Ben. Would. But to our business, madam.—My father is dead, and
I have a mind to inherit his estate.

Mrs Man. You put the case very well.

Ben. Would. One of two things I must choose—either to be a lord
or a beggar.

Mrs Man. Be a lord to choose:—though I have known some that
have chosen both.

Ben. Would. I have a brother that I love very well; but, since one of
us must want, I had rather he should starve than I.

Mrs Man. Upon my conscience, dear heart, you're in the right on't.

Ben. Would. Now your advice upon these heads.

Mrs Man. They be matters of weight, and I must consider.—
[*Drinks.*] Is there a will in the case?

Ben. Would. There is; which excludes me from every foot of the
estate.

Mrs Man. That's bad.—Where's your brother?

Ben. Would. He's now in Germany, in his way to England, and is
expected very soon.

Mrs Man. How soon?

Ben. Would. In a month or less.

Mrs Man. O ho! a month is a great while! our business must be
done in an hour or two. We must—[*Drinks.*] suppose your brother to
be dead; nay, he shall be actually dead—and, my lord, my humble
service t'ye!

The Beaux' Stratagem

This excerpt from Farquhar's The Beaux' Stratagem *(1707) is a delightful exposition of the connoisseur of real ale.*

Bon. Not in my life, sir. I have fed purely upon ale. I have eat my ale, drank my ale, and I always sleep upon ale.

[*Enter* TAPSTER *with a bottle and glass, and exit.*]

Now, sir, you shall see!—[*Filling it out.*] Your worship's health.— Ha! delicious, delicious! fancy it burgundy, only fancy it, and 'tis worth ten shillings a quart.

Aim. [*Drinks.*] 'Tis confounded strong!

Bon. Strong! It must be so, or how should we be strong that drink it?

Aim. And have you lived so long upon this ale, landlord?

Bon. Eight-and-fifty years, upon my credit, sir—but it killed my wife, poor woman, as the saying is.

Aim. How came that to pass?

Bon. I don't know how, sir; she would not let the ale take its natural course, sir; she was for qualifying it every now and then with a dram, as the saying is; and an honest gentleman that came this way from Ireland made her a present of a dozen bottles of usquebaugh—but the poor woman was never well after. But, howe'er, I was obliged to the gentleman, you know.

Aim. Why, was it the usquebaugh that killed her?

Bon. My Lady Bountiful said so. She, good lady, did what could be done; she cured her of three tympanies, but the fourth carried her off. But she's happy, and I'm contented, as the saying is.

The Ale Woman or Bean an Leanna

This is a fine drinking song, alleged to be of Connacht origin.

Tá bean rua ar an mbaile seo in aice na ceárta
Síor-dhéanamh lionn a reaca is ag creachadh daoine áirithe,
Dá n-ólfainn-se mo 'rapper' agus paiste den chába,
Ní bhfaighinn braon ar maidin in aisce ná ar cairde.

Is mairg a mbíonn póca air, is a thóin (do) bheith folamh
Tart ar a scóig is é triall go tigh an leanna,
Tráth shíl sí mo stór is mo lón a bheith caite
Bhí tairní sean-bhróige in mo phóca dá gcraitheadh.

D'éirigh mé ar maidin mo scraiste as an ngríosaigh
'S d'iarr mé ar bhean-an-leanna mo channa do líonadh,
'Níl braon agam ar maidin is téirigh abhaile go hoíche,
Téifidh mé ar maidin is tarraigh Dé hAoine.'

D'ólfainn is d'ólfainn is d'ólfainn do shláinte
'S dá mbeinn ar bord loinge d'ólfainn ní b'fhearr í.
Dá mbeinn-se mo bhean altraim d'oilfinn do pháiste
Chuirfinn crios ceangal air is bindealán fáiscthe.

* * *

There is a red-haired woman in this village, near the forge,
Ever-doing the selling of ale, and ruining certain people.
Though I were to drink my wrapper (in her house) and a patch off
    my cape
(Yet) I would not get a drop the (next) morning (from her) either
    gratis or on 'tick'.

It is a pity of the man who has a pocket and its bottom to be empty,
Thirst on his throat and he travelling to the ale-house

When she thought that my wealth and provision were spent
I had the nails of an old brogue musically rattling in my pocket (to
    deceive her).

I rose up in the morning a miserable-creature out of the embers,
And I asked the ale-woman to fill my can.
'I haven't a drop this morning and go home till night,
I'll heat (brew) in the morning and do you come on Friday.'

I would drink, I would drink, and I would drink your health,
And if I were aboard a ship I would drink it better.
If I were my (*i.e.*, a) nurse I would rear you a child,
I would put a binding-girdle on him and a squeezing-wrapper.

Burns in Ulster

This extract from a story in Lynn C. Doyle's An Ulster Childhood,
*originally published in 1921, relates the poetry of Burns to both
Bacchanalian behaviour and subsequent remorse. Doyle died in 1961.*

The Bacchanalian poems of Burns, however, appealed to him
strongly. Though Paddy could not fairly be called a heavy drinker it
must be admitted that in the matter of porter he was prone to
occasional steppings aside; and thirsty, mellow, or repentant, his
mood was reflected in our readings. When the convivial element
began to predominate I knew that Paddy would shortly go on the
spree; and I knew, too, that when the spree was over we would read
largely in Rabbie's penitential psalms. Paddy used them as a kind of
moral soda-water just as the hapless author must have done. But,
however effective they proved as a cure, as a preventative they failed
utterly, and at last after an unusually heavy spree Paddy betook
himself to 'the clergy' and solemnly renounced drink. He did not
renounce Burns though; and it was with misgiving that I enjoyed his
spirited delivery of 'John Barleycorn', some months later. I was

justified by the event; for Paddy having occasion to go to the fair of C____ allowed himself to be persuaded by some casuist that lager beer was within the limits of his pledge, and was found that evening by a ganger of the local railway peacefully sleeping in the track of an oncoming train. I think at first he felt himself ill-used in this affair; for I remember that he subsequently recited the stanzas ending:

> But if I must afflicted be
> To suit some wise design,
> Then man my soul with firm resolves
> To bear and not repine

as one rather bowing beneath the visitation of Providence than suffering from his own errors; but his remorse did not endure long; for a few nights after he read me 'Scotch Drink' with a good deal of gusto, remarking cheerfully at the close that 'Rabbie was no reading for a Temperance man'; and so far as I know he never renewed his pledge.

Cocktails

This extract is taken from As I Was Going Down Sackville Street *by Oliver St John Gogarty, published in 1937.*

What more could I do? But I was all the more interested in watching McLoren.

'I want you to meet Mrs Kelner, Miss Babette Vyse, Kelner. And now we will go in and have lunch at last…Hold on: I was told to ask you if you'd care for a cocktail.'

The mixed drink of a mixed race and yet more characteristic than the drink of any other nation save, perhaps, absinthe or the vodka of the Russians and the butter tea of Thibet…And yet how preferable to any of these!…

'Yes, a cocktail.'

'What kind?'

'Oh, the yellow one with lemon juice in it...it has a faintly green look. I used to get it in New York.'

'You have been in New York?'

'Yes. And what surprises me is that I am able to answer that embracing question which someone is sure to ask: What do you think of New York?'

Irony, however slight, is either not understood or misunderstood and the subject of suspicion to an American.

'I was going to ask that very question,' said Mrs Kelner. 'Well, what do you think of it?'

'Seen from the air, or from over the Hudson in the evening purple, it is by far the loveliest city I have beheld. It rises like fabulous Troy...there is no city in the world to compare with it...It is greater than Troy not only in its buildings, but also in the beauty of its Helens. The most characteristic thing in America, mechanical America, is that it can make poetry out of material things. America's poetry is not in literature, but in architecture. But one must have seen the sun from the East River on the dark, silvery pinnacle of the Singer Building, to believe it. I lived with a friend for weeks in Number Two Beekman Place, and I saw, through the clear winter morning, that marvellous sight. Like newly-cut lead the pointed roof shone...The sight was as new to me as my first sight of the slender pillar of a mosque...'

'Where did you see a mosque?'

'When I went to Crete...the pillar stood out against a calm, apple-green sky. It was unusual, and full of alien romance to me.'

'Yes. It is refreshing to get away from our traditions for a while...They are apt to be overwhelming if they are not interrupted occasionally. Getting away from them accounts for the popularity of touring, and that itself is a new development of the last twenty years.'

'Do you think that explains why Germany went off Christianity this year?'

'I don't get you.'

'To assist her tourist traffic. I can imagine hundreds of clergymen rushing there in mufti.'

The way a waiter sticks up conversation with a dish is most annoying. That is one reason why I hate food. It interrupts good talk, and just as I was making an impression (whether favourable or not does not matter), or just as I thought I was doing well with my 'reactions' to architecture, the waiter hisses, 'Sauce tartare?' I must have shown my temper on my face...Is it any wonder I prefer drink to food? It promotes, or at least does not hinder, conversation. And it limits the waiters' chances of asking questions. A man can give an order. The initiative is with him. He is not at the mercy of a man who has to fill him up with comestibles within a limited time.

When he had smeared my plate and departed, I said: 'Sorry I interrupted you,' to one of the ladies. It was I who had been interrupted, but in the pause it occurred to me that I was probably talking too much and taking advantage of other people's weakness for food.

'We were talking about the wine list.'

Splendid!

'It would be an awful thing if the ancient drinks were forgotten during the tyranny of the chocolate-makers, Quakers, or whoever they were who dried a great nation. Gin is the enemy of good drink. I suppose no American can remember what good claret tasted like. To whom would he go to recover the lost information? If there was one good drinker left in London, and if he were endowed by the American Senate to come over and to preach on the merits of Château Latour, that would not help: you cannot tell people about taste, any more than you can explain light to the blind. Now, before you forget its flavour, drink thoroughly of some red or amber wine.'

McLoren said, 'I prefer a whiskey-and-soda.'

That is one of Dublin's famous inventions—soda. It was invented in Sackville Street. The well is under Nelson's Pillar. It is a temperance drink, but it is fated to be associated with whiskey until the end of time. A perfect proof that not only is there a Providence, but that Providence disapproves of teetotallers.

'Large or small?' interrupted the waiter.

I had a dear old friend who detested that disastrous question. He often rebuked the fool who asked it, with, 'There is no such thing as a *large* whiskey.' He could always imagine and drink a larger one; but a small whiskey did exist, to the detriment of all good drinkers...

'What are you drinking?'

'Oh, something from the Valley of the Moselle. It is one of the loveliest valleys of the world. I always think of that quotation from Claudian when I drink Moselle:

'Immemorial vines embower the white houses,
The earth yields to the labour of the slaves;
The incense rises from the temples where the distant Emperor is honoured:
Fortune is seldom invoked, for men desire no change.'

That shows that there was at least one period in the world's history when people knew they were well off.

St Patrick and Lager Beer

This is a portion of a story by Lynn C. Doyle from his A Bowl of Broth *of 1945.*

But there was one provision in the pledge which puzzled Anne a good deal, and made her uneasy. Father B____, as became his office, had been more merciful than I, and had allowed Paddy liberty to drink lager beer. He was not acquainted with the properties of this beverage himself; nor was Paddy, at first hand. But a friend of large experience in liquors had told Paddy that it was as good as teetotal, that a man could consume a hogshead of it and still walk a single rail, and that, so far as he was concerned he would near as soon drink water; and Father B____ hearkened to this expert. I put it to Anne that Father B____ must be supposed to know more than either of us (though privately I am afraid I smelt Catholic laxity) and Anne agreed. Nevertheless, she told me, she would be easier in her mind when the first set-day was over.

St Patrick's Day was the next public holiday; and Paddy, according to his custom, put on his Sunday clothes and set out for the town of C____. He did not take formal farewell of Anne, but as he left the farmyard he waved his hand toward the kitchen-door of the dwelling-house, as if he expected Anne to be there, which indeed she was, with myself peering under her arm. She told me Paddy was coming home by the short-cut along the railway-line, and that she was to meet him at the level-crossing at seven o'clock. Then she asked me would I please walk in the direction of the crossing gates a little after seven. If I saw Paddy and her walking together, and she did not wave her handkerchief, I was to keep away, and let on I didn't see them; but if she waved her handkerchief I was to come over, and stick to them till they came back to the yard. I was a little surprised, because, not long before, Anne had told me with some hesitation that perhaps it would be just as well if I didn't always accompany her when she was going to meet Paddy. Then I became aware that Anne, like myself, thought Paddy (who had been altogether abstemious since Christmas) might try his new drink for the first time that day; and that, in spite of the sanction of the church, she still felt a little uneasy about how the experiment might turn out.

Though we said nothing to each other at the time, Anne and I found the day very long. At a quarter to seven Anne set out along the field-path to the crossing; and ten minutes later I followed. As I turned the last corner and came in sight of the crossing gates here was Anne running toward me along the field path at top speed, and sobbing as she ran.

'Oh, Master L____,' she cried, 'Paddy has got drunk on that queer stuff and is lying snoring on the lines, and won't budge; and the up train is due at a quarter past. Come quick; for he'll listen to *you*.'

But when I went, Paddy would not listen to me, or to anyone else. I don't believe he would have listened to Father B____, or to any other dignitary of the church except the Supreme Pontiff, for whom as an Ulster Catholic he was at all times, but notably in his cups, a potential martyr. Paddy was lying on his back between the rails of the up line. His bran-new overcoat lay beside his head, roughly folded; and he had taken off his boots. He was very red in the face and snoring heavily. Two empty black bottles lay near him. Their contents must have consummated his ruin. And, as Anne had said, he wouldn't budge. Certainly not for me, though I shook him with all my childish might, and holloed in his ear. I don't think he knew me; and I am certain he didn't know Anne, or he would have yielded to her entreaties. But all he would do was to snarl incoherently but angrily, though still keeping his eyes shut.

Mixed Drinks

This cunningly conceived poem is from Lough Derg and Other
Poems *(1946) by Denis Devlin.*

The whiskey's prurience through the inner pipes.
This is the change and leaving of thy name.

If the fungus of drunken breathing
Mist feels at the mirrors
Like doubt turning to anger
In the judge's face.

Blond beer cylinders weave
The waitresses' trays ripple over our heads.
I am alone but the others are with me
Tasting the same food, drink and sleep
After the day of ambush
When anguish made the soul efficient
With bell, book and candle,
When the lie startled like stoats into hiding
In the eyes of butcher, baker and banker,
When death put up a showy magazine front
For officer and ranker.

It is a kind of dream-desecration
Of the most beautiful forms man has imagined:
Yet you feel less defiled than when you see
The uncompetitive horror in the eyes
Of a dying man
A little before death.

A shabby-nosed old drunk
Limns with one loyal, black-gloved hand
The motions of a baton, orchestrating
Out of the oxen heart
The world, the flesh and the devil,
The dare of the trumpets, ivied erosion of theme,
Violin-shell children.

Ether-drinking

The custom of drinking ether was virtually confined to Ulster and particularly to Counties Derry and Tyrone. Kenneth Connell made a study of it which appeared in his Irish Peasant Society *which was published in 1968. The excerpts given below are culled from this study.*

Here—if reports can be trusted—in a thousand square miles almost every house had its ether bottle; some 50,000 people, an eighth of the local population, were 'etheromaniacs'. With the occasional tipplers, they annually consumed some 17,000 gallons: to Cookstown alone the railway brought two tons a year. Some local shebeens sold nothing but ether; in others, bottles of whiskey and ether stood side by side. The atmosphere of Cookstown and Moneymore was 'loaded' with ether; hundreds of yards outside Draperstown a visiting surgeon detected the familiar smell; market days smelt 'not of pigs, tobacco smoke or of unwashed human beings'; even the bank 'stoved' of ether, and its reek on the Derry Central Railway was 'disgusting and abominable'. 'Enter the humblest cabin and you will see decrepit, white-haired men, tottering and feeble, inane as far as brain power is concerned, who have become the miserable wrecks they are— helpless to themselves and loathsome and disgusting to others— through the long-continued use of ether.' 'What guarantee is there against ether drinking spreading the length and breadth of the land and clouding the spirit and sapping the physique of the finest peasantry in the world?' 'What is the case of Ireland today', *The Times* warned, 'may become that of England or Scotland tomorrow.'

* * *

Ether, volatilising at body temperature, tends to escape as gas on contact with mouth and stomach; and, irritating the stomach, it is liable to be ejected by vomiting. But a ritual was evolved enabling the drinker to retain enough of so elusive a beverage to experience its gratifying effects: after 'renching his gums' (washing his mouth with cold water), he drank a little water, then, quickly, holding his nose, swallowed his ether, following it with more water. The mouthfuls of water, before and after the ether, lessened its burning effect; with nose-holding, they made vomiting less likely; but mainly, no doubt, they delayed volatilisation by cooling the mouth and stomach.

The inebriating dose naturally varied with the drinker's constitution and experience. Girls in their early twenties might take a teaspoonful, grown women a little more, men a tablespoonful; a dessertspoonful and 'the full of an egg-cup' were normal doses, the 'range of potation' from half a fluid ounce to the three ounces held by a full-sized wine glass. Every drinker might repeat his dose several times a day. The seasoned toper on each occasion needed a second, even a third, glassful. He might, indeed, take half a pint with no alarming effect; withstand a pint in the heroic debauch, or a steady ten ounces day after day. He scorned, too, the ordinary man's ritual, simply gulping and relishing his ether, increasing his dose to offset the greater loss of gas from his uncooled stomach.

To the novice ether offered no immediate pleasure of palate or stomach. Self-experimenters had difficulty in swallowing it at all: 'the eyes water, the mouth closes on it, and there is an absolute kind of revulsion to the whole thing which seems to shut it out.' The taste was 'highly provocative of vomiting'; so, too, was the contraction of the walls of the stomach as ether irritated the lining. If the ether were retained, its volatilisation was accompanied by 'violent eructations', by 'great dissipation of wind', and by a sensation in the stomach variously likened to warmth or burning, to 'a ball of ice', or 'the feeling you have when you grasp a piece of lead'.

In a few minutes, given an appropriate dose, the drinker's pulse quickened, his face flushed, a wave of perhaps hysterical excitement yielded to a calmer mood, and 'he dreamed himself into his personal paradise'. He was in fairyland. Cares vanished in 'blithesome gladness'; his pulse beat with joy, his eye glistened with love. French initiates likened their state to Champagne drunkenness: they were in paradise, listening to delicious music as they danced at the ball and walked on the clouds. In Ireland, too, 'you always heard music, and you'd be cocking your ears at it…Others would see men climbing up the walls and going through the roof, or coming in through the roof and down the walls, nice and easy.' The erotic appeal of ether was stressed more by Continental than by Irish observers. Elsewhere, men, hoping for 'strange voluptuousness', were rewarded by visions of 'lascivious situations' and 'beautiful women'; but in Ireland (where ether-inebriation was a regional more than a personal problem) the drinkers' dreams were said to be 'light' and 'refined'.

In folklore, if not in physiology, the agreeable effects of one day's ether might be recaptured the next, simply by drinking a glass of water. But the ether-drinker's 'luxurious advantage' was that, half-a-dozen times a day, he might pass through 'the drama of intoxication'. Within the hour—in twenty minutes, some said—he might be sober, helplessly drunk, and sober again. Recovering, he was a little depressed, needing a repetition of his pleasurable experience, and denied it by none of the spirit-drinker's headache or vomiting.

* * *

To the critic, the pleasure of drinking ether was ephemeral—pleasurable, indeed, only to the taste it warped; its cost grotesquely great, damaging the drinker's body and mind, threatening his life, imperilling society and posterity. Blindness and digestive troubles were laid at its door, and a 'low brooding melancholy', nervous prostration, sleeplessness, insanity itself. Young girls had to be restrained from harming themselves; adult drinkers, 'made free of their minds', shone their teeth, and laughed hysterically; they shouted, danced, acted like maniacs; suffered, even, convulsions like an epileptic, falling down, writhing and foaming at the mouth. 'The poisonous influence of the destroying agent was shown by an antedated shrivelling up of the living frame': one 'etheromaniac' in his early forties was already 'a wizened, beat, decrepit and tottering old man; a battered and lonely hulk cast up on the shores of existence—a hopeless and despairing human wreck'.

These bodily 'evils' of ether-drinking recall the teetotaller's 'evils of alcohol': some thought that, as the brutish pleasure was similar, so too must be the cost; and others, fearing the cumulative effects of the new drink, invented or inflated evils to diminish its appeal. The criticisms are not easily disproved: relatively few people drank ether;

they did it, for the most part, when medical research was uncertain, where systematic observation was difficult; and the fact that the heavy drinker commonly had long experience of alcohol made the effects of ether harder to isolate. Significantly, however, medical observers were mostly the milder critics. That the ether-drinker was peculiarly prone to digestive troubles doctors generally conceded; but, one suggested, only the 'hardened toper' suffered acutely, and so long only as he clung to his indulgence. As to ills more grave or lasting, Richardson readily attributed gout, fatty degeneration, paralysis, and cirrhosis to alcohol, but none—nor other organic trouble—simply to ether; nor, in his observation, was it a cause of blindness. 'The aythur is putting the people asthray, an' desthroyin' their heads': clergy and journalists certainly accepted the popular view; so, too, did the odd doctor. Richardson, however, was sceptical, and his doubts were confirmed by physicians from Derry and Tyrone asylums who, though treating patients who took ether, in no case attributed their troubles to its agency. Indeed, mental imbalance in the inveterate ether-drinker was plausibly said to precede rather than follow his addiction. Whether ether, when drunk, was strictly a drug of addiction, was a matter medical observers disputed: most, according to a French inebriologist, felt it was not; but to some, 'addiction was its greatest danger'; the taste for ether was speedily acquired, 'and when acquired the craving was as strong as ever it could be for alcohol'.

* * *

Ether-drinking, though less harmful physically and mentally than the alarmists alleged, was not without risk—the risk, when a man was stupefied by ether, of his freezing by the wayside; of his dying from starvation when it too long lulled his hunger; of his being suffocated asleep by the fumes from a broken bottle. It was the more menacing in that the margin between an intoxicating and a fatal dose was uncomfortably small, and in the hurry of so disagreeable a dosing, the odd drop might 'go the wrong way', causing spasm, obstruction and suffocation. Even going the right way, the ether 'would kill or bust you if you didn't rift'—explosive volatilisation, too slowly released, might fatally constrict the heart. But the greatest peril was of fire:

mixed with air, ether vapour is highly explosive; creeping along the floor, it ignites on contact with flame or fire. The drinker, consequently, must choose the direction of his explosive eructation: 'it wouldn't do to rift into the fire…or the flames would travel down your throat.' He must mingle with care the pleasures of ether and tobacco: a farmer at Bellaghy, lighting his pipe, ignited his breath: 'I knew a man that was always dhrinkin' it, and won day after a dose uv it, he wint to light his pipe and the fire cot his breath, and tuk fire inside, and only for a man that was carryin' in a jug of wather wud some whiskey to the kitchen, he'd a lost his life. He just held him down at wanst, as quick as he could, and poured down the wather down his throat.'

Observers of ether-drinking—even leaders of the campaign against it—blamed it for little social evil. The drinker's craving, and the vendor's ready acceptance of stolen goods, led to petty thieving, to husbands returning from work to find meal and potatoes traded for ether. Some dwelt on the power ether gave 'designing, unscrupulous persons for immoral purposes'. Regular Sunday sessions of Cookstown drinkers were the scene of 'great' (but unspecified) demoralisation. Occasionally, ether roused the desire to fight: the odd blow might be exchanged; but the drinker was sober again, or senseless, before he could do much harm. So transient, indeed, was the effect of ether, that, however boisterous the drinker, the constable was loath to arrest him lest he should be sober before being charged.

Confessions of an Irish Ether-drinker

It is appropriate that this poem should be by a Northern poet, since the habit of drinking ether was virtually confined to the North. It is from Michael Longley's 1973 publication, An Exploded View.

It freezes the puddles,
Films the tongue, its brief lozenge
Lesions of spittle and bile,
Dispersals of weather—

Icicles, bones in the ditch,
The blue sky splintering,
Water's fontanel
Closed like an eyelid.

II

My dialect becomes
Compactings of sea sounds,
The quietest drifts,
Each snowed-under
Cul-de-sac of the brain—
Glaucoma, pins and needles,
Fur on the tongue:

Or the hidden scythe
Probing farther than pain,
Its light buried in my ear,
The seed potatoes
Filling with blood—
Nuggets of darkness,
Silence's ovaries.

Sloe Gin

Seamus Heaney has a renowned talent for extracting the essence of rurality from practically anything. This poem from his 1984 collection Station Island *does it with consummate ease, reminding us that sloes are, indeed, the essence of rurality.*

The clear weather of juniper
darkened into winter.
She fed gin to sloes
and sealed the glass container.

When I unscrewed it
I smelled the disturbed
tart stillness of a bush
rising through the pantry.

When I poured it
it had a cutting edge
and flamed
like Betelgeuse.

I drink to you
in smoke-mirled, blue-black,
polished sloes, bitter
and dependable.

Bulmer

This poem from Bernard O'Donoghue's Poaching Rights *of 1987 is more than just a poem in praise of cider (or woodpeckers).*

How do you know but every bird
That beats the gladsome air
Is an immense world of delight,
Closed by your senses five?

Into Tesco's with me, eight a.m.,
And, cider bottle under my oxter,
Out with a light step, fearing no one.

Sitting on the bridge, I watch them
Haring by, buses, briefcases,
God knows what. You'd be sorry

For the poor misfortunes, with their work
And their temper, but what can you do?
They'd only think they knew better.

One day I saw a woodpecker
Above in the tree: as clear
As I see you now, and as green

As the one on the bottle. I called
In a whisper to this fellow going by,
But he dodged around me, and nearly

Hit the wall. 'You'd only drink it',
He said. Leave him at it. Green
As deep as the kingfisher's blue.

Once I sat for hours, talking
To a little foxy girl, a student
In a duffle coat. There was nothing

She didn't know about birds.
Spring again now, and the sun
Is warm enough to dry the green

Of winter off the bark. I thought
I'd head for London to see
What they make of things down there.

Confused or Embarrassing Drinking

She Stoops to Conquer

This excerpt from Goldsmith's She Stoops to Conquer *of 1773 is typical of the confusion created by Tony Lumpkin's trick of pretending to Hastings and Young Marlow that his stepfather's house is an inn; Hardcastle, who is an old friend of Young Marlow's father, is rather surprised to find his house being used as if it were an inn.*

Enter HARDCASTLE.

Hard. I no longer know my own house. It's turned all topsy-turvy. His servants have got drunk already. I'll bear it no longer, and yet, from my respect for his father, I'll be calm. (*To him.*) Mr Marlow, your servant. I'm your very humble servant. (*Bowing low.*)

Mar. Sir, your humble servant. (*Aside.*) What's to be the wonder now?

Hard. I believe, sir, you must be sensible, sir, that no man alive ought to be more welcome than your father's son, sir. I hope you think so?

Mar. I do, from my soul, sir. I don't want much entreaty. I generally make my father's son welcome wherever he goes.

Hard. I believe you do, from my soul, sir. But though I say nothing of your own conduct, that of your servants is insufferable. Their manner of drinking is setting a very bad example in this house, I assure you.

Mar. I protest, my very good sir, that is no fault of mine. If they don't drink as they ought, they are to blame. I ordered them not to spare the cellar. I did, I assure you. (*To the side-scene.*) Here, let one of my servants come up. (*To him.*) My positive directions were, that as

I did not drink myself, they should make up for my deficiencies below.

Hard. Then they had your orders for what they do? I'm satisfied!

Mar. They had, I assure you. You shall hear from one of themselves.

Enter SERVANT, *drunk.*

Mar. You, Jeremy! come forward, sirrah! What were my orders? Were you not told to drink freely, and call for what you thought fit, for the good of the house?

Hard. (*Aside.*) I begin to lose my patience.

Jeremy. Please your honour, liberty and Fleet Street for ever! Though I'm but a servant, I'm as good as another man. I'll drink for no man before supper, sir, d____ me! Good liquor will sit upon a good supper, but a good supper will not sit upon—hiccup—upon my conscience, sir.

Mar. You see, my old friend, the fellow is as drunk as he can possibly be. I don't know what you'd have more, unless you'd have the poor devil soused in a beer-barrel.

Hard. Zounds! he'll drive me distracted, if I contain myself any longer. Mr Marlow, sir, I have submitted to your insolence for more than four hours, and I see no likelihood of its coming to an end. I'm now resolved to be master here, sir, and I desire that you and your drunken pack may leave my house directly.

Mar. Leave your house!—Sure you jest, my good friend! What! when I'm doing what I can to please you!

Hard. I tell you, sir, you don't please me; so I desire you'll leave my house.

Mar. Sure you cannot be serious? at this time of night, and such a night? You only mean to banter me.

Hard. I tell you, sir, I'm serious! and now that my passions are roused, I say this house is mine, sir; this house is mine, and I command you to leave it directly.

Mar. Ha! ha! ha! A puddle in a storm. I shan't stir a step, I assure you. (*In a serious tone.*) This your house, fellow! It's my house. This is my house. Mine while I choose to stay. What right have you to bid me leave this house, sir? I never met with such impudence, curse me; never in my whole life before.

Hard. Nor I, confound me if ever I did. To come to my house, to call for what he likes, to turn me out of my own chair, to insult the family, to order his servants to get drunk, and then to tell me, 'This house is mine, sir.' By all that's impudent it makes me laugh. Ha! ha! ha! Pray, sir (*bantering*), as you take the house, what think you of taking the rest of the furniture? There's a pair of silver candlesticks, and there's a fire-screen, and here's a pair of brazen-nosed bellows; perhaps you may take a fancy to them.

Mar. Bring me your bill, sir; bring me your bill, and let's make no more words about it.

Hard. There are a set of prints, too. What think you of the 'Rake's Progress' for your own apartment?

Mar. Bring me your bill, I say; and I'll leave you and your infernal house directly.

Hard. Then there's a mahogany table that you may see your own face in.

Mar. My bill, I say.

Hard. I had forgot the great chair for your own particular slumbers, after a hearty meal.

Mar. Zounds! bring me my bill, I say, and let's hear no more on't.

Hard. Young man, young man, from your father's letter to me, I was taught to expect a well-bred modest man as a visitor here, but now I find him no better than a coxcomb and a bully; but he will be down here presently, and shall hear more of it. [*Exit.*]

Mar. How's this? Sure I have not mistaken the house. Everything looks like an inn; the servants cry 'Coming'; the attendance is awkward; the barmaid, too, to attend us. But she's here, and will further inform me. Whither so fast, child? A word with you.

Drinking in the Wardrobe

This brief description of teenage drinking is from The Pineapple Tart *(1992) by Anne Dunlop.*

There was one day when we were fourteen and fifteen when she decided she wanted to be drunk, and invited me along to drink a bottle of brandy with her. She sold her book-token—a Sunday school prize—to buy the bottle. She had got the top prize for memorising Isaiah 53. The book-token was valuable because we didn't get pocket money—bad for children, my parents said.

We started drinking in the attic wardrobe after Saturday lunch because Laura felt we needed the entire afternoon: we might get 'overhangs' and we had to have recovered before dinner. I can't say I appreciated the burn as I swallowed the first mouthful but once started we didn't stop. Gordons don't start a thing and then give up. The brandy warmed all my organs, in fact I was sure my toes were curling in the heat. Laura said she could feel her fingernails growing. A few more mouthfuls and suddenly there were two Lauras. Everything she said caused me to collapse in helpless giggles. I felt as if I had a huge bubble inside my head and I was so light I could float. Laura was swimming breast stroke along the dusty floor and I was barking like a dog when mummy caught us.

Laura promptly stopped swimming, sat bolt upright and vomited rings round her. There seemed to be carrots everywhere, and I was sure we had no carrots for lunch. In the deadly silence that followed I hiccuped really loudly but nobody laughed. We were dosed with a pint glass each of Andrews Liver Salts.

'Drink it when it's fizzing,' mummy said. 'It's no good unless it's fizzing.'

We were put to bed to await our hangovers and our punishment when daddy came in for tea and I lay quaking in case he would shout at me. The drunkenness had worn off and a blinding headache had begun.

The Red Telephone

This extract from The Red Telephone *by Kathleen O'Connor, published in 1993, describes the mysterious temporary disappearance of Peggy O'Grady and her subsequent embarrassing discovery by the Sergeant, whose son has just married her daughter Grainne.*

'We had better ring Dad,' she suggested, picking up the phone. Hugh knew immediately that there was something wrong, when he heard Alana's voice.

'Mum is missing.'

The words hit him like a ton of bricks. He got the biggest shock of his life. 'Missing! What do you mean?'

'Well, she didn't come home from Mass this morning.'

This wasn't at all like his wife. She loved her home, and she was always there. 'Have you searched everywhere?'

'Yes, and there's not trace nor tidings of her.'

'That's extraordinary. Did you ring the Guards?' The very thought of it made him shudder.

'No, we were waiting and hoping she would come every minute.'

'Ring them straight away. I'll be home in about an hour.' His mind was in a state of turmoil. Something must have upset her, but he couldn't figure out what it could be. She had been through a lot, but she always stood her ground, and she was great to bounce back.

As Peggy was walking into the church that morning, Madge Murphy tapped her on the shoulder.

'Did you see the paper?' Her face was flushed with excitement.

'No, not yet, I'll get it on my way home.'

'Look at this.' She held up the photograph of Grainne and Eoin, and the big write-up about them. Peggy was elated as she flicked quickly through the report. It was perfect, absolutely to her liking.

'Eoin, only son of Sergeant and Mrs O'Dowd, and Grainne, nee O'Grady, of the well-respected family in Glenbeg, well known among the legal profession being secretary to the State Solicitor. The happy couple left from Shannon to honeymoon in New York.'

That was the bit she was waiting for, and she was delighted that they had put it in.

She hardly said a prayer at Mass, thinking about what she had just read. The well-respected family, that sounded well, and of course the reference to Grainne's involvement with the legal profession. She was a bit sorry that they didn't mention Hugh, the great athlete who won a gold medal for running. He would have been thrilled with that. Still it was wonderful, and she couldn't wait to get home and read it in every detail.

She always sat at the end of the church, about four seats from the door, with Kate Moloney and Mamie Cremin. Madge Murphy and Molly Hegarty preferred to go up a bit nearer the altar, but this morning as soon as Mass was over, they all gathered together in one seat, and Peggy was the centre of attraction. The little meeting was in full swing when Father Seamus approached them, looking none too pleased.

'This is the house of God, ladies, and not the place for gossiping.'

They scattered immediately.

'I think we should go somewhere and celebrate,' Mamie Cremin suggested as soon as they were outside the door.

'A very good idea.' Kate Moloney was in no humour for going home. This chin-wag was much more entertaining than a bit of dirty washing.

Madge Murphy was a bit reluctant. 'I have a lot of work to do, and—'

Molly Hegarty interrupted her abruptly. 'Yerra, for God's sake, Madge, the house will be after you. Sure, there's not a speck of dirt in it. Don't be such a spoil-sport.'

'Where will we go?' Peggy was anxious to prolong the conversation.

'We'll go to Paudie Flynn's,' Molly replied. 'The little room that used to be the snug is fine and cosy, and very private too. Sure, nobody will be a bit the wiser.'

Peggy wasn't very happy with that. 'I don't go into pubs,' she protested, but they persuaded her to come along.

'It's only once in a lifetime that Glenbeg gets into the news,' Kate Moloney said, 'and we may as well make the most of it.'

Paudie Flynn's eyes almost popped out of his head when he saw the five women walking in.

'What's this all about?' he asked. 'Did one of you win the sweep or something?'

'We're celebrating this.' Mamie Cremin showed him the paper.

'Oh begor, you must be the proud mother.' He shook Peggy's hand. 'Your daughter did well for herself, all right.'

Peggy was slightly indignant. 'And her husband did very well for himself too.'

Paudie realised he had put his two big feet in it and tried to redeem himself. 'Sure, she's the catch of the season, and I'm going to give you all a drink on the house. What will it be?'

'A glass of orange for me,' Peggy replied, and the others rose up in revolt.

'Ah, come on! You can't let the side down. You'll have something stronger.'

'No, I had a few drops of sherry at the wedding, and I'm not right since.'

'This will cure you.' Paudie put a large glass of port in front of her. 'Did you ever hear tell of the hair of the dog that bit you?'

The drinks were coming one after another, the conversation was pleasant and stimulating, and nobody took any notice of the clock.

'Times are changing aren't they? Imagine going to America on your honeymoon. It's like something you'd read about.' Kate Moloney couldn't get over it at all.

Madge Murphy thought it was a waste of money. She would much prefer to buy nice things for the house. Peggy was quick to enlighten her.

'Eoin and Grainne have a beautiful new house at Blossom Grove Heights with the very best of everything in it. They even have a washing machine.'

Mamie Cremin wasn't very impressed. 'I wouldn't have one of them things in me way. There's nothing like the oul wash board.'

'Where did you go on your honeymoon, Mamie?' Peggy asked her.

'I went to Killarney for the weekend and we stayed in a caravan that belonged to Frankie's uncle. I'll never forget it to me dying day. Everywhere I looked there were spiders, real big ones, and I was petrified. I thought I'd never get me two legs out of it.'

'You did better than I did,' Madge Murphy said. 'Jack and meself took the train to Youghal for the day, and we had a picnic on the beach. He brought a flask of porter for himself, and he was as drunk as a skunk going into the merries after. Me heart was up in me mouth with him in the bumpers. He crashed into every car in sight, and I came out with a split lip. People thought he gave me a beating. They weren't far out, God knows. Tis many a time I got a black eye from him after that.'

She noticed the surprise on all the faces. 'Me tongue is getting loose now from the whiskey and all me secrets are coming out.'

'Don't worry about that,' Molly Hegarty said. 'You're among friends, and sure, there's nobody perfect. Look at me with two husbands planted, and I never had a honeymoon at all. Vincent took me to Blarney for a day, and we went for a spin in a side car. Dan and meself spent a few days in his friend's house in Cork. He took me to the pictures in the Assembly Rooms one night, and we had milk and cakes after in Kelly's Kitchen.'

'What about Eric and yourself? Where will ye go?' Mamie Cremin asked.

'We won't be going anywhere for the moment anyway. I couldn't leave poor Rosie's kids. Eric said he'll throw a big party for them instead.'

'Well, I'm one up on all of ye,' Kate Moloney boasted, 'because believe it or not, I went abroad,' and she laughed heartily as she continued. 'Dinny took me with him on one of his trips to Fishguard, and we dined in style at the captain's table. I never tasted anything like the food before or since, but sure the seagulls got it after, because it was a very rough crossing and I spent an hour on deck throwing up.'

Peggy hadn't much to boast about her honeymoon.

'I was lucky to be married at all,' she said, 'not to mention a honeymoon. Will I ever forget it? It was surely the worst day of my life.'

'Ah, but we had a great hooley after in Number Nine,' Madge Murphy added. 'With John Joe Murphy playing the melodeon and all of us dancing around the kitchen. God rest poor Neil O'Grady's soul, but there was no one like him. He made sure that we all had plenty to eat and drink. You wouldn't get craic like that in New York.'

They continued to talk on and on, reminiscing about the good old days, and they hadn't a care in the world. They didn't hear the front door opening, nor did they notice the Sergeant coming in.

'Good day to you, Paudie,' he said.

'Hello, Sergeant O'Dowd. What brings you in here in uniform?'

'I'm looking for a little group of ladies, in particular Peggy O'Grady. I believe they're here.'

Paudie pointed to the little door on the left of the counter, puzzled.

'You'll find them in there, Sergeant. There's nothing wrong, I hope.'

'Not a bit in the world, but don't say a word for a while,' the Sergeant whispered. 'Can I use your phone?'

'To be sure. It's over there on the wall.'

Hugh answered and the girls were all standing behind him.

'Hello!'

'I have good news for you, Hugh. We have located the good woman, and she's alive and well.'

He breathed a sigh of relief. 'Thank God and His Blessed Mother! Where did you find her?'

'You'll never guess.'

'I won't even try. Tell me.'

'Down at Paudie Flynn's, with four other neighbours.'

Hugh couldn't understand for the life of him what she was doing there. Didn't she hate the sight of pubs?

'What brought them in there?' he asked.

'From what I can gather, there was a little celebration to mark the photograph of Eoin and Grainne which appeared in this morning's paper. Did you read it?'

'No, she usually brings the newspaper herself.'

'Ah well, the poor woman didn't do anything out of the way. I know you all got a bit of a fright, but all is well that ends well. I'll bring her home right away.'

Peggy couldn't believe her eyes when she saw Sergeant O'Dowd walking into the little room. Imagine Grainne's father-in-law catching her in a pub drinking.

'Good afternoon, ladies. I see you're enjoying yourselves.'

They lost the use of their tongues and suddenly they just looked in amazement from one to another, and back to the Sergeant. Peggy finally recovered sufficiently to speak.

'I hope you haven't got the wrong impression of me, Sergeant O'Dowd. I'm not a drinking woman at all. Would you believe I was never in a pub before? It was just that my neighbours insisted that I join them, and I didn't like to refuse.'

He was smiling to himself as he spoke. He knew quite well what had happened. 'Think nothing of it. I'm delighted to see you all having such a nice time together. That's what neighbours are all about. It's just that the family were a bit worried about you,' he said, pulling out a large gold watch from his pocket. 'Four-thirty in the afternoon is a bit late to be coming from ten o'clock Mass.'

No Mouse

This is a sensitive portrayal of one man's attempt to assist a less fortunate fellow human; the fact that it is set initially in a pub helps us, perhaps, to misunderstand the situation. In fact Big Dan is trying to help the boy overcome his incontinence. It is taken from Bryan MacMahon's The Tallystick *of 1994.*

When the huge craggy-faced man entered the crossroads bar, conversation ceased at once. The three or four customers seated on stools at the long counter seemed to bend lower over their drinks.

Kicking the legs of a bar stool into place, while his eyes covertly roved left and right, the newcomer conveyed a truculent challenge to those present.

From behind the bar the publican turned with a muscular smile. He raised his eyebrows in unspoken query to confirm what the newcomer wanted.

Receiving an almost undetectable but contemptuous gesture of the big man's hand, the publican began to pull a pint of stout. From time to time his eyes looked up from the froth-filling glass to glance at his latest customer.

The man was seated alone; his face glowered as he turned his powerful calloused hands over and over as if to ponder the clefts and creases on his palms and fingers. From under his frayed shirt-cuff the blue-splayed flukes of a tattooed whale protruded on to the back of his hand. Now and again the flukes offered a semblance of movement as the big man clenched and unclenched his fist.

The almost-filled pint glass was placed aside for its froth to subside. At last, the filled glass before him, the big fellow threw some coins on the counter: receiving his change he began to chink the coins between his fingers with a sound that conveyed menace.

Still no overt conversation. The man took the first slug of his drink.

The door leading to the kitchen at the end of the bar suddenly burst open and the face of a Down's Syndrome boy appeared. He seemed to be about thirteen years of age. His widely-spaced eastern eyes surveyed the scene. Suddenly recognising the latest customer his head jerked, and in an uncoordinated way he shambled forward, launching himself at the big man now with such violence as almost to dislodge him from his stool. The craggy head swivelled sideways and the craggy face broke into an ill-fitting but indulgent smile.

'Big Dan,' the boy chortled. 'Dirty man. Wash he face, fryin' pan.'

The expression on the weather-beaten features grew a shade more indulgent. Big Dan kicked a second bar stool into place beside him. The boy clambered awkwardly and sat upon it. Nonchalantly the man lifted his pint glass and placed it under the boy's jaws. The boy buried his nose in the glass and gulped and swallowed noisily. He wore a broad moustache of cream-coloured froth when Big Dan indicated that he had had enough.

The boy settled his bottom comfortably on the stool.

A query creased his face. 'Fishin'?' he said.

'Show me you,' the big man growled.

The boy began to cringe. He tightened his body and bunched his shoulders forwards so as to hide the tell-tale spread of dampness on the flies of his trousers.

Big Dan would have none of it. With rough gentleness and determined tuggings he disentangled the lad's legs so as to reveal the wide stain of which the boy was ashamed.

'Why d'ya do it? You're a big boy now?' Big Dan growled in a low voice.

'We go fishin'?'

'I won't take you fishin' if you keep wettin' yourself like a bloody baby. You hear me?'

'Up at the bridge—fishin'.'

'I'll throw you into the goddam river if you do it again. Forty times I told you to unzip your flies, take it out, and piss. Let me show you.'

'No, No!' in great agitation. 'He bite you.'

The publican took no notice. The other drinkers didn't even glance around. A newcomer who had entered the bar and had stopped to watch the odd pair was subjected to a fusillade of stares from all present.

Big Dan had his mouth close to the boy's ear. He spoke in a hoarse whisper, 'Listen, you stupid little bastard, get this into your head. You must take it out and slash your water against a ditch or a wall—into the river or anywhere except down your trousers. If you do it again I'll give you a belt in the ear that you'll bloody well feel.'

The boy was sulking. Head down, he eyed the man with an odd upward glance.

'Your lesson,' Dan said. He spilled froth from his pint out the counter. Smoothed it out to make a little plaque of froth. With his forefinger he wrote C...a...t on the cream blackboard. 'C...a...t,' he said, 'Wha' word is that?'

'Cat,' the boy said in a surly tone.

Dan traced the outline of a cat's head on the froth. The boy grew gleeful at once. His lips worked. 'Cat kill 'im.' he said.

'Kill who?'

The boy's eyes were on his wet fork. 'Kill 'im bad,' he muttered. 'All blood, his head.'

Big Dan's stare roamed from the boy's face to the water stain. His eyes gradually registered awareness and realisation.

'Who say?' he whispered in the lad's ear.

'Nanna, Mamma Kate, Josee.'

'Go upstairs. Wash yourself. Change your trousers. We'll go fishin'. I've the rod at the house.'

The gentle boy shambled gleefully back into the kitchen. 'I go fishin', Big Dan,' he shouted as he thundered up the stairs.

The man waited until the noise of the lad's boots had died away. He got up suddenly and kicked the half open kitchen door fully in. The womenfolk inside, the grandmother, the mother and the yard woman all looked up. Concern was written on their faces.

'What kind of stupid bitches are ye?' Dan shouted. He called on Christ and the Mother of God to punish them. 'Why did ye tell him to call it that?'

The grandmother spoke, 'Not to shame us in front of the people,' she said with trembling bravery.

'Could ye get another name for it?'

'What will we call it so?' from the mother.

'What d'ye call it is it? Call it prick, dick, mickie, Patsy Fagan, John Willie, number one or penis.'

'Penis!' the grandmother said with scorn.

'Any bloody thing ye like except what you call it. That frightens him out of his wits. The same fright is on an elephant or a stabled stallion. If ye call it that again, ye'll answer to me.'

No one stirred. Dan crashed his way back to the bar. Standing, he gulped the remnants of his drink, wiped his mouth and turned to growl at the other customers. All were listening although no one turned.

'If ye see me at a gateway or behind the bushes with the boy don't get any wrong ideas in yeer heads. All I'm tryin' to do is teach him. Before Jesus, if I find one of ye sniggerin' behind my back he'll pay for his snigger with a mouthful of broken teeth.'

Still no one appeared to take notice. The publican blandly worked on. If he did glance up it was at the moving flukes on Big Dan's uplifted wrist below the rock that was his fist.

Deaths and Wakes

The Last of Mrs Murphy

The end of this story from Brendan Behan's After the Wake *(1981)*
describes the fruitless attempt to convey Mrs Murphy to the 'Refuge
of the Dying'.

She brought me into Mrs Murphy, and the two of them talked and
laughed about it while I didn't look at them but sat in the corner
playing with Minnie Murphy who, if she was vicious enough to
scrawb you if she thought she'd get away with it, didn't make you feel
such a fool. When my mother went I wanted to go too but my mother
said Mrs Murphy was sick and I could mind her till she came back.

Mrs Murphy called me to the bedside and gave me a pinch of snuff,
and had one herself, and the new baby went out of our heads.

The doctor came and said she'd have to go to the Refuge of the
Dying. He told her that years ago.

Mrs Murphy didn't know whether she'd go or not. I hoped she
would. I heard them talk about it before and knew you went in a cab,
miles over the city and to the southside. I was always afraid that they
might have got me into another school before she'd go for, no matter
how well you run out of them or kick the legs of the teacher, you have
to go sometime.

She said she'd go and my granny said that she'd order a cab from
the Roto to be there in the morning.

We all got into the cab. Mrs Murphy was all wrapped up in
blankets. She didn't lean on my head, but was helped by the jarvey,
and off we went.

Going past a pub on the corner of Eccles Street, she said she didn't
like to pass it, for old times' sake. My granny and Long Byrne and
Lizzie MacCann all said they'd be the better of a rozziner. And the
jarvey came in with the rest of us. On the banks of the other canal we

went in and had another couple. We stopped there for a long time and my granny told the jarvey she'd make it up to him.

Glasses of malt she ordered, and Mrs Murphy called on Long Byrne for a bar of a song.

The man in the pub said that it wasn't a singing house, but Mrs Murphy said she was going into the Refuge and it was a kind of a wake.

So Long Byrne sang, 'When the Cock, Cock Robin, comes hop, hop, hoppin' along', and *On Mother Kelly's Doorstep*, and for an hour it was great and you'd wish it could go on forever, but we had to go or the Refuge would be shut.

We left in Mrs Murphy and waited in the hall. Long Byrne said you get the smell of death in it.

'It's the wax on the floors,' said my granny.

'It's a very hard-featured class of a smell, whatever it is,' said Lizzie MacCann.

'We'll never see her again now, till we come up to collect her in the box,' said Long Byrne.

'For God's sake, whisht up out of that, you,' said my granny, 'people's not bad enough.' She fumbled with her handkerchief.

'All the same, Christina,' said Lizzie MacCann, 'you'd feel bad about leaving the poor devil in a place like this.'

The jarvey was trying to smoke without being caught. 'It's a very holy place,' he said, but not looking too sure about it.

'Maybe it's that we're not that holy ourselves,' said Lizzie MacCann. 'We might sooner die medium holy, like.'

'It's not the kind of place I'd like to leave a neighbour or a neighbour's child,' said Long Byrne.

'Oh, whisht your mouth,' said my granny, 'you'd make me feel like an—an informer or something. We only do the best we can.'

A very severe looking lady in a white coat came out and stood in front of us. The jarvey stuck the pipe in his pocket and straightened his cap.

'Whars in charge of the peeshent?' she says in a very severe tongue.

My granny stood up as well as she could. 'I am, with these other women here. She's a neighbour of ours.'

'There are no admissions here after five o'clock. The patient arrived here in an intoxicated condition.'

'She means poor old Murphy was drunk,' says Long Byrne.

'The poor old creature had only about six halves, the couple of glasses of malt we had to finish up, and the few bottles we had over in Eccles Street,' said Lizzie MacCann, counting on her fingers, 'God forgive them that'd tell a lie of an old woman, that she was the worse for drink.'

'And I get a distinct smell of whiskey here in this very hall,' said the woman in the white coat.

'How well you'd know it from the smell of gin, rum or brandy,' said Long Byrne, 'Ah well, I suppose practice makes perfect.'

The woman in the white coat's face got that severe that if she fell on it she'd have cut herself.

'Out,' she put up her hand, pointing to the door, 'Out, at once.'

There was a shuffling in the back of the hall, and Mrs Murphy came out, supported by two nurses.

'I wouldn't stop where my friends aren't welcome,' said Mrs Murphy.

'Come on so,' says my granny.

When they got back to Jimmy the Sports, they had a few and brought some more over to Mrs Murphy's while they put her to bed.

Long Byrne said herself and Lizzie MacCann would look after her between them.

My granny liked laziness better than she did money and said she'd bunce in a half a bar towards their trouble.

'And it won't break you,' says Long Byrne, 'damn it all, she's not Methuselah.'

Finnegan's Wake

This is probably one of the best-known Irish street ballads—at least by name—to feature a wake. (In the last line of this example 'thanam o'n dhoul' represents Irish 'Anam an Diabhail'—'by the devil's soul'.)

Tim Finnegan liv'd in Walkin Street
    A gentleman Irish mighty odd.
He had a tongue both rich and sweet,
    An' to rise in the world he carried a hod,
Now Tim had a sort of tipplin' way
    With the love of the liquor he was born,
An' to help him on with his work each day,
    He'd a drop of the craythur ev'ry morn.

Chorus:
Whack fol the dah, dance to your partner
    Welt the flure yer trotters shake,
Wasn't it the truth I told you,
    Lots of fun at Finnegan's wake.

One morning Tim was rather full,
    His head felt heavy which made him shake,
He fell from the ladder and broke his skull,
    So they carried him home his corpse to wake,
They rolled him up in a nice clean sheet,
    And laid him out upon the bed,
With a gallon of whiskey at his feet,
    And a barrel of porter at his head.

His friends assembled at the wake,
    And Mrs Finnegan called for lunch,
First they brought in tay and cake,
    Then pipes, tobacco, and whiskey punch.

Miss Biddy O'Brien began to cry,
    'Such a neat clean corpse, did you ever see,
Arrah, Tim avourneen, why did you die?'
    'Ah, hould your gab,' said Paddy McGee.

Then Biddy O'Connor took up the job,
    'Biddy,' says she, 'you're wrong, I'm sure,'
But Biddy gave her a belt in the gob,
    And left her sprawling on the floor;
Oh, then the war did soon enrage;
    'Twas woman to woman and man to man,
Shillelagh law did all engage,
    And a row and a ruction soon began.

Then Micky Maloney raised his head,
    When a noggin of whiskey flew at him,
It missed and falling on the bed,
    The liquor scattered over Tim;
Bedad he revives, see how he rises,
    And Timothy rising from the bed,
Says, 'Whirl your liquor round like blazes,
    Thanam o'n dhoul, do ye think I'm dead?'

After the Wake

This, the title story from Brendan Behan's After the Wake *(1981),
describes a woman's death by cancer and the relationship between
her widower and the narrator.*

The night before she went into hospital we had a good few drinks—
the three of us together.

We were in a singing house on the Northside and got very sob-
gargled between drinking whiskey and thinking of the operation.

I sang *My Mary of the Curling Hair* and when we came to the Gaelic chorus, *'siúl, a grá'* ('walk, my love'), she broke down in sobbing and said how he knew as well as she that it was to her I was singing, but that he didn't mind. He said that indeed he did not, and she said how fearful she was of this operation, that maybe she'd never come out of it. She was not sorry for herself, but for him, if anything happened her and she died on him, aye, and sorry for me too, maybe more sorry, 'Because, God help you,' she said to me, 'that never knew anything better than going down town half-drunk and dirty rotten bitches taking your last farthing.'

Next day was Monday, and at four o'clock she went into the hospital. She was operated on on Thursday morning and died the same evening at about nine o'clock.

When the doctor talked about cancer, he felt consoled a little. He stopped his dry-eyed sobbing and came with me into a public-house where we met his mother and hers and made arrangements to have her brought home and waked in her own place.

She was laid out in the front room on their spare single bed which was covered in linen for the purpose. Her habit was of blue satin and we heard afterwards that some old ones considered the colour wrong - her having been neither a virgin nor a member of the Children of Mary Sodality.

The priest, a hearty man who read Chesterton and drank pints, disposed of the objection by saying that we were all Children of Mary since Christ introduced St John to Our Lady at the foot of the Cross— Son, behold thy Mother; Mother, behold Thy Son.

It is a horrible thing how quickly death and disease can work on a body.

She didn't look like herself, any more than the brown parchment-thin shell of a mummy looks like an Egyptian warrior; worse than the mummy, for he at least is dry and clean as dust. Her poor nostrils were plugged with cotton-wool and her mouth hadn't closed properly, but showed two front teeth, like a rabbit's. All in all, she looked no better than the corpse of her granny, or any other corpse for that matter.

There was a big crowd at the wake. They shook hands with him and told him they were sorry for his trouble; then they shook hands with his and her other relatives, and with me, giving me an understanding smile and licence to mourn my pure unhappy love.

Indeed, one old one, far gone in Jameson, said she was looking down on the two of us, expecting me to help him bear up.

Another old one, drunker still, got lost in the complications of what might have happened had he died instead of her, and only brought herself up at the tableau—I marrying her and he blessing the union from on high.

At about midnight, they began drifting away to their different rooms and houses and by three o'clock there was only his mother left with us, steadily drinking.

At last she got up a little shakily on her feet and, proceeding to knock her people, said that they'd left bloody early for blood relatives, but seeing as they'd given her bloody little in life it was the three of us were best entitled to sit waking—she included me and all.

When his mother went, he told me he felt very sore and very drunk and very much in need of sleep. He felt hardly able to undress himself.

I had to almost carry him to the big double bed in the inner room.

I first loosened his collar to relieve the flush on his smooth cheeks, took off his shoes and socks and pants and shirt, from the supply muscled thighs, the stomach flat as an altar boy's, and noted the golden smoothness of the blond hair on every part of his firm white flesh.

I went to the front room and sat by the fire till he called me.

'You must be nearly gone yourself,' he said, 'you might as well come in and get a bit of rest.'

I sat on the bed, undressing myself by the faint flickering of the candles from the front room.

I fancied her face looking up from the open coffin on the Americans who, having imported wakes from us, invented morticians themselves.

Larry M'Farland's Wake

This extract from one of the stories in William Carleton's Traits and
Stories of the Irish Peasantry *(1843) shows some of the difficulties
experienced by poitín makers and their customers.*

'For heaven's sake, Sally,' says Art, 'don't exaggerate him more nor
he is; the boy is only stunned—see, he's coming to: Dick, ma bouchal,
rouse yourself—that's a man: hut! he's well enough—that's it,
allanah[1]: here, take a slug out of this bottle, and it'll set all right—or,
stop, have you a glass within, Sally?' 'Och, musha, not a glass is
under the roof wid me,' says Sally; 'the last we had was broke the
night Barney was christened, and we hadn't one since—but I'll get
you an egg-shell[2].' 'It'll do as well as the best,' says Art. And to make
a long story short, they sat down, and drank the bottle of whiskey
among them. Larry and Sally made it up, and were as great friends as
ever; and Dick was made drunk for the bating he got from his father.

What Art wanted was to buy some oats that Larry had to sell, to run
in a private Still, up in the mountains, of coorse, where every Still is
kept. Sure enough, Larry sould him the oats, and was to bring them up
to the still-house the next night after dark. According to appointment,
Art came a short time after night-fall, with two or three young boys
along with him. The corn was sacked and put on the horses; but before
that was done, they had a dhrop, for Art's pocket and the bottle were
ould acquaintances. They all then sat down in Larry's, or, at laste, as
many as there were seats for, and fell to it. Larry, however, seemed to
be in better humour this night, and more affectionate with Sally and the
childher: he'd often look at them, and appear to feel as if *something
was over him*[3]: but no one observed that till afterwards. Sally herself
seemed kinder to him, and even went over and sat beside him on the
stool, and putting her arm about his neck, kissed him in a joking way,
wishing to make up, too, for what Art saw the night before—poor
thing—but still as if it wasn't *all* a joke, for at times she looked
sorrowful. Larry, too, got his arm about her, and looked often and often
on her and the childher, in a way that he wasn't used to do, until the
tears fairly came into his eyes.

'Sally, avourneen,' says he, looking at her, 'I saw you when you had another look from what you have this night; when it wasn't asy to fellow you *in* the parish or *out* of it;' and when he said this he could hardly spake.

'Whisht, Larry, acushla,' says she, 'don't be spaking that way—sure we may do very well yet, plase God: I know, Larry, there was a great dale of it—maybe, indeed, it was all—*my* fault; for I wasn't to you, in the way of care and kindness, what I ought to be.'

'Well, well, aroon,' says Larry, 'say no more; you might have been all that, only it was my fault: but where's Dick, that I struck so terribly last night? Dick, come over to me, agra—come over Dick, and sit down here beside me. Arrah, here, Art, ma bouchal, will you fill this egg-shell for him?—Poor gorsoon! God knows, Dick, you get far from fair play, acushla—far from the ating and drinking that other people's childher get, that hasn't as good a skin to put it in as you, alannah! Kiss me, Dick, acushla—and God knows your face is pale, and that's not with good feeding, any how: Dick, agra, I'm sorry for what I done to you last night; forgive your father, Dick, for I think that my heart's breaking, acushla, and that you won't have me long with you.'

Poor Dick, who was naturally a warm-hearted, affectionate gorsoon, kissed his father, and cried bitterly. Sally herself, seeing Larry so sorry for what he done, sobbed as if she would drop on the spot: but the rest began, and betwixt scoulding and cheering them up, all was as well as ever. Still Larry seemed as if there was something entirely very strange the matter with him, for as he was going out, he kissed all the childher, one after another; and even went over to the young baby that was asleep in the little cradle of boords that he himself had made for it, and kissed it two or three times, asily, for fraid of wakening it. He then met Sally at the door, and catching her hand when none of the rest saw him, squeezed it, and gave her a kiss, saying, 'Sally, darling!' says he.

'What ails you, Larry, asthore?' says Sally.

'I don't know,' says he; 'nothing, I bleeve—but Sally, acushla, I have thrated you badly all along; I forgot, avourneen, how I loved you *once*, and now it breaks my heart that I have used you so ill.'

'Larry,' she answered, 'don't be talking that way, bekase you make me sorrowful and unasy—don't, acushla: God above me knows I forgive you it all. Don't stay long,' says she, 'and I'll borry a lock of meal from Biddy, till we get home our own *meldhre*, and I'll have a dish of stirabout ready to make for you when you come home. Sure, Larry, who'd forgive you, if I, your own wife, wouldn't? But it's I that wants it from you, Larry; and in the presence of God, and ourselves, I now beg your pardon, and ax your forgiveness for all the sin I done to you.' She dropped on her knees, and cried bitterly; but he raised her up, himself a choaking at the time, and as the poor crathur got to her feet, she laid herself on his breast, and sobbed out, for she couldn't help it. They then went away, though Larry, to tell the thruth, wouldn't have gone with them at all, only that the sacks were borried from his brother, and he had to bring them home, in regard of Tom wanting them the very next day.

The night was as dark as pitch—so dark, faiks, that they had to get long pieces of bog fir, which they lit, and held in their hands, like the lights that Ned there says the lamp-lighters have in Dublin to light the lamps with.

At last, with a good dale of trouble, they got to the still-house; and, as they had all taken a drop before, you may be sure they were better inclined to take another now. They, accordingly, sat down about the fine rousing fire that was under the still, and had a right good jorum of strong whiskey that never seen a drop of water. They all were in very good spirits, not thinking of to-morrow, and caring at the time very little about the world as it went.

When the night was far advanced, they thought of moving home; however, by that time they weren't able to stand: but it's one curse of being drunk, that a man doesn't know what he's about for the time, except some few, like that poaching ould fellow, Billy M'Kinny, that's cunninger when he's drunk than when he's sober; otherwise they would not have ventured out in the clouds of the night, when it was so dark and severe, and they in such a state.

---

[1] My child.

[2] The ready wit of the Irish is astonishing. It often happens that they have a whiskey when neither glasses nor cups are at hand; in which case they are never at a loss. I have seen them use not only egg-shells, but pistol barrels, tobacco boxes, and scooped potatoes, in extreme cases.

[3] This is precisely tantamount to what the Scotch call 'fey'. It means that he felt as if some fatal doom were over him.

The Party Fight and Funeral

This extract describes the funeral which, inevitably, followed the
faction fight. The generosity of the Irish peasants described in
William Carleton's Traits and Stories of the Irish Peasantry *of 1843*
is astounding.

While these ceremonies were going forward, the churchyard
presented a characteristic picture. Beside the usual groups who
straggle through the place, to amuse themselves by reading the
inscriptions on the tombs, you might see many individuals kneeling
on particular graves, where some relation lay—for the benefit of
whose soul they offered up their prayers with an attachment and
devotion which one cannot but admire. Sometimes all the surviving
members of the family would assemble, and repeat a *Rosary* for the
same purpose. Again, you might see an unhappy woman beside a
newly-made grave, giving way to lamentation and sorrow for the loss
of a husband, or of some beloved child. Here, you might observe the
'last bed' ornamented with hoops, decked in white paper, emblematic
of the virgin innocence of the individual who slept below;—there, a
little board-cross informing you that 'this monument was erected by a
disconsolate husband to the memory of his beloved wife.' But that
which excited greatest curiosity was a sycamore tree, which grew in
the middle of the burying-ground.

It is necessary to inform the reader, that in Ireland many of the
churchyards are exclusively appropriated to the interment of Roman
Catholics, and, consequently, the corpse of no one who had been a
Protestant would be permitted to pollute or desecrate them. This was
one of them: but it appears that, by some means or other, the body of
a Protestant *had* been interred in it—and hear the consequence! The
next morning heaven marked its disapprobation of this awful
visitation by a miracle; for, ere the sun rose from the east, a full-grown
sycamore had shot up out of the heretical grave, and stands there to
this day, a monument at once of the profanation and its consequence.
Crowds were looking at this tree, feeling a kind of awe, mingled with

wonder, at the deed which drew down such a visible and lasting mark of God's displeasure. On the tombstones near Kelly's grave, men and women were seated, smoking tobacco to their very heart's content; for, with that profusion which characterises the Irish in everything, they had brought out large quantities of tobacco, whiskey, and bunches of pipes. On such occasions it is the custom for those who attend the wake or the funeral to bring a full pipe home with them; and it is expected that, as often as it is used, they will remember to say, 'God be merciful to the soul of him that this pipe was over.'

The crowd, however, now began to disperse; and the immediate friends of the deceased sent the priest, accompanied by Kelly's brother, to request that we would come in, as the last mark of respect to poor Denis's memory, and take a glass of wine and a cake.

'Come, Toby,' said my brother, 'we may as well go in, as it will gratify them; we need not make much delay, and we will still be at home in sufficient time for dinner.'

'Certainly you will,' said the Priest; 'for you shall both come and dine with me to-day.'

'With all my heart,' said my brother; 'I have no objection, for I know you give it good.'

When we went in, the punch was already reeking from immense white jugs, that couldn't hold less than a gallon each.

'Now,' said his Reverence, very properly, 'you have had a decent and creditable funeral, and have managed every thing with great propriety; let me request, therefore, that you will not get drunk, nor permit yourselves to enter into any disputes or quarrels; but be moderate in what you take, and go home peaceably.'

'Why, thin, your Reverence,' replied the widow, 'he's now in his grave, and, thank God, it's he that had the dacent funeral all out—ten good gallons did we put over you, astore, and it's yourself that liked the dacent thing, any how—but sure, Sir, it would shame him where he's lyin', if we disregarded him so far as to go home widout bringing in our friends, that didn't desart us in our throuble, an' thratin' them for their kindness.'

While Kelly's brother was filling out all their glasses, the priest, my brother, and I, were taking a little refreshment. When the glasses were filled, the deceased's brother raised his in his hand, and said,—

91

'Well, gintlemen,' addressing us, 'I hope you'll pardon me for not dhrinking your healths first; but people, you know, can't break through an ould custom, at any rate—so I give poor Denis's health that's in his *warm* grave, and God be marciful to his sowl.'

The priest now winked at me to give them their own way; so we filled our glasses, and joined the rest in drinking 'Poor Denis's health, that's now in his warm grave, and God be merciful to his soul.'

When this was finished, they then drank ours, and thanked us for our kindness in attending the funeral. It was now past five o'clock; and we left them just setting into a hard bout of drinking, and rode down to his Reverence's residence.

Drink and Fighting

The Battle of the Factions

William Carleton's Traits and Stories of the Irish Peasantry *of 1843 is a work not always totally complimentary to those whose 'traits' are described in its pages. These extracts, however, are vastly entertaining.*

I remember the fair-day of Knockimdowney well: it has kept me from griddle-bread and tough nutriment ever since. Hard fortune to Jack Roe O'Hallaghan! No man had better teeth than I had till I met with him that day. He fought stoutly on his own side; but he was *ped* then for the same basting that fell to me, though not by my hands, if to get his jaw dacently divided into three halves could be called a fair liquidation of an old debt—it was equal to twenty shillings in the pound, any how.

There had not been a larger fair in the town of Knockimdowney for years. The day was dark and sunless, but sultry. On looking through the crowd, I could see no man without a cudgel; yet, what was strange, there was no certainty of any sport. Several desultory skrimmages had locality, but they were altogether sequestered from the great factions of the O's. Except that it was pleasant, and stirred one's blood to look at them, or occasioned the cudgels to be grasped more firmly, there was no personal interest felt by any of us in them; they therefore began and ended, here and there, through the fair, like mere flashes in the pan, dying in their own smoke.

The blood of every prolific nation is naturally hot; but when that hot blood is inflamed by ardent spirits, it is not to be supposed that men should be cool; and, God he knows, there is not on the level surface of this habitable globe, a nation that has been so thoroughly inflamed by *ardent spirits* of all kinds as Ireland.

Up till four o'clock that day, the factions were quiet. Several relations on both sides had been invited to drink by John and Rose's families, for the purpose of establishing a good feeling between them. But this was, after all, hardly to be expected, for they hated one another with an ardency much too good-humoured and buoyant; and, between ourselves, to bring Paddy over a bottle is a very equivocal mode of giving him an anti-cudgelling disposition. After the hour of four, several of the factions were getting very friendly, which I knew at the time to be a bad sign. Many of them nodded to each other, which I knew to be a worse one; and some of them shook hands with the greatest cordiality, which I no sooner saw than I slipped the knot of my cravat, and held myself in preparation for the sport.

I have often had occasion to remark—and few men, let me tell you, had finer opportunities of doing so—the differential symptomatics between a Party Fight, that is, a battle between Orangemen and Ribbonmen, and one between two Roman Catholic Factions. There is something infinitely more anxious, silent, and deadly, in the compressed vengeance, and the hope of slaughter, which characterise a *party fight*, than is to be seen in a battle between *factions*. The truth is, the enmity is not so deep and well-grounded in the latter as in the former. The feeling is not political nor religious between the factions; whereas, in the other, it is both, which is a mighty great advantage; for when this is adjuncted to an intense personal hatred, and a sense of wrong, probably arising from a too intimate recollection of the leaded black-thorn, or the awkward death of some relative, by the musket or the bayonet, it is apt to produce very purty fighting, and much respectable retribution.

In a party fight, a prophetic sense of danger hangs, as it were, over the crowd—the very air is loaded with apprehension; and the vengeance burst is proceeded by a close, thick darkness, almost sulphury, that is more terrifical than the conflict itself, though clearly less dangerous and fatal. The scowl of the opposing parties, the blanched cheeks, the knit brows, and the grinding teeth, not pretermitting the deadly gleams that shoot from their kindled eyes, are ornaments which a plain battle between factions cannot boast, but which, notwithstanding, are very suitable to the fierce and gloomy silence of that premeditated vengeance which burns with such intensity in the heart, and scorches up the vitals into such a thirst for

94

blood. Not but that they come by different means to the same conclusion; because it is the feeling, and not altogether the manner of operation, that is different.

Now a faction fight doesn't resemble this, at all, at all. Paddy's at home here; all song, dance, good-humour, and affection. His cheek is flushed with delight, which, indeed, may derive assistance from the consciousness of having no bayonets or loaded carabines to contend with: but, any how, he's at home—his eye is lit with real glee—he tosses his hat in the air, in the height of mirth—and leaps, like a mountebank, two yards from the ground. Then, with what a gracious dexterity he brandishes his cudgel! what a joyous spirit is heard in his shout at the face of a friend from another faction! His very 'whoo!' is contagious, and would make a man, that had settled on running away, return and join the sport with an appetite truly Irish. He is, in fact, while under the influence of this heavenly *afflatus*, in love with every one, man, woman, and child. If he meet his sweetheart, he will give her a kiss and a hug, and that with double kindness, because he is on his way to thrash her father or brother. It is the *acumen* of his enjoyment; and woe be to him who will adventure to go between him and his amusements. To be sure, skulls and bones are broken, and lives lost; but they are lost in pleasant fighting—they are the consequences of the sport, the beauty of which consists in breaking as many heads and necks as you can; and certainly when a man enters into the spirit of any exercise, there is nothing like elevating himself to the point of excellence. Then a man ought never to be disheartened. If you lose this game, or get your head good-humouredly beaten to pieces, why you may win another, or your friends may mollify two or three skulls as a set-off to yours; but that is nothing.

When the evening became more advanced, maybe, considering the poor look up there was for anything like decent sport—maybe, in the early part of the day, it wasn't the delightful sight to see the boys on each side of the two great factions, beginning to get frolicksome. Maybe the songs and the shouting, when they began, hadn't melody and music in them, any how! People may talk about harmony; but what harmony is equal to that in which five or six hundred men sing and shout, and leap and caper at each other, as a prelude to neighbourly fighting, where they beat time upon the drums of each other's ears and heads with oak drumsticks? That's an Irishman's music; and hard fortune to the *garran** that wouldn't have friendship and kindness in him to join and play a *stave* along with them! 'Whoo! your sowl! Hurroo! Success to our side! Hi for the O'Callaghans! Where's the blackguard to—,' I beg pardon, decent reader; I forgot myself for a moment, or rather I got new life in me, for I am nothing at all at all for the last five months—a kind of nonentity I may say, ever since that vagabond Burgess occasioned me to pay a visit to my distant relations, till my friends get that last matter of the collar-bone settled.

The impulse which *faction* fighting gives to trade and business in Ireland is truly surprising; whereas *party* fighting depreciates both. As soon as it is perceived that a *party* fight is to be expected, all buying and selling are nearly suspended for the day; and those who are not *up*, and even many who are, take themselves and their property home as quickly as may be convenient. But in a *faction* fight, as soon as there is any perspective of a row, depend upon it, there is quick work at all kinds of negociation; and truly there is nothing like brevity and decision in buying and selling; for which reason faction fighting, at all events, if only for the sake of national prosperity, should be encouraged and kept up.

---

* A horse; but it is always used as meaning a bad one—one without mettle. When figuratively applied to a man, it means a coward.

The Contractors

This is a short extract from the novel of that name by John B. Keane,
published in 1993, telling of the experiences of Dan Murray from
Ballynahaun in the Irish building contractor's world in London. In
this extract he tastes for the first time the wilder and more vicious
aspects of this life.

'The mood I'm in at the moment needs a large quantity of intoxicating drink before it can be disposed of,' Sylvester suggested. 'Do you feel like coming along?'

'I suppose a drink wouldn't poison us,' Dan concurred.

'Nor affect the general tenor of our lives to any alarming degree,' Sylvester asseverated.

'Oh sure,' said Dan.

'And so long as we don't make pigs of ourselves. That's most important.' Sylvester sounded so serious that Dan looked to see if he meant it.

'I mean,' Sylvester spoke convincingly, 'it's all right for a man to have a drink or two but any more is an affront to those saints and martyrs who thought up the seven deadly sins. A man who stuffs himself with intoxicating liquor is no better than an animal. Better his right cobble were cut from where it hangs with its fellow or that his penis be guillotined at its maximum erection. I say to you,' and here Sylvester pointed an apocalyptic finger at Dan, 'I say to you put your appetite behind you and go forth in the nude to the well of the spring water or a day will come when you will call from the flames of hell to the holy in heaven for a drop, a single drop of water. Now let's go forth and get truly pissed.'

'What about the Shillelagh?' Dan asked.

'I have every third Friday night free,' Sylvester assured him.

'And Sandra?'

'Sandra is babysitting for a friend. I can see you are determined to put obstacles in my way.'

'You are already half drunk,' Dan reminded him.

'That's a terrible state to be in. Let's go.'

They started off at the Crown in Cricklewood but the place became crowded in a short time so they left and took a taxi to a pub in Kilburn High Road. This was not so crowded but it was noisier and there were two sing-songs going at the same time.

'These are not my normal haunts,' Sylvester told Dan, 'but I imagine it will appeal to you with your tender years and your appetite for life. This is alleged to be the best pub in London for the "crack" as the Paddies euphemistically call that vulgar mixture of Irish gossip, dirty stories, news of cushy jobs and the silent migrations of the ever-transient whore population of this great city. In short it's the buck navvy's paradise. Here he can drink and mate and fight. What more does a red-blooded man want? Here he will hear the sagas of the legendary long-distance men and the tough tales of the present-day ones who cannot stay for more than a season in the same place. If you are a buck navvy and want to stay a buck navvy this is the place to be. If you never want to possess the price of a down-payment on a decent house for your wife and family let this be your hang-out because your fellows are here.'

Sylvester did not sound bitter but it was obvious that he was not happy in their present surroundings.

'We can leave if you like,' Dan suggested.

'No. No,' his friend was adamant, 'tonight won't be too bad. We'll stick around while we can. Enjoy the scene. These are our own people and yet they are a people apart. I wouldn't come here tomorrow night for all the money in the Bank of England.'

'It seems all right,' was Dan's rejoinder. 'They may be a bit rough and ready,' he went on defensively, 'but they seem to be a good-natured lot.'

'You will insist on learning the hard way,' Sylvester smiled ruefully. 'Listen Dan, the odds are ten to one on that there will be a serious fight in this pub tomorrow night. A number of people will be hurt. Most of the customers come here for no purpose other than the settling of old scores. Here they are away from the supervision of parents and parish priests. In their own townlands and parishes they numbered only a handful. They were suppressed easily and the violence rarely surfaced. Here they number hundreds. They are a force to be reckoned with. They fight amongst each other for recognition the same way a colony of artists might try to outpaint or outwrite or outsculpt each other. The art forms here are the fist, the duster and the boot. Tomorrow night when they have exhausted themselves the Black Marias will haul them to jail.'

They stayed till closing time. A somewhat intoxicated Sylvester held forth on matters relating to the building industry, 'I don't know what I'd do without the bustle of a site now and then. I need it to sustain me, to comfort me. Whatever else there may be on a building site there is no loneliness. There's camaraderie and there's pride and there's life but, best of all, there are the sounds.'

He swallowed from his glass and would have said no more but he noted Dan's intentness. The younger man had been listening, really listening.

'Sounds of the site,' Sylvester spoke half to himself, half to Dan, 'the song of the site I call it,' Sylvester continued. 'It's not to be heard at its best on the site itself or too near the site. Like the bagpipes.'

Sylvester's hands were extended now as he forgot his surroundings, 'the chorus of the site is enhanced by distance. It is a chorus beloved of contractors. They spend all their waking hours with their ears tuned to it, ears that have been developed for nothing else. You too Master Dan will develop an ear for it as I have. In the early days on my way to work I would park the van at the requisite distance. Then, in with me to the nearest field where I would listen in peace to the opening notes, the jibes, the catcalls and the whistles of the labourers setting up for the day, then the chippies joining in with tipping, tapping and thumping of hammer on joist and beam and hardboard. Every hammer-blow says we're here, we the chippies are here, the cockerels of every site, we begin, let others follow. Then the deafening drillers now muted by distance, then the churning mixers and the scraping shovels and the clinking and the clanking, and the chugging of the dumpers and the dying of human voices as the chorus strengthens and all the sounds are one.'

Dan turned his ear to the pub noises, the singing, the bustle, the drunken staggering, the joviality of the various groups, the apparent good-fellowship at every table. Behind the counter a squad of coatless barmen were pushed almost beyond their capabilities to meet the

99

demand for pints of black and tan, mild and bitter and in-between nips of the hard stuff. Not once did Dan hear anybody question the price of a round of drinks. Every so often a charge-hand swept the tills clear of larger notes. In jig time the tills were filled again. Dan had never seen the equal of it.

In the toilet there was a man with his coat off and his shirt outside his trousers. The coat was wet from the urine which spattered from the white-tiled channels. He did not seem to notice. He stood swaying with his legs apart.

'I'm rough,' he was saying. 'I'm tough. I'm Irish.' He kept repeating the phrase.

'Bait,' Sylvester whispered.

'Hardly,' Dan was inclined to disagree.

'Bait,' Sylvester whispered secondly, 'although I doubt if he's party to it.'

'Let's get out of here,' Dan urged, 'before one of us brushes against him accidentally.'

'Excellent idea,' Sylvester assented. He led the way, carefully avoiding the swaying drunk.

'O, sweet memorable John Joseph Jesus!' The exclamation came from Sylvester when he opened the door of the toilet and looked into the bar.

'What's the matter?' Dan called from behind him.

'What isn't?' from Sylvester.

Dan peered over his shoulder. The bar was a broiling mass of crazed humanity. Women screamed and men yelled. Bottles flew and glasses were smashed. A man came staggering toward them with a broken corrugated glass clutched by the handle in his hand. It was discoloured with a mixture of beer, foam and blood.

'Get out of my bastardin' way,' he shouted.

Dan and Sylvester moved to one side. The man with the glass disappeared into the toilet.

'What are we going to do?' Dan asked.

'Follow me,' Sylvester said. With his back to the wall he edged his way towards the door. Dan followed close by.

When they were half-way towards their destination a man dashed from the outskirts of a rough and tumble where everybody was trying to strike everybody else. He recognised Sylvester.

'You're the dirty bastard that had me barred from the Green Shillelagh,' he shouted. He swung a powerful fist which caught Sylvester on the side of the face. Sylvester covered his head with both hands as his assailant made ready to strike him again. Before he had time to deliver a second blow Dan struck him a flush on the jaw. The man dropped without a sound.

'Come on,' Dan called, 'before his pals get us.'

He pushed Sylvester towards the door and out on to the street where the fighting was worse. Several of the combatants lay on the ground or were crouched in a huddled position holding their stomachs. Some moaned with pain. Others were unable to do so. Dan warded off a blow from a youngster who was determined to fight someone so that he could make a name for himself. Sylvester slumped against the balustraded window of the pub. His hands still covered his head. Dan was forced to turn his full attention to the youth who was endeavouring to strike him.

'Go away,' Dan said, 'I don't want any trouble.'

'Fight you coward,' the youth called mockingly.

Again Dan was forced to move quickly in order to avoid the swinging fists. Then suddenly and quite unexpectedly the youth turned and ran. Dan was mystified. At the same time a crowd came pouring out of the pub. They did not seem to want further fighting. Their only aim seemed to be to get as far away as possible from the disaster area. Dan was perplexed by such odd behaviour but when two large black vans drew up at the kerb, from opposite directions he guessed that these must be the infamous Black Marias. He lifted Sylvester to his feet as about twenty policemen with drawn batons emerged from the vans.

Suddenly he felt his left hand go limp. He turned to see a policeman with a baton in his hand attempting to strike him again.

'I'm only trying to help this man,' Dan explained and pointed at Sylvester.

'Effing Paddies,' the policeman snarled, 'can't take a drink like civilised people.'

He struck Dan a sharp blow on the head. The blow made him lose consciousness. He reeled for a moment or two and then fell to the ground alongside Sylvester.

The powerfully-built man Dan had seen in the toilet seemed to be immune to the baton blows that rained on his head and shoulders. Eventually they managed to hold him down. Sylvester, who saw what was happening, was certain that the man was in for a terrific beating but the police seemed content to lift him bodily into the van.

When Dan came round and opened his eyes he discovered that he had an excruciating pain in his head. Sylvester lay beside him but he was fast asleep, snoring drunkenly in much the same condition as when Dan first met him on the train from Fishguard. They were in a cell. That much was obvious from the iron bars in front of him. There were two other occupants. One was the man Dan struck in the pub and the other the burly fellow the police had been unable to render unconscious. Both were sleeping soundly. There was some congealed blood on the big man's face but otherwise he looked in good shape.

Dan was unable to sleep. The pain in his head was a real discomfort. The hours passed. From another cell, in another part of the building came a drunk singing 'Down by the Glenside' and in the circumstances Dan found it weird. It affected him in the oddest manner possible. He felt as though he must weep. At first he put this down to drink but as the verses dragged on he found it was something more. The song rang out hollowly, eerily and lamentably. It literally chilled him although really it was no more than a lonely, poorly-sung melody but Dan felt an overpowering loneliness for his home, for his brother and his parents. Suddenly the singing stopped. It was followed by a grunt and he guessed that his captors were less appreciative of the song's value.

In the morning they were whisked away to a courthouse where a magistrate was disposing of similar cases at a speed which left Dan somewhat giddy.

Drinking Songs and Toasts

The Bould Thady Quill

This is a Munster sportsman's drinking song written in the early part of the twentieth century; Thady Quill is rumoured to have lived in the Mushra Mountains near Macroom, Co. Cork.

Ye maidens of Dunhallow who are anxious for courting,
    A word of advice I will give unto ye.
Go down to Banteer to the athletic, sporting,
    And hand in your name to the club committee.
But do not commence any sketch of your progress,
    Till a carriage you see coming over the hill,
And down thro' the valleys and hills of Kilcorney,
    With that Muskerry sportsman, the bould Thady Quill.

Chorus:
For rambling or bowling, for football or coursing,
    For emptying a bowl just as fast as you'd fill,
In all your days roving you'll find none so jovial,
    As the Muskerry sportsman, the bould Thady Quill.

At the great hurling match between Cork and Tipperary,
    'Twas played in the Park, on the banks of the Lee.
Our own darling boys were afraid of being beaten,
    So they sent for bould Thady to Ballinagree.
He hurled the ball right and left in their faces,
    And showed the Tipperary boys action and skill,
If they touched on our lines he did manfully brave them,
    And they put in the paper the praise of Thade Quill.

Repeat Chorus

Our Thady is famous in a great many places,
   At the athletic races held down in Cloughroe,
He won the long jump without throwing off his waistcoat,
   Going twenty-four feet from the heel to the toe.
And at throwing the weight, with Dublinman foremost,
   Our own darling Thady, exceeded him still,
And all round the field went the loud swinging chorus,
   Long life and success to the bould Thady Quill.

Repeat Chorus

At the Cork Exhibition there was a fair lady
   Her fortune exceeded a million or more,
But a bad constitution had ruined her completely,
   And medical treatment had failed o'er and o'er.
Yerrah, mamma, says she, sure I know what will heal me
   And cure the disease that is certain to kill.
Give over your doctors and medical treatment,
   Let me have a stroll out with bould Thady Quill.

Repeat Chorus

She Stoops to Conquer

This song, sung in the play by Tony Lumpkin, is from Goldsmith's
She Stoops to Conquer *of 1773.*

Let schoolmasters puzzle their brain,
   With grammar, and nonsense, and learning;
Good liquor, I stoutly maintain,
   Gives *genus* a better discerning.
Let them brag of their heathenish gods,
   Their Lethes, their Styxes, and Stygians,
Their qui's, and their quae's, and their quods,
   They're all but a parcel of pigeons.
                Toroddle, toroddle, toroll.

When methodist preachers come down,
   A-preaching that drinking is sinful,
I'll wager the rascals a crown,
   They always preach best with a skinful.
But when you come down with your pence,
   For a slice of their scurvy religion,
I'll leave it to all men of sense,
   But you, my good friend, are the pigeon.
               Toroddle, toroddle, toroll.

Then come, put the jorum about,
   And let us be merry and clever,
Our hearts and our liquors are stout,
   Here's the Three Jolly Pigeons for ever!
Let some cry up woodcock or hare,
   Your bustards, your ducks, and your widgeons;
But of all the birds in the air,
   Here's a health to the Three Jolly Pigeons.
               Toroddle, toroddle, toroll.

The Duenna

These two drinking songs are both from Sheridan's The Duenna *of 1775. The first is sung by Isaac, Don Ferdinand and Don Jerome. The second by Father Paul, Father Francis and Father Augustine with a chorus of other friars.*

A bumper of good liquor
Will end a contest quicker
Than justice, judge, or vicar;
   So fill a cheerful glass,
   And let good humour pass.
But if more deep the quarrel,
Why, sooner drain the barrel
Than be the hateful fellow
That's crabbed when he's mellow.
   A bumper, etc.

              * * *

GLEE AND CHORUS

This bottle's the sun of our table,
　His beams are rosy wine:
We, planets, that are not able
　Without his help to shine.

Let mirth and glee abound!
　You'll soon grow bright
　With borrow'd light,
And shine as he goes round.

The School for Scandal

This splendid drinking song is from Sheridan's The School for Scandal *of 1777. In the play it is sung by Sir Harry Bumper.*

Here's to the maiden of bashful fifteen;
　Here's to the widow of fifty;
Here's to the flaunting extravagant quean,
　And here's to the housewife that's thrifty.

Chorus:
Let the toast pass,—
Drink to the lass,
I'll warrant she'll prove an excuse for a glass.

Here's to the charmer whose dimples we prize;
　Now to the maid who has none, sir;
Here's to the girl with a pair of blue eyes,
　And here's to the nymph with but one, sir.

Chorus:
Let the toast pass,—
Drink to the lass,
I'll warrant she'll prove an excuse for a glass.

Here's to the maid with a bosom of snow:
    Now to her that's as brown as a berry:
Here's to the wife with a face full of woe,
    And now to the damsel that's merry.

Chorus:
Let the toast pass,—
Drink to the lass,
I'll warrant she'll prove an excuse for a glass.

For let 'em be clumsy, or let 'em be slim,
    Young or ancient, I care not a feather;
So fill a pint bumper quite up to the brim,
So fill up your glasses, nay, fill to the brim,
    And let us e'en toast them together.

Chorus:
Let the toast pass,—
Drink to the lass,
I'll warrant she'll prove an excuse for a glass.

Ode to Whiskey

This has been ascribed to Carolan and has been described as 'one of the finest Bacchanalian songs in any language'.

A h-uiscí chroidhe na n-anamann,
    Leagan tú ar lár mé,
Bím gan chéill, gan aithne,
    'Sé an t-eachrann do b'fhearr liom!
Bíonn mo chóta stracaighthe,
Agus caillim leat mo charabhat,
Is bíodh a ndeárnais maithte leat,
    Acht teangmhaigh liom amárach!

* * *

D'Alton's translation:

Why, liquor of life! do I love you so,
When in all our encounters you lay me low?
More stupid and senseless I every day grow,
    What a hint—if I'd mend by the warning.
Tattered and torn you've left my coat,
I've not a cravat—to save my throat,
Yet I pardon you all, my sparkling doat,
    If you'll cheer me again in the morning!

Kean O'Hara

*This little drinking song was composed by Carolan for Cian Ó
h-Eaghra of Nymphsfield, Co. Sligo, who was born c.1657.*

Dá mbeinn thiar i n-Árainn
    Nó i gCáirlinn na séad,
Mar ngluaiseann gach sár-long
    Le claireid is le méad,
B'fhearr liom gan amhras
    Mar shásadh dhom pféin
Cupán geal Uí Eaghra
    Bheith láimh le mo bhéal!

* * *

Were I blessed in Sweet Aran
    Or Carlingford shade,
Where ships swiftly sailing
    With claret and mead,
Diffusing soft pleasure
    And glee to each heart,
Still the cup of O'Hara
    Would greater impart.

Health to the Whiskey

This is another song by Carolan in praise of whiskey—always credited with being his favourite drink!

Sláinte an fuisce tá fial breá folláin
  Is ioma croí marbh a thógfas sé,
Ón rí go dtí an bacach ba mhian leo bheith 'n aice
  Dá mhéid a dtaithí ba mhóide a spéis.

  Cearant' nó 'Curfá:
  Má chastar an sagart ort
  Buail ar an mala é,
  D'ólfadh an bodach
  A sháith é féin!

Fóill! arsa an chailleach, 's í ag éirí ar maidin
  Triall chun an aifrinn nó dul go tigh Dé
Muna mbeadh 'gam ach pighin do bhéarfainn ar naigín (í)
  Seo dhuit mo phaidrín lán mo bhéil.

  Má chastar an sagart ort
  Buail ar an mala é
  D'ólfadh an bodach
  A sháith é féin!

Dul faoi an gcorrach duit bain faoi go socair
  Ní fhearr dhuit ar fhlocas ná ar leaba do luí,
Do luí ins an lathaigh ó oíche go maidin
  Ól gloine fuisce, 's bí slán 'na dhiaidh.

  Má chastar an sagart ort
  Buail ar an mala é
  D'ólfadh an bodach
  A sháith é féin.

Health to the whiskey, that's generous, fine, and wholesome;
    It's many the dead heart it raises up.
From the king to the beggar, they'd like to be near it;
    The more they frequent it the greater their love.

        Chorus:
        If the priest meets you
        Strike him on the forehead—
        The churl would drink
        Enough of it himself.

'Easy!' says the hag, and she rising in the morning,
    Journeying to Mass or going to the house of God,
If I hadn't but one penny I'd give it for a naggen;
    That's my Rosary—the full of my mouth (of it).

        If the priest meets you, etc.

Going through the Curragh, if you attack it quietly,
    'Twere no better for you to be lying on a flock-couch or a bed
        (than on the Curragh with your bottle).
(After) your lying in the mud from morning till evening
    Drink a glass of whiskey, and be well after it.

        If the priest meets you, etc.

A Drinking Song

Although this is its title, this poem from The Green Helmet and Other
Poems *(1910) by W. B. Yeats is difficult to construe as a simple
drinking song.*

        Wine comes in at the mouth
        And love comes in at the eye;
        That's all we shall know for truth
        Before we grow old and die.
        I lift the glass to my mouth,
        I look at you, and I sigh.

The Holy Ground

*At every gathering of Irish drinkers—male or female—this song is
certain to be performed, at least once.*

A dieu my fair young maiden,
Ten thousand times a dieu,
We must bid good bye to the Holy Ground,
And the girls that we love true,
We will sail the salt sea over,
And return again for sure,
To seek the girls who wait for us,
In the Holy Ground once more,
You're the girl I do adore
And still I live in hopes to see,
The Holy Ground once more.

(*Spoken*) Fine girl you are!

Oh the night was dark and stormy,
You scarce could see the moon,
And our good old ship was tossed about,
And her rigging all was torn:
With her seams agape and leaky,
With her timbers dozed and old,
And still I lived in hopes to see,
The Holy Ground once more,
You're the girl I do adore
And still I live in hopes to see,
The Holy Ground once more.

Fine girl you are!

And now the storm is over,
And we are safe on shore,
Let us drink a health to the Holy Ground
And the girls that we adore:

We will drink strong ale and porter
Till we make the tap room roar
And when our money all is spent
We will go to sea for more.
You're the girl I do adore
And still I live in hopes to see,
The Holy Ground once more.

Fine girl you are!

The Monks of the Screw

In September 1779, the social and political club known as 'The Monks of the Order of St Patrick', better known as 'The Monks of the Screw', was founded. Its charter song was written by John Philpot Curran.

When St Patrick our Order created and called us the Monks of the Screw
Good rules he revealed to our Abbot to guide us in what we should do.
But first he replenished his fountain with liquor, the best in the sky,
And he swore by the word of his Saintship that fountain should never run dry.
My children, be chaste till you're tempted. While sober be wise and discreet,
And humble your bodies with fasting whene'er you have nothing to eat.
There be not a glass in the convent except on a festival found
And this rule to enforce I ordain it a festival all the year round.

An Orange Toast

This Orange association, described by Sir Jonah Barrington in his Personal Sketches of his own Times, *published in 1827, had its own toast.*

This organisation, constituted near a century before, remained, I fancy, quite unaltered at the time I became a member. To make the general influence of this association the greater, the number of members was unlimited, and the mode of admission solely by the proposal and seconding of tried *aldermen.* For the same reason, no class, however humble, was excluded—equality reigning in its most perfect state at the assemblies. Generals and wig-makers—king's counsel and hackney clerks, &c. all mingled without distinction as brother-aldermen:—a lord mayor was annually appointed; and regularity and decorum always prevailed—until, at least, towards the *conclusion* of the meetings, when the aldermen became more than usually noisy and exhilarated,—King William's bust being placed in the centre of the supper-table, to overlook their extreme loyalty. The times of meeting were monthly; and every member paid sixpence per month, which sum (allowing for the absentees) afforded plenty of eatables, porter and punch, for the supping aldermen.

Their charter-dish was *sheeps' trotters* (in allusion to King James's running away from Dublin):—rum-punch in blue jugs, whiskey-punch in white ones, and *porter* in its *pewter*, were scattered plentifully over the table; and all regular formalities being gone through, and the eating part of the ceremony ended, the real *business* began by a general chorus of 'God save the King!' whereupon the grand engine, which, as a loyal and facetious shoemaker observed, would *bind* every *sole* of them together, and commemorate them *all* till the end of time, was set at work by order of the *lord mayor.* This engine was the charter-toast, always given with nine times nine! and duly succeeded by vociferous acclamations.

The 1st of July, (anniversary of the battle of the Boyne) was the favourite night of assembly: then every man unbuttoned the knees of his breeches, and drank the toast on his bare joints—it being pronounced by *his lordship* in the following words, composed

113

expressly for the purpose in the year 1689; afterwards adopted by the Orange Societies generally; and still, I believe, considered as the charter-toast of them all.

This most ancient and unparalleled *sentiment* runs thus:—

ORANGE TOAST.

'The glorious,—pious,—and immortal memory of the great and good King William:—not forgetting Oliver Cromwell, who assisted in redeeming us from popery, slavery, arbitrary power, brass-money, and wooden shoes. May we never want a Williamite to kick the **** of a Jacobite!—and a **** for the *Bishop of Cork!* And he that won't drink this, whether he be priest, bishop, deacon, bellows-blower, grave-digger, or any other of the fraternity of *the clergy*;—may a north wind blow him to the south, and a west wind blow him to the east! May he have a dark night—a lee shore—a rank storm—and a leaky vessel, to carry him over the river Styx! May the dog Cerberus make a meal of his r—p, and Pluto a snuff-box of his scull; and may the devil jump down his throat with a red-hot harrow, with every pin tear out a gut, and blow him with a *clean* carcase to hell! *Amen!*'

The extraordinary zeal wherewith this toast was drunk, could only be equalled by the enthusiasm with which the blue and white jugs and pewter pots were resorted to, to ascertain the quality of the potation within: both processes serving to indicate the quantity of loyalty entertained by every alderman towards the King, Doctor Duigenan, and the Protestant Religion!—they then rebuttoned the knees of their breeches (trousers had not come into fashion), and sat down *to work* again in downright earnest. Mr Powell, a jolly apothecary, (till he was killed, by *singing* I suppose,) led, in my time, the vocal band; and after a dozen speeches, accompanied by numerous replenishments of the jugs, &c. every body who had *any thing to do in the morning* generally withdrew, leaving the rest of the loyalists to finish the last drop.

The idea of 'Orange Societies' arose, in my opinion, from this association. I believe it exists still; but has, I understand, degenerated into a sort of *half-mounted* club;—not exclusive enough for gentlemen, and too fine for wig-makers: it has sunk into a paltry and unimportant corporate utensil.

114

Hangovers

More Drink than Bite

In this extract from Christy Brown's novel of 1982, A Promising
Career, *a hangover and its progress are delicately portrayed.*

They sat round a low glass-topped table near the open terrace window,
sipping gin and tonic, a welcome light breeze on their faces. Simon,
annoyed with the latecoming of his two guests and petulantly
determined to let them know it, sat a little apart, pretending to be
listening with half-closed eyes to the muted sounds of the stereo, but
stealing surreptitious glances at them when he thought they were not
looking, rather like a sly master trying to catch his pupils out in a
childish misdemeanour. This subterfuge was quite lost on Art,
however, who bore a ravaged appearance, the unwise festivities of the
night before spiderwebbing his face, eyes sunk far back in his head,
hunched on the edge of his seat, gripping the square chunky glass in
both hands. The stop at a pub in Earl's Court on the way over in the
minicab had apparently not produced the desired effects, nor was the
second gin and tonic now in his hand weaving any magical formula so
far. He wished to Christ they would shut off that bloody music, stop
the small talk and just put the gin bottle on the table without further
ado, but the social niceties had to be observed, though he was more
than content to let Janice make most of the verbal running, which she
was doing anyway and with a vivacity that was unusual in her, he
noted in the midst of his hangover misery. She sat just as rigid as
himself, her face strained, nervous, devoid of makeup, a bit
bedraggled-looking in her corduroy jacket and jeans, talking over-
loudly at times, vying with the music as if to compensate for his
bilious silence. The stop at the pub had in fact been a bit of a disaster,
for they had done nothing but quarrel for the ten minutes or so that
they were there, and the drink itself had been a dead loss as far as a

cure was concerned, so all in all he concluded the day had little or nothing to offer him and he resigned himself to wait for Marcie to offer him a refill as he quietly died in the meantime. He had a vague idea that Simon had some kind of business proposition to put, but he could remember only bits of their conversation yesterday and had not the strength or inclination to think about it now. All he wanted at the moment was another bloody gin and let the rest take care of itself. He moped in limbo.

At least the lounge was cool, the beige and oatmeal-toned walls giving it a spacious airy elegance. Strips of vivid Peruvian rugs broke the glazed dark-brown surface of the woodblock floor; some prints lined the walls, sparse abstracts and samples of poster art in the Beardsley fashion, with here and there one or two originals Simon had got or bullied or otherwise wheedled out of small covens of artistic dilettantes whose style, or lack of it, plainly reflected his own. Plants in terracotta pots threw pleasant green shades across the tiles of the terrace outside. Simon soaked in all this comfort like a sponge, igniting a brief envy in Art before it waned and was submerged in a renewed flood of post-bacchanalian ennui and self-pity.

Marcie, cool and efficient as ever in an oriental-type gown with high prim collar, long sleeves ending in tight-wristed cuffs and with a hip-reaching slit up one side, found herself once more pitying the other girl, her pinched scared defiance as if she felt there was some sort of unvoiced conspiracy brewing between Simon and her husband but was determined to push it from her mind and be cordial to everyone. The late arrival of the two had not affected Marcie in the slightest; she knew it had not really upset her lover either, and that he was only making a silly fuss of it because he felt it incumbent on him as a sort of elder statesman to show his displeasure at the ill grace of the younger generation. She was amused by this, but she also rather despised him for pretending to harbour a grievance he did not really feel in order just to make them uncomfortable and assert his authority. Whatever sympathies she had were entirely on the side of the supposed miscreants, and she thought Simon patently ludicrous in his false injured dignity and bloated pomposity, lingering over his diluted gin, a fat spoilt boy.

Becoming aware at last of her amused eyes on him as she passed between him and the table, he shifted uneasily in his chair, then gave a sheepish grin and drew closer to the others.

'Oh hell,' he said, expansive, laying a paternal hand upon Art's shoulder, 'let's all have a refill, my dears!'

'I was about to do just that,' said Marcie, returning with a large glass jug holding gin and iced tonic.

As she quietly poured, Simon pulled his chair closer and loosened his jacket, looking at Art in sly merry old-boy camaraderie. 'Who was a naughty boy last night then, eh?' He swivelled his head and winked hugely round at the women. 'Drenched in wine and smothered in roses, eh?' He blinked, as if surprised at his own wit, and slapped his knee. 'That's it, eh—drenched in wine and smothered in roses!' He leaned back in the chair and laughed in great gusts at his ingenuity of phrase until his eyes streamed and he fished out the copious handkerchief again to wipe away the moisture. 'And we in our innocence thinking you'd gone straight back to your trusting little wife here!'

In the laying down and lifting of a glass, it seemed, Simon was transformed from a glowering sullen host brooding in a dark niche into a beaming avuncular teddy bear, florid and jolly, dispensing largesse with a bland wave of his soft plump hand, his eyes moist with conviviality sunk in the creased suet layers of his face. Marcie sat down and surveyed him over the rim of her glass, distrusting his sudden spurt of mellifluous hilarity.

Art grinned weakly, the gin slowly working the hoped-for miracle; he was far from cured yet but his misery was becoming more bearable. 'That's about the size of it, Simon,' he confessed, contritely eyeing Janice. 'Went for a bite and a drink somewhere—God knows where—and ended up having more drink than bite.'

Delirium Tremens

*This ballad by the hugely popular singer Christy Moore remains
extremely funny, despite the fact that so many of the references are to
the mid 1980s.*

I dreamt a dream the other night I couldn't sleep a wink
The rats were tryin' to count the sheep and I was off the
   drink.
There were footsteps in the parlour and voices on the stairs,
I was climbin' up the wall and movin' round the chairs.
I looked out from under the blanket and up at the fireplace,
The Pope and J. F. Kennedy were starin' me in the face.
Suddenly it dawned on me I was gettin' the old DTs,
When the Child o' Prague began to dance around the
   mantelpiece.

Goodbye to the Port and Brandy, to the Vodka and the Stag,
To the Schmiddick and the Harpic, the bottle draught and
   keg.
As I sat looking up at the Guinness ad I could never figure
   out
How your man stayed up on the surfboard after fourteen pints
   of stout.

Well I swore upon the Bible I'd never touch a drop,
My heart was palpitatin' I was sure 'twas goin' to stop.
Thinkin' I was dyin' I gave my soul to God to keep,
A tenner to St Anthony to help me get to sleep.
I fell into an awful nightmare and got a dreadful shock,
When I dreamt there was no duty-free at the airport down in
   Knock.
George Seawright was sayin' the rosary and SPUC were on
   the pill,
Frank Patterson was gargled and singin' Spancel Hill.

I dreamt that Mr Haughey had recaptured Crossmaglen
Then Garret got re-elected and gave it back again.
Dick Spring and Roger Casement were on board the Marita-
Ann
As she sailed into Fenit they were singing Banna Strand.
I dreamt Archbishop McNamara was on Spike Island for
three nights
Havin' been arrested for supportin' travellers' rights.
I dreamt that Ruairi Quinn was smokin' marijuana in the Dáil
And Barry Desmond handin' Frenchies out to the scuts in
Fianna Fail.

I dreamt of Nell McCafferty and Mary Kenny too
The things that we got up to but I'm not tellin' you.
I dreamt I was in a jacuzzi along with Alice Glenn
'Twas then I knew I'd never drink again.

Goodbye to the Port and Brandy, to the Vodka and the Stag,
To the Schmiddick and the Harpic, the bottle draught and
keg.
As I sat looking up at the Guinness ad I could never figure
out
How your man stayed up on the surfboard after fourteen pints
of stout.

Willie Wickham

The description of Willie's hangover in John Broderick's The Flood
of 1990 *is vastly convincing.*

Willie Wickham, Willie Willie Wick as ever was, naked and sweating
whiskey, was lying on the floor, face downward, with his eyes
gummed together. 'I'm honey-eyed, I am', he used to say gaily, just
before the booze took over and deprived him of coherent speech. He

was literally floored this time, after five days and nights of steady, relentless drinking. Maud Daly had refused him again, and he wanted to anaesthetise every aching thought of her. In and out of the hotel he swayed, like a large chunk of music played out of tune; in and out of a dozen pubs in Church Street, pausing only to vomit on the way. But eventually, hands shaking, knees crumpling, morose and tearful, he shouldered his way back to The Duke of Clarence, where he always ended up. There his treasure lay, a great deal of it in Mrs Daly's bar till, and a few grains of finest gold in the heart of her daughter.

Donie had put him to bed in the Lock Hospital for three nights: another night was lost behind Willie's glazed eyes.

Now, hearing as from a great abyss, at the bottom of which mighty waters beat against the rocks, he had become aware that Donie was no longer in the room. A little while later he managed to roll off the bed and lie on his stomach on the floor where, with his nose in the carpet, he felt some relief from the burning of his body. But the thick, dusty pile soon warmed under him as it always did, so he crawled slowly under the bed, where it was cooler than the rest of the room. But even this haven, an algid creek in a coastline ravaged by the sun, quickly became stifling, and dimly in his mind, while his body burned, he began to thirst for water. Sluglike, sniffling and turning his baked head from side to side, he began the long, long trek on hands and knees over the parched desert of the carpet, towards the oasis of the distant bathroom.

Once, in his apprentice days, when he had not yet achieved the status of a bottle-a-day man, and two or three when on the twist, a barber in Dublin (round the corner from the Hibernian Hotel) took pity on him, and applied the end of an ice-cold towel to the throbbing veins behind Willie's ears. That sensation, the keenest he had yet experienced in a fairly sheltered life—drink was as respectable as going to church—had caused him to rear up in the chair and gasp with relief and pleasure.

'O Mother of God,' he moaned, shivering indecently, and wriggling his feet two inches over the floor.

'Steady on there now, auld son,' said the barber, who knew his trade from the inside out and, more importantly, from the outside in: it was worth half-a-crown from this well-dressed and innocent eejit.

Now, nine years on, Willie paused at the bathroom door for breath. The treasure of the Indies, the gold of King Solomon's mines, the diamonds of Kimberley, the spices of Asia and all the tin in Colombia were as nothing to him beside the imminent prospect of cold water on his face, neck and wrists.

He put his head against the door which, fortunately, opened. There was a sound of gurgling water, splashing, running, rejoicing in its own half-human language, which got straight through to Willie's befuddled mind as quickly as a new theory of healing might penetrate and flower in the brain of a hyper-intelligent medical scientist.

In he went on all fours across the rubber floor—a great innovation, and one that all Bridgeford longed to see—until he reached the haven of the washbasin. This was a magnificent Victorian piece in mahogany with florid but indestructible ironwork. Clutching it, and whimpering with thirst, Willie managed to haul himself to his feet, supporting his sagging knees by gripping the edge of the basin. Then slowly, trembling like a nervous dog, he managed to turn the big brass handle of the cold water tap. It seemed to him that the effort took every drop of strength out of him, and for a few minutes he stood there, wobbling and hanging on to the porcelain rim, gazing through sticky lids at the life-giving water.

A few minutes later, after groping about for the plug, he plunged his hands into the miraculous spring and panted with relief. He dipped his arms in as far as they would go. He soaked a face towel which, also miraculously, was laid across the side of the basin: he applied it to the backs of his ears, his burning nose and cheeks, and his half-sealed eyes.

Almost immediately he felt relief. If only the water were colder, cooler, icy. He was still shaking in every limb, but at least he could see, and the wet towel, if not as burning cold as he would wish, was as welcome as a ham sandwich to a starving man. Then he looked up and, with the courage of the condemned, peered at his image in the glass. It was slightly damp, and Willie knew that his sight was not quite perfect yet, as he had many times had the experience of seeing himself reflected in a glass twice, even using only one eye. But the double or triple image had at least always been that of himself: what he was seeing now bore no resemblance to himself at all. It was the face of a man, much older, with something on his head which Willie in the heat and cold of the moment took to be a pair of horns.

His voice had not always come when called at this stage of a hangover, but he did make a weak, hoarse sound, and hanging onto the basin, poised on the very brink of Hell, he began to mutter his prayers. At last it had happened. His soul had left his body and he was *damned*, devil and all, down in the deepest pit where he would burn forever as he was burning now. The cold towel would be taken away and the torture would begin.

'Jesus, Mary and Joseph and Holy John the Baptist—'

'Please,' said a voice with a very high-toned whine, 'there is no need to curse.'

'Curse! Oh Sacred Heart, I'm only saying my prayers.'

'Oh, I see.' The voice was quite sympathetic, even kind.

But the shock of finding himself where he thought he was had sobered up Willie a great deal: it was at least as good as a large pot of black coffee, raw eggs and Fernet Branca, aspirin and a teaspoon of poteen, the black syrup the chemist down the street sold, and the pound of raw beef that Mrs Daly had once made him swallow. Where was she now? Where was his own mother in his hour of need? Why didn't somebody do something?

Suddenly, as intimations of death and immortality flitted through his subconscious, always muddily stirred up by booze, Willie became aware that he was facing the devil stark naked. He groped wildly on either side and grasped the towel hanging on the rim of the basin. O blessed towel, more than Adam had to cover his shame. He dragged it over his stomach, making him respectable at least in the presence of Lucifer, Son of the Morning, far fallen, but still a prince.

'I'm awfully sorry old boy, but I'm afraid that's my towel.'

Moaning, Willie thrust it from him in the general direction of the evil one, then bringing back his hand with great effort, his fingers touching more towelling material, he grabbed it and pulled it in front of his loins. The sweat was pouring down the inside of his legs, and his back felt like a wet tent.

'Sorry again, old man, I'm afraid that's mine too. It's a bore, quite a mix-up. But there *is* a hotel towel—of sorts—just below the other side of the basin, on a rail. Fine piece of Victoriana, that washstand, wouldn't mind bidding for it, but that's only a passing temptation.'

'Temptation?' croaked Willie, finding the towel on the rail at last, and wrapping it round his middle. It felt coarse, rasping and prickly—was this the sort of thing they wore down here?

'I always resisted it. I always said my prayers. I never gave into anything at once. O God, temptation isn't my fault.'

Instead of an answer, Willie was conscious of a splashing noise and the movement of something large and pinkish, a bit blurred along the edges, and for a moment seeming to possess two right arms. But what was clearly evident, even to Willie's befuddled eyes, was the fact that this man or devil or apparition or whatever he was, was bare naked also.

Inept or Excessive Drinking

A Political Philosopher

This rather sad extract is from Brinsley MacNamara's The Clanking of Chains *(1920).*

Somebody was whispering at his elbow:

'I saw you playing Robert Emmet th'other night, Michael, and it was grand, grand. But, of course the mouths that you were playing it for didn't understand, but I understood, so I did, because I read in the history of Ireland everything about him, and before I forgot it entirely I had off his speech by heart, and could sound it out, aye, nearly as well as yourself, Michael. And it would bring me a power of drink, too, this accomplishment of mine, whenever I'd go to a decent town where the blood of Fenianism still stirs in a few veins, but of course, condemned as I am to live in this sorrowful place, where there's scarcely a mother's son with a bit of blood in him, for want of exercise it went out of my mind, including most of my knowledge of ancient and modern history through having to be looking at them day after day, the narrow, miserable crew...Will you give me the lend of tuppence, Michael? I hadn't e'er a drink yet this blessed day?'

Michael turned to look at Kevin Shanaghan, one of the strangest figures in Ballycullen. A man who, still not without a certain glimmer of intellect, lived from pub to pub, and from drink to drink. He might be about fifty, but neglect and hunger and drink had added to his years, and the unshaven grey stubbles upon his white, wasted face, gave him the look of a man who had descended past all hope. And the look in his eyes, too, was one from which hope had fled. It was a sad, wistful, famished look, and might be that of a man who, at some time in his life, had been stricken by a great misfortune from which he had never since recovered. But there was one great day in Ballycullen, and Kevin Shanaghan had been a great man that day. It was the day the meeting had been held to celebrate the triumph of the people in the Land War even in this part of Ireland.

The throngs that marched four deep came like detachments of victorious armies down every road into Ballycullen, with their banners blazing in the sun. And Kevin Shanaghan rode at the head of all after they had passed into one great company, and, with the staff laid proudly across his shoulder, he carried a huge green flag with a gold harp on it.

My First Taste of Porter

This extract from Flann O'Brien's At Swim-Two-Birds *of 1939 describes, among other things, the initiation of one into the art of drinking porter and the almost inevitable consequences.*

Biographical reminiscence, part the first: It was only a few months before composing the foregoing that I had my first experience of intoxicating beverages and their strange intestinal chemistry. I was walking through the Stephen's Green on a summer evening and conducting a conversation with a man called Kelly, then a student, hitherto a member of the farming class and now a private in the armed forces of the King. He was addicted to unclean expressions in ordinary conversation and spat continually, always fouling the flowerbeds on his way through the Green with a mucous deposit dislodged with a low grunting from the interior of his windpipe. In some respects he was a coarse man but he was lacking in malice or ill-humour. He purported to be a medical student but he had failed at least once to satisfy a body of examiners charged with regulating admission to the faculty. He suggested that we should drink a number of *jars* or pints of plain porter in Grogan's public house. I derived considerable pleasure from the casual quality of his suggestion and observed that it would probably do us no harm, thus expressing my whole-hearted concurrence by a figure of speech.

Name of figure of speech: Litotes (or Meiosis).

He turned to me with a facetious wry expression and showed me a penny and a sixpence in his rough hand.

I'm thirsty, he said. I have sevenpence. Therefore I buy a pint.

I immediately recognised this as an intimation that I should pay for my own porter.

The conclusion of your syllogism, I said lightly, is fallacious, being based on licensed premises.

Licensed premises is right, he replied, spitting heavily. I saw that my witticism was unperceived and quietly replaced it in the treasury of my mind.

We sat in Grogan's with our faded overcoats finely disarrayed on easy chairs in the mullioned snug. I gave a shilling and two pennies to a civil man who brought us in return two glasses of black porter, imperial pint measure. I adjusted the glasses to the front of each of us and reflected on the solemnity of the occasion. It was my first taste of porter. Innumerable persons with whom I had conversed had represented to me that spirituous liquors and intoxicants generally had an adverse effect on the senses and the body and that those who became addicted to stimulants in youth were unhappy throughout their lives and met with death at the end by a drunkard's fall, expiring ingloriously at the stair-bottom in a welter of blood and puke. Indian tonic-waters had been proposed to me by an aged lay-brother as an incomparable specific for thirst. The importance of the subject had been impressed upon me in a school-book which I read at the age of twelve.

Extract from Literary Reader, the Higher Class, by the Irish Christian Brothers: And in the flowers that wreathe the sparkling bowl, fell adders hiss and poisonous serpents roll—Prior. What is alcohol? All medical authorities tell us it is a double poison—an irritant and a narcotic poison. As an irritant it excites the brain, quickens the action of the heart, produces intoxication and leads to degeneration of the tissues. As a narcotic, it chiefly affects the nervous system; blunts the sensibility of the brain, spinal cord and nerves; and, when taken in sufficient quantity, produces death. When alcohol is taken into the system, an extra amount of work is thrown on various organs, particularly the lungs. The lungs, being overtaxed, become degenerated, and this is why so many inebriates suffer from a peculiar form of consumption called alcoholic phthisis—many, many cases of which are, alas, to be found in our hospitals, where the unhappy victims await the slow but sure march of an early death. It is a well-established fact that alcohol not only does not give strength but lessens it. It relaxes the muscles or instruments of motion and consequently their power decreases. This muscular depression is often followed by complete paralysis of the body, drink having unstrung the whole nervous system, which, when so unstrung leaves the body like a ship without sails or ropes—an unmovable or unmanageable thing. Alcohol may have its uses in the medical world, to which it should be relegated; but once a man becomes its victim, it is a terrible and a merciless master, and he finds himself in that dreadful state when all will-power is gone and he becomes a helpless imbecile, tortured at times by remorse and despair. Conclusion of the foregoing.

On the other hand, young men of my acquaintance who were in the habit of voluntarily placing themselves under the influence of alcohol had often surprised me with a recital of their strange adventures. The mind may be impaired by alcohol, I mused, but withal it may be pleasantly impaired. Personal experience appeared to me to be the only satisfactory means to the resolution of my doubts. Knowing it was my first one, I quietly fingered the butt of my glass before I raised it. Lightly I subjected myself to an inward interrogation.

Nature of interrogation: Who are my future cronies, where our mad carousals? What neat repast shall feast us light and choice of Attic taste with wine whence we may rise to hear the lute well touched or artful voice warble immortal notes or Tuscan air? What mad pursuit? What pipes and timbrels? What wild ecstasy?

Here's to your health, said Kelly.

Good luck, I said.

The porter was sour to the palate, but viscid, potent. Kelly made a long noise as if releasing air from his interior.

I looked at him from the corner of my eye and said:

You can't beat a good pint.

He leaned over and put his face close to me in an earnest manner.

Do you know what I am going to tell you, he said with his wry mouth, a pint of plain is your only man.

Notwithstanding this eulogy, I soon found that the mass of plain porter bears an unsatisfactory relation to its toxic content and I became subsequently addicted to brown stout in bottle, a drink which still remains the one that I prefer the most despite the painful and blinding fits of vomiting which a plurality of bottles has often induced in me.

I proceeded home one evening in October after leaving a gallon of half-digested porter on the floor of a public-house in Parnell Street and put myself with considerable difficulty into bed, where I remained for three days on the pretence of a chill. I was compelled to secrete my suit beneath the mattress because it was offensive to at least two of the senses and bore an explanation of my illness contrary to that already advanced.

Buff-coloured Puke

Extracted from Flann O'Brien's At Swim-Two-Birds *is this description of the conversion of stout into buff-coloured puke.*

That same afternoon I was sitting on a stool in an intoxicated condition in Grogan's licensed premises. Adjacent stools bore the forms of Brinsley and Kelly, my two true friends. The three of us were occupied in putting glasses of stout into the interior of our bodies and expressing by fine disputation the resulting sense of physical and mental well-being. In my thigh pocket I had eleven and eightpence in a weighty pendulum of mixed coins. Each of the arranged bottles on the shelves before me, narrow or squat-bellied, bore a dull picture of the gas bracket. Who can tell the stock of a public-house? Many no doubt are dummies, those especially within an arm-reach of the snug. The stout was of superior quality, soft against the tongue but sharp upon the orifice of the throat, softly efficient in its magical circulation through the conduits of the body. Half to myself, I said:

Do not let us forget that I have to buy *Die Harzreise*. Do not let us forget that.

Harzreise, said Brinsley. There is a house in Dalkey called Heartrise.

Brinsley then put his dark chin on the cup of a palm and leaned in thought on the counter, overlooking his drink, gazing beyond the frontier of the world.

What about another jar? said Kelly.

Ah, Lesbia, said Brinsley. The finest thing I ever wrote. How many kisses, Lesbia, you ask, would serve to sate this hungry love of mine?—As many as the Libyan sands that bask along Cyrene's shore where pine-trees wave, where burning Jupiter's untended shrine lies near to old King Battus' sacred grave:

Three stouts, called Kelly.

Let them be endless as the stars at night, that stare upon the lovers in a ditch—so often would love-crazed Catullus bite your burning lips, that prying eyes should not have power to count, nor evil tongues bewitch, the frenzied kisses that you gave and got.

Before we die of thirst, called Kelly, will you bring us *three more stouts*. God, he said to me, it's in the desert you'd think we were.

That's good stuff, you know, I said to Brinsley.

A picture came before my mind of the lovers at their hedge-pleasure in the pale starlight, no sound from them, his fierce mouth burying into hers.

Bloody good stuff, I said.

Kelly, invisible to my left, made a slapping noise.

The best I ever drank, he said.

As I exchanged an eye-message with Brinsley, a wheezing beggar inserted his person at my side and said:

Buy a scapular or a stud, Sir.

This interruption I did not understand. Afterwards, near Lad Lane police station a small man in black fell in with us and tapping me often about the chest, talked to me earnestly on the subject of

Rousseau, a member of the French nation. He was animated, his pale features striking in the starlight and voice going up and falling in the lilt of his argumentum. I did not understand his talk and was personally unacquainted with him. But Kelly was taking in all he said, for he stood near him, his taller head inclined in an attitude of close attention. Kelly then made a low noise and opened his mouth and covered the small man from shoulder to knee with a coating of unpleasant buff-coloured puke. Many other things happened on that night now imperfectly recorded in my memory but that incident is still very clear to me in my mind. Afterwards the small man was some distance from us in the lane, shaking his divested coat and rubbing it along the wall. He is a little man that the name of Rousseau will always recall to me. Conclusion of reminiscence.

Rathard

This unwonted display of drunkenness is from Sam Hanna Bell's December Bride, *published in 1951.*

There was little that the men could do in this weather, so they stayed indoors and sat about in Sarah's road. Hamilton nursed the fire in his lap, as Sarah said crossly, whittling eternally with his knife. He cut teeth for the new-fangled horse rake and then he made a butter-print for the girl, a cow in relief on a shamrock. She scoffed at the crude figures, but he was content for he saw that she was pleased. Frank lay smoking all day, turning the yellowed leaves of a natural history book. Sometimes he threw himself fully clothed on his bed, and Sarah found rinds of mud on the blankets. When she scolded him he threw the book away, fluttering and shedding leaves, and went outside. He came back in a few minutes and lounged about in a hangdog way. 'I'm going down tae Sampson's—is there anything ye want?' he asked at last. Sarah lifted the paraffin jar and shook it. 'There is,' she answered, thrusting it into his hand. 'And ask Agnes tae get me half a dozen candles and a loaf o' baker's bread from Skillen's shop.' He put on his hat and drew a sack over his shoulders and went out.

They were seated at their evening meal when he came back. Sarah rose when she heard his feet on the close, and lifting his plate from the hearth, blew the embers from the rim with her breath. They heard him fumbling at the latch, and then he came in with a little rush. Regaining his balance, he stared at them foolishly for a moment, blinking his eyes in the light. He lurched again as he set the oil-jar in the corner. Skimming his sodden hat across the room where it left a mark on the crocus-yellow wall, he crossed over to the table and sat down. His lips were wet and quivering, and his hair, darkened with the rain, tumbled on his brow so that Sarah's heart suddenly yearned to him. 'Fetch us down a couple o' glasses, Sarah!' he shouted and drew a half-pint of whiskey from his pocket. He set the bottle down with a thump among the tea-things and little trills of laughter ran through him as he peered at the bright amber liquor. Then he raised it between his eyes and the lamp. Shaken thus, the liquid released whorls of light that rose slowly up the bottle, melting and reforming again in spirals and flecks of golden fire. The light penetrating the liquid cast an aureate glow on the drunken face held close to the bottle. He sucked a great breath into his mouth. 'God, but it's a wonderful lovely thing,' he said. The sober awe in his voice startled and shocked Sarah. 'Ye drunken crature!' she cried, 'did ye ask Agnes tae get the groceries?' He stared at her dumb and outraged, then waved her impatiently aside. He turned to his brother. 'Hami, will ye have a wee drop?' There was a pleading note in his voice. Hamilton shook his head without looking up. 'Noan for me,' he mumbled.

The young man stared angrily at the other two bent over their plates. The cork squealed as he drew it from the bottle. Still they did not look up. He tilted the bottle over his cup and looked at them again. Their heads were low over their plates and their lips were scarcely moving. To his drunken mind they seemed to be saying grace. He drove the cork back again with his fist and set it down with a crash on the dresser. His actions were wanton, violent; he wanted the others to look up and speak to him. The meal finished in silence and towards the end of it Hamilton stole a glance at his brother. His face was sober and sullenly turned away. He looked at the bottle on the dresser. The golden liquor glowed like an idol. He was uneasy and perplexed. It was the first time that strong drink had ever been in Rathard.

The whiskey bottle sat on the dresser for some days and Sarah lifted it to dust under it each day. Then by that inexplicable process that activates household articles it was moved to the window ledge behind the bowl of shamrock. After a time it was carried down to the parlour and at last it came to rest, still untouched, in the darkest corner of the camphor-scented press in the sideboard.

Mr McCann

This extract from Patrick Boyle's Like Any Other Man *of 1966 is an object—and abject—lesson in how to get drunk.*

McCann, drinking at the bar counter with two fishermen, peered around the crowded, smoke-laden room. She was not to be seen. On the pretext of being in need of a leak, he went out to the kitchen, glancing into the empty drinking-room on the way past. The kitchen, too, was empty.

A sour ball of anger and disappointment rose in his throat. He hurried back to the bar where he ordered a fresh round of drinks.

'And I'll have a Gold Label this time,' he added. 'A large one.'

Hannah was very distressed.

'You've a right to stick to the Guinness, Mr McCann,' she pleaded. 'You know the way whiskey affects you after stout?'

'Give the man his pleasure,' one of the fishermen said.

'It's all right, Hannah,' said McCann. 'It was the empty stomach sickened me before. I have a gutful of food in me now.'

She served up the whiskey. He threw it back and ordered another round.

'Och, Mr McCann!' she protested. But she dished up the double whiskey nevertheless.

McCann took longer over this drink. He swirled the whiskey round in the glass, relishing the feeling of warmth and well-being that pervaded him. With each sip the clamour in the room lessened until at last—his glass emptied—the mouthing, wild-eyed, gesticulating figures made no more noise than the subdued, conversational hum of a cluster of feeding dung flies. When he spoke, his own voice sounded muffled. Disembodied.

'One more large whiskey, Hannah, and I'll go back to the stout.'

With a reproachful look, she filled out the drink. She said: 'You've a right to take the stout first and leave the whiskey for later.'

'Pull a stout, so,' he said.

As she was pouring out the stout, he downed the whiskey, puffing noisily after each mouthful.

'You're making a bog hole of your poor stomach, Mr McCann.' She shook her head disapprovingly as she placed the tumbler of stout at his elbow.

Her moving lips added no meaning to the muted buzz going on all round him. It was as if, stunned and stricken by the heat, he rested for a moment, head hanging like an exhausted beast, while around him the irrelevant murmur of insect life rose and fell in a ceaseless dirge. The heat was intense. Beating down on skull and shoulders. With little hope of bettering his lot, he took a long slug of stout. Sighed deeply. Replaced the glass. The walls of the room had closed in. The ceiling become depressed and threatening. Smoke swirled and eddied around dim moving figures.

He started to mop his steaming forehead and smarting eyes but the handkerchief slipped through his nerveless fingers and fluttered to the floor. Stooping to retrieve it, he felt a warning spasm of nausea rise in his throat. He straightened up, gripping the swaying counter.

'Must...go...out,' he explained to the heedless company in noiseless fishlike gasps. 'Air...Air...Want...fresh...air.'

He plunged towards the door.

'Are you all right, Mr McCann?' Hannah called after him.

Outside on the road, he began to feel better. The threatened nausea did not recur. Soothed by the cool night air, he set off up the cliff path, walking silently on a grass verge—moonlit, calcified, alien. When a cloud slid across the moon, he stopped, suspicious of the perilous half-dark. In fits and starts he reached the cliff-top where he flung himself down in the long grass.

He lay there—supine—head pillowed on forearms, savouring the safety of solid earth. Not till the night sky had ceased swaying and plunging did he lift his head to look around.

Drunkard

This poem is from Patrick Kavanagh's Complete Poems *of 1972.*

From your wine-cask I fill
My glass again
And I will drink to all
The happy men.

And I will drink to those
Dark passionate
Children who dance unto
Death's rusty gate.

And I will drink to every
Dog that goes
Bravely to that far country
No one knows.

The Royal Iris

These extracts are from Hugh Leonard's Home Before Night *of 1979; they describe a notable outing.*

'If you're bold,' his mother said to him, 'I'll give you back to your mother.'

They were on the *Royal Iris*, on one of the evening cruises around Howth, and he was looking at Lambay Island. 'There she is,' his mother said, 'coming for to get you,' and real as real he saw a tall woman in black clothes on the edge of the cliffs. Her face was dark because she knew he was safe from her on the *Royal Iris*, but she would get him yet.

Later on when he grew up and got sense he would suppose that it was one of the times his mother, not his real one, but the one he called mammy, had drink on her, or why else would she frighten him? Sure enough, a man asked her up to dance with him to the melodeon band, and she went—that was proof—and he and his da sat on one of the life rafts and watched. His da said nothing then, but he must have been jealous. He had a temper; he was short with red hair and in his time had played tug-o'-war. And he had gone into a rage that day when Jack stuck his head into a Jewman's car on the Barrack Road to find out what the driver could see in the mirror.

The Jewman was off up the Alley Lane collecting payments, but his dog was in the car and it sprang up and swung out at Jack's lip. One woman ran out of her house with iodine and another with Lourdes water, and when his da came home from work Jack was wearing a moustache of sticking plaster and cotton wool and belching from the whole bottle of Taylor-Keith lemonade the Jewman had poured into him outside the hospital. 'Now, Nick,' was all his mother had time to say before his da began jumping up and down, munching his tongue and giving an imitation of a boy skipping like a lunatic along the footpath, which was how he thought Jack had cut his lip. 'He won't be marked,' his mother said as the clay from his da's boots

135

hit the Blessed Virgin like sleet. 'Acting the go-boy, acting the go-boy,' his da sang, doing a war dance. 'You old madman,' his mother said, 'a dog bit him.' 'A nawg mih me,' Jack said, with his top lip starched into a sneer, and even when his da at last understood he was too headstrong to own himself in the wrong, but instead went jazz-dancing out into the yard and up a heap of coal. When he came back in he was in a good humour but pale from the shock. He looked at Jack on the edge of the big double bed, and said: 'Do you know what I'm going to tell you? The Kerry Blue and the alsatian is treacherous animals.'

On the *Royal Iris*, however, he watched Jack's mother waltzing with the man to 'Gold and Silver' and held his tongue. The times she had a drop taken, she was like uncle Sonny: she would go for you if you vexed her, so maybe it was as well to be jealous in your mind and not to her face. Except at Myra Kinsella's wedding, Jack had never seen her dance before. She was small and stout, like two Christmas puddings, one sitting on top of the other, with a weenchy little one on top of them again. Her hair was long and black and done up in a bun under her hat with the wide mauve band and the not-real rose. She was light on her feet. The sea was choppy, and empty stout bottles skithered up and down the wet deck, with the dancers kicking at them accidentally on purpose. A man and a girl fell, and a woman called out 'He can't wait,' whatever that meant. Jack wondered if the man would bring his mother back to them, then he looked out across the sea to Lambay Island, and away again quickly before he could see his real mother where the cliffs began. His da's red whiskers shivered in the wind.

When the dancing stopped, a man got up to sing 'Smilin' Through' and Jack's mother came back. She wasn't too bad: you could only tell if you knew her, because the eyes were queer. She would put you in mind of that woman in the pictures who always acted the mother and had the same look in her eyes, only nobody in the picture with her ever let on they noticed. When Jack saw that look—on a Holy Thursday when she came in from doing the Seven Churches, or in Christmas week, or on a bank holiday like now—he would go sulky and be cool with her. That was always the start, and she knew the signs in him as well as he knew them in her. Now, coming through the crowd on the deck, she caught sight of his face and his da's. She began to hum to show them she had not a care in the world and they were only begrudgers. Instead of sitting with them on the life raft, she plucked her handbag from between them and went off to the lav. Jack knew there was a Baby Power in the handbag, but it would be another four or five years before he would get up the nerve to open her bag at such times and pour the whiskey down the shore in the yard.

'There's Ireland's Eye, son,' his da said.

* * *

When she came back from the lav they were passing the Bailey lighthouse. Lambay Island had gone behind Howth, and he could look out at the sea now with his two eyes, instead of keeping the near one shut like when he would run past the red Sacred Heart lamp in the window of the room where Biddy Byrne had died. 'We thought you got stuck,' his da said to his mother, to make a joke. 'No fear of me,' she said, as cold as rain. She was black out with the pair of them, and gave Jack a quick look with her bright, not-well eyes to let him know that he was a cur and she was done with him. 'The day held out fine, after all,' his da said, to be sociable. 'If a body was let enjoy it,' she said. The words fell out of her mouth the way you would chop logs with a hatchet. His da said she was a comical woman and stood Jack up on the life raft to see Dublin.

The sun was in their eyes and Dublin was as jet black as the mountains, but you could see Dun Laoghaire harbour and make out Dalkey by the island and the three hills. Home was a long way.

His mother nearly turned her ankle getting off the *Royal Iris* at Butt Bridge. Jack was with his da at the bottom of the gangway. 'Come on, Mag,' his da said. Instead, she gave a scalding look to a man who was behind her with a bottle of stout in his fist, and said: 'Don't you push me, you pup.'

The man could not believe she meant him. 'I never laid hand nor glove on you missus,' he said. The pair of them were blocking the gangway, with the crowds of the world trying to get past. The people who were already off the boat and on the quay turned to gawk. 'You're a liar and a blasted one,' his mother said.

The man had black hairs all over his face and a nose that would cut butter. He was up from the country, and all he could think of to say was: 'Who's a liar?' A high-up sailor in a peaked cap said for the passengers to move along now, please. The crowd behind his mother and the man were muttering and shoving. His da called out 'Mag, Mag,' and Jack felt his insides go empty with shame. This put Marie Dressler in the ha'penny place; it was worse, even, than the day his mother tripped and fell outside Thomas's dairy and her hat rolled along like a hoop.

'Keep your mawsy hands to yourself,' she said to the man. 'How dare you, how dare the ignorant likes of you interfere with me.'

People from off the bogs were always dangerous and would turn on you when riz, and now that the man had got a hold on his senses he went red under the black hairs. 'Don't you call me ignorant, missus,' he said in the sort of sing-song way they talked in the country. 'And I'm no liar neither, so I'm not.'

'Ignorant liar,' she said up into his face, putting the two words together to aggravate him two times over.

The edge of his nose could have stabbed her. A man who was with him caught his shoulder and said: 'Don't put yourself in a passion, Dominic. The woman has drink took.'

'I what? I what?' she said, turning on the other man. 'Say that out loud.' The words were not out of her mouth when the crowd trying to get off the ship gave a heave and pushed the bogman against Jack's mother. It was only a little nudge in the stomach, but she caught hold of the rope on the two sides of the gangway and called out: 'Nick, Nick, he hit me.'

The bogman said 'I did not,' dribbling like a babby, and Jack's mother said 'He hit me in the breast.' The way she held on to the two ropes, you would think the bogman was trying to throw her in the River Liffey.

They were now disgraced to the world. People on the boat began to shout things like 'Hit her another belt' and 'Send for the Guards' and 'Eh, missus, give us a dance,' and a gang of women on the quay sang a song called 'Give the Woman in the Bed More Porter'. Jack's da went tearing up the gangway, shouting 'Did you hit that woman?' He was in a roaring rage. He could not get past her to give the bogman a puck of his fist: she was in his way, and when he pulled at her arm to make her let go of the rope she clung on like a conger eel. She was sobbing now: 'Is there no one to protect a harmless poor creature?' His da kept saying: 'Did you hit that woman?' and 'Mag, let go of the rope.'

Jack's mother had made a show of the bogman, and now he was lepping for fight. He was doing a tap dance on the gangway with his big boots, massacring the air with his fists and wiping his nose with his thumb. He still had a hold of the bottle, and his antrumartins sent the stout gushing out of it in thick foamy spouts over his blue suit. 'Come on,' he said to Jack's da, 'I'm ready for oo. Now oo've met oor match.' The man with him was trying to make peace. 'Mister, nobody is tampering with her. Will you take the decent woman home and let us off the shagging boat?' Jack's da kept shouting: 'Mag, let go.'

Jack wanted to run, run across the bridge and hide in Tara Street station, but there would only be a worse commotion if they thought he was lost. He turned his back on the *Royal Iris* and them and looked at other things: the Customs House, the row of hansom cabs, the lit-up trams on O'Connell Bridge, the Corinthian picture house. He was making himself wonder what picture was on there when a woman bent down to him, a cream-coloured face stooping too low and saying: 'Are you with that lady and gentleman?' He was going to say no; instead he put his fists in his eyes. She pulled one hand down and held a threepenny bit in front of his face. 'Your mammy is only upset,' she said. She wrapped his fist around the threepenny bit. 'Will we wait for them over here?' She led him to the corner of the bridge. It entered his mind that she might be trying to steal him, the way the tinkers on the Barnhill Road would if they caught you, but she looked well-off, so let her.

She was not as old as his mother. 'Will you buy sweets with your threepence?' she asked. He nodded to keep her from annoying him and put his fists back in his eyes. 'What kind of sweets?' He did not think much of her for asking him to belittle his misery with a conversation about sweets; but if ever there was a tomorrow he would buy Scot's Clan: they were his favourites, his mother always bought a bag when they went to the pictures. There was a snot running out of his nose with the crying. The woman took a handkerchief from the pocket of the suit he got last year for his First Holy Communion and wiped his face. A man came out of the crowd; he had a little girl in a harness on his back and a boy by the hand. He was with the woman. The boy looked at Jack as if he had nettles growing out of his ears. 'That's my little boy,' the woman said. 'His name is Cormac. What's your name?' 'Bruce,' Jack said. He thought that Cormac looked a proper little get.

A great jeer went up from the crowd, then there was a grumbling sound like when a concert was over and the clapping had stopped. Then his da came in sight walking quickly, pushing his mother along by the elbow and not minding the people who were looking at them with their eyes out on sticks. His mother's hat was wagging up and down on her head, caught by one hatpin at the back. They looked like Laurel and Hardy, only not funny, with his mother like Hardy in a huff. 'They won't mock and jeer at *me*,' she was saying. 'Bad scran to curs the like of them, may they never have a day's luck.' She made to stop and give a look over her shoulder that would scarify the jeerers, but his da kept pushing her so that while the top half of her was in no hurry the legs were going around like the pedals on a bicycle. You could see that he was raging for having made a show of himself over her.

He stood in their way. Now that they were on the move he did not want them to have to stop and look for him, and maybe call him by his name for the world to hear. When they got close, the woman who had given him the threepence said: 'You're not fit to be in charge of a child. I'm a mother and I—' His da did not even slow down and look at her. He caught hold of Jack the way a snowball would pick up a stone; it was the sort of thing you could not do a second time if they paid you. He was swept along, and the woman was left with the words hanging out of her mouth while the three of them were off across Butt Bridge like hares.

Peculiar Parties

Dramas

This excerpt from Edna O'Brien's Lantern Slides *of 1990 describes a situation when a new shopkeeper arrives in an Irish town; it may appear a little contrived, but it is credible and amusing.*

It was about four o'clock in the afternoon when the disturbance happened. I had gone over there because of being possessed by a mad hope that they would do a reading of the play, and that I would be needed to play some role, even if it was a menial one. I stood in the doorway of the drapery shop across the street, visible if Barry should lift the net curtain and look out. Indeed, I believed he would and I waited quite happily. The village was quiet and sunk in its after-dinner somnolence, with only myself and a few dogs prowling about. It had begun to spatter with rain. I heard a window being raised and was stunned to see the visitors on the small upstairs balcony, dressed in outlandish women's clothing. I should have seen disaster then, except that I thought they were women, that other visitors, their wives perhaps, had come unbeknownst to us. When I saw Barry in a maroon dress, larking, I ducked down, guessing the awful truth. He was calling, 'Friends, Romans, countrymen.' Already three or four people had come to their doorways, and soon there was a small crowd looking up at the appalling spectacle of three drunk men pretending to be women. They were all wearing pancake makeup and were heavily rouged. The actor also wore a string of pearls and kept hitting the other two in jest. Ivan was wearing a pleated skirt and a low-cut white blouse, with falsies underneath. The actor had on some kind of toga and was shouting wild endearments and throwing kisses.

The inflamed owner of the drapery shop asked me how long these antics had been going on.

'I don't know,' I said, my face scarlet, every bit of me wishing to vanish. Yet I followed the crowd as they moved, inexorably, towards the balcony, all of them speechless, as if the spectacle had robbed them of their reason. It was in itself like a crusade, this fanatic throng moving towards assault.

Barry wore a tam-o'-shanter and looked uncannily like a girl. It gave me the shivers to see this metamorphosis. He even tossed his neck like a girl, and you would no longer believe he was bald. The actor warmed to the situation and started calling people 'ducky' and 'Cinders', while also reciting snatches from Shakespeare. He singled people out. So carried away was he by the allure of his performance that the brunette wig he was wearing began to slip, but determined to be a sport about this, he took it off, doffed it to the crowd and replaced it again. One of the women, a Mrs Gleeson, fainted, but more attention was being paid to the three performers than to her, so she had to stagger to her feet again. Seeing that the actor was stealing the scene, Ivan did something terrible: he opened the low-cut blouse, took out the falsies, tossed them down to the crowd and said to one of the young men, 'Where there's that, there's plenty more.' The young man in question did not know what to do, did not know whether to pick them up and throw them back or challenge the strangers to a fight. The actor and Ivan then began arguing and vied with each other as to who was the most fetching. Barry had receded and was in the doorway of the upper room, still drunk, but obviously not so drunk as to be indifferent to the calamity that had occurred.

The actor, it seemed, had also taken a liking to the young man whom Ivan had thrown the falsies to, and now holding a folded scroll, he leaned over the wrought iron, looked down directly at the man, brandished the scroll and said, 'It's bigger than that, darling.' At once the locals got the gist of the situation and called on him to come down so they could beat him to a pulp. Enthused now by their heckling, he stood on the wobbly parapet and began to scold them, telling them there were some naughty skeletons in their lives and that they couldn't fool him by all pretending to be happily married men. Then he said something awful: he said that the great Oscar Wilde had termed marriage bed 'the couch of lawful lust'. A young guard arrived and called up to the actor to please recognise that he was causing a disturbance to the peace as well as scandalising innocent people.

'Come and get me, darling,' the actor said and wriggled his forefinger, like a saucy heroine in a play. Also, on account of being drunk he was swaying on this very rickety parapet.

'Come down now,' the guard said, trying to humour him a bit, because he did not want the villagers to have a death on their hands. The actor smiled at this note of conciliation and called the guard 'Lola', and asked if he ever used his big baton anywhere else, and so provoked the young guard and so horrified the townspeople that already men were taking off their jackets to prepare for a fight.

'Beat me, I love it,' he called down while they lavished dire threats on him. Ivan, it seemed, was now enjoying the scene and did not seem to mind that the actor was getting most of the attention and most of the abuse. Two ladders were fetched and the young guard climbed up to arrest the three men. The actor teased him as he approached. The doctor followed, vowing that he would give them an injection to silence their filthy tongues. Barry had already gone in, and Ivan was trying to mollify them, saying it was all clean fun, when the actor put his arms around the young guard and lathered him with frenzied kisses. Other men hurried up the ladder and pushed the culprits into the bedroom so that people would be spared any further display of lunacy. The french doors were closed, and shouting and arguments began. Then the voices ceased as the offenders were pulled from the bedroom to the room downstairs, so that they could be carted into the police van which was now waiting. People feared that maybe these theatrical villains were armed, while the women wondered aloud if Barry had had these costumes and falsies and things, or if the actors had brought them. It was true that they had come with two suitcases. The Liddy girl had been sent out in the rain to carry them in. The sergeant who now arrived on the scene called to the upper floor, but upon getting no answer went around to the back of the house, where he was followed by a straggle of people. The rest of us waited in front, some of the opinion that the actor was sure to come back onto the balcony, to take a bow. The smaller children went from the front to the back of the house and returned to say there had been a terrible crash of bottles and crockery. The dining-room table was overturned in the fracas. About ten minutes later they came out by the back door, each of the culprits held by two men. The actor was wearing his green suit, but his makeup had not been fully wiped off, so that he looked vivid and startled, like someone about to embark on a great role. Ivan was in his raincoat and threatening aloud to sue unless he was allowed to speak to his solicitor. He called the guards and the people 'rabble'. The woman who had fainted went up to Barry and vehemently cursed him, while one of the town girls had the audacity to ask the actor for his autograph. He shouted the name of the theatre in Dublin to which she could send for it. Some said that he would never again perform in that or any theatre, as his name was mud.

When I saw Barry waiting to be bundled into the van like a criminal, I wanted to run over to him, or else to shout at the locals, disown them in some way. But I was too afraid. He caught my eye for an instant. I don't know why it was me he looked at, except perhaps he was hoping he had a friend, he was hoping our forays into drama had made a bond between us. He looked so abject that I had to look away and instead concentrated my gaze on the shop window, where the weighing scales, the ham slicer and all the precious commodities were like props on an empty stage. From the side of my eye I saw him get into the big black van and saw it drive away with all the solemnity of a hearse.

Jamesy's Father's Party

This is an extract from The Leaves on Grey *(1980) by Desmond Hogan.*

Rain came in November like a deluge, and one evening Jamesy's father threw a party.

Jamesy's home lay outside Dublin, a two storey house by the ocean. It stood upon rocks and always at night the sea seduced, distant lights, noise. One was led to the sea as though to an exterior effect of the house. It assembled lights, colours, an astonishing medley of sounds. Ultimately it told one something of Ireland, this ancient country, always bordering on sea, on sky, an unclear bond between it and other countries.

Music gently eroded the soft breezes the evening of the party, conversation rising and falling near the window-sill, women in black, penitential, the menfolk like bumble bees to a man, bellies swollen with drink.

A lady, Protestant, spoke in an arch voice about her acquaintance with W. B. Yeats. 'The Greatest Irishman,' she said, and a raucous Dublin accent called out, 'What about Eamon de Valera?'

'A stringy French bean,' the Protestant lady issued over a liqueur and the Dublin man said, 'Well we had Matt Talbot and Sean McDermott,' confusing an alcoholic martyr and a young hero, 'And you call your man Yeats great.'

Whereupon the Protestant lady marched to the window, looked upon the ocean and cried as though to the Hill of Howth opposite, 'And great art beaten down.' The Dublin man, an actor, began singing 'Kelly the boy from Killane' when a Hollywood starlet walked in past the swimming-pool, a little black cape about her wasp-like shoulders. She smiled, hiding a multitude of complicity under the umbrella of her smile. A journalist veered towards her, a lady journalist, and nearly fell in the swimming-pool. Benny Goodman began to play up, saxophone music from New York troubling the night, the moon that had just emerged from the clouds, standing above Dublin bay like a Roman sovereign.

Mrs Nesbitt, Jamesy's mother, held a glass of sherry as though she was outstretching an antique thimble. She stood. People looked at her. She had certain airs, graces, blown at her from the Twelve Pins in Connemara. Daughter of an Anglo-Irish family, many of her relatives gathered, astonishing ancient men like jaded Irish wolfhounds, ladies from the mansions of Connemara or Wicklow, lichen virtually grown into their manners, their chins uneven, chins that told of an iron dominance of Ireland for 900 years.

Jamesy's mother spoke to Sarah, Christine in that order. She spoke to Liam, to me, civilised conversation with Jamesy's new-found friends. Sarah would have been impressive, Sarah in white, Sarah holding a handbag. The mixture of coquette and saint.

I perceived Liam in a black blazer and white shirt, the shirt singularly white, his hair the colour of daffodils before opening, green upon yellow. Odd moments I looked and he was there, totally there, there like the oak tree of old, holding out somehow, against time. He was totally present that evening, the sound of a New York saxophone edging in upon his silhouette against the darkening Irish Sea.

Someone entered and spoke of snow.

Someone else entered and told about a hungry protesting mob he'd seen.

A woman with a yellow scarf dotted with red still on her head entered, one flake clinging to her scarf, and her Anglo-Irish voice rebounding in the room, telling of a Catholic group she'd seen in O'Connell Street, bearing flame and pictures of prelates behind the Iron Curtain.

A parson with a voice rich as British vegetables spoke about the *I Ching*.

A dotty old professor muttered about Archimedes.

The film star had her picture taken.

As if as an afterthought Jamesy's father announced it was his birthday. A birthday cake entered as though on a magic carpet. It was in fact borne by a maid. The Hollywood starlet got upset, began crying. A birthday serenade was sung.

Sarah sat by the swimming-pool discussing Troubadour poetry with a young academic from Cambridge. Christine and the Dublin actor were singing 'Carrickfergus' in a corner. Liam was moping about, fingering porcelain, china, holding it as he had held little snails wrapped in their nuggets of shells as a child. The parson was loudly telling ghost stories, witches, ogres, poltergeists seen in Wicklow, when I discovered Jamesy with his trousers down making love to an older woman.

First time I'd ever seen anyone making love. I reckoned that evening it was a Protestant, Anglo-Irish thing to do. I'd drunk too much. I was aware of friends floating, each on their own journey. I now knew the illusion of togetherness between us but I didn't wish to think about it. I knew the unalterable gap that lay between people.

The moon re-emerged and the Hollywood starlet could be seen standing on rocks, holding a glass of rosé, looking towards the Hill of Howth as though to Hollywood's lost illusions and Jamesy's father spoke of Hollywood, time he'd played an Irish priest in a film and a young American actor entered the confessional and said—the lines weren't in the script—'Father, I don't make love. I masturbate.' A woman who looked like a wedding cake, layer upon layer of her, sang an aria by the piano and Jamesy's mother in the absence of Jamesy, talked of Connemara, the mountains, the beauty, days on white horses among rhododendron bushes.

Someone addressed Jamesy's father. 'Mr Nesbitt, how come you never played Hamlet, always Polonius?' whereupon Jamesy's father recited the last lines of Othello, forgetting the very end, lapsing into Molière, then standing on a table, drunk out of his mind, taking down his trousers, waving them in the air, crying, 'A glass of wine, a loaf of bread—and thou, thou, thou.'

No more was seen of the Hollywood starlet. People presumed she'd taken a boat to sea. The parson said what Ireland needed was the royal family. Jamesy's mother had found a titled gentleman among the crowd, a relation of the Queen of England. Her husband was wandering around in his knickers, his balls bulging and his knickers huge like a child's nappy. An English lady screamed that she'd seen a mouse and a leading Irish poet entered, accompanied by his cohorts, danced with a rounded Anglo-Irish lady, stuffed himself with English cheddar, accused everyone of being 'a shower of fucking bejaysus wankers,' put an arm about Liam's shoulders and said, 'I can tell you've got sense.'

Liam walked away. He was quite drunk. I could suddenly tell his head was swimming with drink. His eyes were glazed. He made for the swimming-pool and jumped in. There was horror. People stopped. Jamesy's father who had fetched a photograph of himself with Lady Gregory was silenced.

One could see that Liam had disappeared to the bottom of the pool. I knew what was happening, recognised the glaze in his eyes from a long time ago. I jumped in, in my clothes.

I caught Liam. I knew that he was trying to drag himself down, that again it was a long time ago and a woman was weighting herself down to the bottom of a river. 'Liam,' I screamed. I caught him by his blond hair, tugged him up. His shirt was torn half off. He lay unconscious by the pool. A man gave him artificial respiration. Sarah knelt beside him. She didn't touch him. Just looked.

Mind That 'Tis My Brother

This is an extract from the novel of that name by Gaye Shortland;
her book is slightly unusual in that the narrator, Tony, is cremated
and in an urn.

It gave me a queer feelin goin inta the club that night. Like I'd a lump
in me throat. Especially when I saw Mothur ensconced in his usual
position, cigarette ensconced in its usual position. Our club is a great
place—a bit makeshift as far as furniture goes, with wooden benches
like, but tis all decked out with scenury an bits a lightin and stuff
robbed from the Everyman an othur theatres an places round the city.

Mothur's an artist an does well for himself—no shortage a dosh but
he spends a ferocious amount. His real name is Denis, by the way,
Denis Harte. Yeh mighta heard a him or seen him on RTE or seen his
pictures. Lean-lookin man—piercin blue eyes. Nice-lookin. At *least*
ten years oldur than us—maybe more like fifteen. Bit of a beard, or a
berd as the ould folk would say, just very little, y'know the kinda
thing—brownyfair.

Anyway, as I was sayin, most a the scenury was swiped an half of
it from RTE an the Eurovision Song Contest years ago an brought
down from Dublin in the back of a van.

When we went in they were all dancin *mad* as usual.

The clones an chickuns were there in full force an the place was
full a women too—the dykes an the hoors an the fag-hags an the odd
woman chancin her arm with a man. A lot a the lads bring their sisturs
with em—y'see this is a kinda traditional thing to do by way of havin
a woman to parade yerself with. We had ta shouldur our way through
em all to get to Mothur's table. The noise wasn't exactly disco-level
because we don't have the equipment like but twas deafenin enough.
He looked up at us through the usual cloud a smoke, a bevy a rings on
his fingurs an a bevy a pints before him. Plus a bottle a Paddy, three-
quarters full. The pints would be ones he'd bought for othur people—
he only drank whiskey an vodka an white an gins an tonics an the like
himself. Jay, twas great to see him. He was flanked (that's a grand

word for it) by Mad Mary an one a his favourite chickuns who looked right sulky to see us. The chickuns, in case yeh don't know, are a whole troop a lads who keep appearin out a nowhere (an endless supply, Mothur says) newly gay, newly decked out in their gay attire, all around seventeen an eighteen. They're very wild, at least some of em are.

'Benedicite,' said Dec. Chapter 63, that is. *Whenever the brethren meet, let the junior ask the senior for a blessing.*

'Daaaahlings! How are you! Liam! How good to see you!' An they both got kissed. 'Declan, come sit here next to me and hold my hand. I'm *most* depressed, *hideously* depressed!'

Dec glared at Mad Mary, who was in drag as usual that night, till he made room for him next to Mothur.

'Where's your boa?' said Dec, lookin down his nose at Mad Mary's legs. 'Shouldn't you be out on the floor flaunting yourself?'

'Fuck aafff, baaoy!' I'm guessin now but I'd say Mad Mary didn't know what boa or flauntin meant.

'Pardon me now, Mr Harte, but your catamite is giving me terrible abuse. Don't you evur correct him? If I were you I'd take him home and *ledder* him for his own good. It's this liberal upbringing that has the youth of this country ruined...'

'Oh, please, please, *please*, I *beg* of you, don't start squabbling—I couldn't stand it tonight! Liam—but you're looking absolutely marvellous, my dear! And how is the Great Metropolis? Seething in Sin as usual, I trust? Excellent, excellent.' He distributed pints a Murphy's from the fleetful in fronta him. 'Declan, *what* are you *doing* to me? My flat is in a *disgusting* state—like the proverbial rubbish-tip. It's no wonder I'm depressed. Now it's *your* fault, dear boy—you know it is. *Why* haven't you been by? You *know* I depend on you!' Dec has been cleanin Mothur's flat for years.

'Didn't they tell you I was away?' asked Dec, a bit aggressive like.

'They may have, they may have...perhaps they did...it may be I didn't absorb the information...' Mothur was a *ferocious* drinker. 'But where *were* you, daahling?'

'Swansea.'

'*Swan*sea?'

'On my way to London. But I turned back.'

'London! But you mustn't *dream* of leaving Cork! I cannot survive without you—I would *recidivate*!'

Recidivate. That's what he said, I'm sure of it. I don't know what it means. But I can guess. He meant that him an his flat would go to the dogs.

'You're right there, girl,' said Liam. 'That flat was shaggin awful before Regina started workin for yeh—a total wreck like.'

'He changed my life! Will I ever forget it? That happy day! Here's my list before I start, said he to me, handing me this *lengthy* document—a veritable *catalogue* of cleaning equipment. Ah, blessed words if I did but know it at the time!' Mothur seemed a bit distracted. He kept lookin at the door an the fact that he was talkin so much an wavin his hands about meant he was nervous.

'Yeah, an then he went out an spent the money on drink an he had to wait for dole-day to buy the cleanin stuff!'

'But he *did* buy it,' said Mothur. 'And came—'

'With my little magic wand,' said Dec.

'Oh, he's a wonder…' said Mothur.

Tis true. I've seen him at it. Like he'd go in an he'd be *scrubbin mad*, gettin the whole place spick an span an throwin things out. An then he'd say 'If you're lookin for anything now tis out in the bin' an that kinda thing. An then when he'd be finished Mothur would produce a bottle a whiskey an they'd sit down an they'd polish it off between em. He's done it for a few people besides Mothur too.

'And how he pampers me!' said Mothur. 'Cooking and running after me with cups of coffee, making me sit down, telling me "not to budge now". I need it, I need it, my *soul* needs it.'

'But doesn't Mad Mary do all that for yeh?' asked Liam slyly.

'Fuck aafff!' said Mad Mary.

'Mary has his own function, dahling, and it has little to do with the kitchen.' Mad Mary smirked at this, twirlin his long black hair—well, his hair-piece like—around his fingurs.

'That's *his* mistake. There's more powur in the kitchen,' said Dec. That's why wherevur I was I'd wangle my way into the kitchen by hook or by crook. And anothur thing,' eyein Mad Mary. 'I wouldn't be seen *dead* in a mini-skirt if I had knobbly knees like that. Which I haven't, thanks be to God.'

'Declan! Please! I really cannot *stand* bitchiness tonight. Listen to me—tell me, must chaos come again? Have you deserted me?'

'Will you stop *moaning*? I'll be down tomorrow. A dab of Pledge behind the ears and I'll sort you out in no time. Shur, I have your place now to a fine art.'

'Thank you, thank you, thank you!' An he filled a glass up to the top with whiskey for Dec. He was gazin at the door again. I saw Liam takin that in an smilin inta his pint. 'Really! Liam, dear, could you go and ask them to put on some decent music? One can only take so much of that dance stuff. Ask them to play Annie Lennox perhaps.'

'Why not some Joan Suthurland?' said Dec. 'Tell them there's a request for the quartet from *Rigoletto*.'

No soonur did he say that but the speakurs began to blare out Hammur's *U Can't Touch This* an twas like a signal for everybody to clear the floor. All the clones an chickuns lined up for this kind of dance-competition they do. The clones were all decked out in rap gear. The original clones were back a bit, in the late 70s maybe— they'd all dress the same, very sharp, in suits, an if they were a bit butch they'd have a moustache. They useta fox-trot with each othur all night an do this kinda jivin off each othur. An now we call the Hammur crowd 'clones' because they all dress the same too.

'Oh, Good Lord, No! It's Spanner-time!' Mothur was definitely cranky tonight. He usually liked watchin the chickuns in action.

Music hits me so hard, rapped Hammur with the chickuns an clones backin him.

Makes me say oh my Lord!

'Don't ye want to dance?' said Dec to Mad Mary an the chickun, real aggressive. He didn't like Mary an he didn't approve a the chickuns at all. He was always givin out about them bein too young, sayin twas immoral altogethur—which was queer because he was on the game himself since he was fourteen—on the game, not just on the scene like. Although he always said he nevur took money—that he done it because he *liked* doin it. Maybe. Anyway, like me, in the early days he'da been scared a his mothur.

Wedlocked

This description of a house-warming party is from Emma Cooke's
novel of that name published in 1994.

Their name is Daly. He is an Irishman and his wife, Sophia, is Greek.
Last night they gave a house-warming party. Everyone in the
neighbourhood was invited. Sophia Daly is petite, glamorous, a great
cook. Long tables held selections of rainbow-coloured dainties.
Andrew Daly mixed lethal cocktails with a heavy hand. Everyone
quickly got drunk and hilarious. It was Andrew's birthday. He was
thirty years old, the big three 0. Decorations gave a carnival
atmosphere. I felt older than I wanted to be. I wished we could turn
back the clock. I wished we hadn't married so young. I wished I could
rewind my life as if it was a tape. I'd had enough to drink to make it
seem like a reasonable proposition.

It seemed so long since I'd been at a party! I couldn't always live
the way I had lived over the past months, in a knot, eating my heart
out over the cruelty of Peter's death.

'Don't push me around.' I heard Ruth's voice out in the hall.
Turning, I saw her enter with Alan behind her.

I didn't greet them. I was here to enjoy myself. I was in no mood
for Ruth and her troubles as I wondered what Andrew Daly used as
the base for his special pink punch cocktail.

'Please, Alan!' I heard her voice. She sounded tearful.

I couldn't avoid seeing him pinch her arm. I was forced into
remembering how he had been on that Sunday afternoon. I was
looking into a cold yawning hole and Ruth lay at the bottom with a
dark destroyed look on her face. The party was just a façade, we had
no business here.

'Leave her alone,' I said sharply.

He looked sullen then stepped towards me, caught my arm and
twisted the skin between his hands so that it burned. In spite of the
cocktails I'd drunk I could smell the whiskey on his breath.

'Shut up or I'll make you squeal again,' he said and I had a glimpse of Ruth's terror-stricken existence. I wanted to run away and hide but his grip was too strong for me to wriggle free.

'OK, sweetie, how about another of these?'

Andrew Daly was beside us, all aftershave and hair mousse, another tumbler of his pink concoction in his hand.

'You two know each other?' he smiled. He could have advertised toothpaste to good effect.

'Too long. Back in the bad old days she used to be a good fuck, pardon my French, now she's turned into a right bitch,' said Alan loudly.

The people near us had stopped talking. The Dalys had invited everybody in the neighbourhood and so it was a mixed bunch of young and old, butterfly glasses, teased hair, blue rinses, jeans, dark suits, mini skirts and pussycat bows. I watched as they merged into a collage of modern suburbia.

'How about Paris. Remember that time in Paris?' Alan prodded.

'Oh, Paris,' Andrew Daly picked up the name like a crow grabbing a breadcrumb. 'Great place. Sophia and I just love it. Do you enjoy Paris, Dixie—Mrs Molloy?'

I saw by his expression that he was terrified that a row was about to start.

'Sure,' I said. 'It's terrific. The Champs Élysées and all that.'

'I remember you in that big old wooden bed and squatting on the bidet beside the fireplace in that dump behind the Galeries Lafayette,' Alan snorted. 'God, you were mad for it! I always knew Clive was only half a man. Couldn't give you what you wanted. Am I right?'

I heard a titter. I stole a glance towards Ruth. She was watching with her fist screwed up against her lips. I perceived that Clive was standing beside her.

'I don't know what you're getting at,' I managed haughtily. Then, I hiccuped.

Piped music suddenly swelled through the room masking my discomfort. Sophia had tactfully turned up the volume of the speakers. People turned to talk to each other too loudly and too fast. The house began to hum like a beehive.

I helped myself to a savoury from a passing tray and crammed it into my mouth. It was covered with some sort of burning peppery sauce. I took a swig from my glass which made me splutter as Clive moved in saying, 'You've drunk too much of that stuff.' He was having a plain soda water himself.

My palate was on fire and tears sprang to my eyes. It was all so unjust, so unfair.

'You might think of Ruth before starting a scene,' he said coldly.

The flames I had swallowed turned into a raging furnace. 'You're as thick as the wall,' I said. 'You can't even see what he does to her. He rapes her, rapes her, I'm telling you. Don't think that it's because you're sexy that she fancies you. It's always because she wants to get away from him, nothing else. Alan's right about that. You're not the answer to a maiden's prayer by a long shot, you never were. You can't even hold a candle to Brendan Collins.'

I suppose if you want to say something unforgivable to your husband or your partner you might as well say it in front of as many people as possible. No matter how atrociously you behave there will always be one or two in a large crowd who will sympathise and see themselves as kindred spirits.

No thunderbolt struck me down on the thick cream carpet, instead Sophia was by my side. 'It's Andrew's mixtures, I'm afraid that they trigger people off,' she explained with a little laugh. Then she was pressing my arm and leading me off to another room where some people were dying to meet me.

Irish Dissipation in 1778

A quite remarkably convivial gathering is described in this extract from Sir Jonah Barrington's Personal Sketches of his own Times, *published in 1827.*

Close to the kennel of my father's hounds, he had built a small cottage, which was occupied solely by an old huntsman, his older wife, and his nephew, a whipper-in. The chace, and the bottle, and the piper, were the enjoyments of winter; and nothing could recompense a suspension of these enjoyments.

My elder brother, justly apprehending that the frost and snow of Christmas might probably prevent their usual occupation of the chace, determined to provide against any listlessness during the shut-up period, by an uninterrupted match of what was called 'hard going', till the weather should break up.

A hogshead of superior claret was therefore sent to the cottage of old Quin the huntsman; and a fat cow, killed, and plundered of her skin, was hung up by the heels. All the windows were closed to keep out the light. One room, filled with straw and numerous blankets, was destined for a bed-chamber in common; and another was prepared as a kitchen for the use of the servants. Claret, cold, mulled, or buttered, was to be the beverage for the whole company; and in addition to the cow above mentioned, chickens, bacon and bread were the only admitted viands. Wallace and Hosey, my father's and my brother's pipers, and Doyle, a blind but a famous fiddler, were employed to enliven the banquet, which it was determined should continue till the cow became a skeleton, and the claret should be on its stoop.

My two elder brothers;—two gentlemen of the name of Taylor (one of them afterwards a writer in India);—a Mr Barrington Lodge, a rough songster;—Frank Skelton, a jester and a butt;—Jemmy Moffat, the most knowing sportsman of the neighbourhood;—and two other sporting gentlemen of the county,—composed the *permanent* bacchanalians. A few visitors were occasionally admitted.

As for myself, I was too unseasoned to go through more than the first ordeal, which was on a frosty St Stephen's day, when the '*hard goers*' partook of their opening banquet, and several neighbours were invited, to honour the commencement of what they called their '*shut-up pilgrimage*'.

The old huntsman was the only male attendant; and his ancient spouse, once a kitchen-maid in the family, now somewhat resembling the amiable Leonarda in Gil Blas, was the cook; whilst the drudgery fell to the lot of the whipper-in. A long knife was prepared to cut collops from the cow; a large turf fire seemed to court the gridiron; the pot bubbled up as if proud of its contents, whilst plump white chickens floated in crowds upon the surface of the water; the simmering potatoes, just bursting their drab surtouts, exposed the delicate whiteness of their mealy bosoms; the claret was tapped, and the long earthen wide-mouthed pitchers stood gaping under the impatient cock, to receive their portions. The pipers plied their chants; the fiddler tuned his cremona; and never did any feast commence with more auspicious appearances of hilarity and dissipation, appearances which were not doomed to be falsified.

I shall never forget the attraction this novelty had for my youthful mind. All thoughts but those of good cheer were for the time totally obliterated. A few curses were, it is true, requisite to spur on old Leonarda's skill, but at length the banquet entered: the luscious smoked bacon, bedded on its cabbage mattress, and partly obscured by its own savoury steam, might have tempted the most fastidious of epicures; whilst the round trussed chickens, ranged by the half dozen on hot pewter dishes, turned up their white plump merry-thoughts exciting equally the eye and appetite: fat collops of the hanging cow, sliced indiscriminately from her tenderest points, grilled over the clear embers upon a shining gridiron, half drowned in their own luscious juices, and garnished with little pyramids of congenial shalots, smoked at the bottom of the well-furnished board. A prologue of cherry-bounce (brandy) preceded the entertainment, which was enlivened by hob-nobs and joyous toasts.

Numerous toasts, in fact, as was customary in those days, intervened to prolong and give zest to the repast—every man shouted forth his fair favourite, or convivial pledge; and each voluntarily surrendered a portion of his own reason, in bumpers to the beauty of his neighbour's toast. The pipers jerked from their bags appropriate planxties to every jolly sentiment: the jokers cracked the usual jests and ribaldry: one songster chanted the joys of wine and women; another gave, in full glee, the pleasures of the fox-chase: the fiddler sawed his merriest jigs: the old huntsman sounded his horn, and thrusting his fore-finger into his ear (to aid the quaver), gave the *view holloa!* of nearly ten minutes' duration; to which melody *tally ho!* was responded by every stentorian voice. A fox's brush stuck into a candlestick, in the centre of the table, was worshipped as a divinity! Claret flowed—bumpers were multiplied—and chickens, in the garb of spicy spitchcocks, assumed the name of *devils* to whet the appetites which it was impossible to conquer!

My reason gradually began to lighten me of its burden, and in its last efforts kindly suggested the straw-chamber as my asylum. Two couple of favourite hounds had been introduced to share in the joyous pastime of their friends and master; and the deep bass of their throats, excited by the shrillness of the huntsman's tenor, harmonised by two rattling pipers, a jigging fiddler, and twelve voices, in twelve different keys, all bellowing in one continuous unrelenting chime—was the last point of recognition which Bacchus permitted me to exercise: for my eyes began to perceive a much larger company than the room actually contained;—the lights were more than doubled, without any virtual increase of their number; and even the chairs and tables commenced dancing a series of minuets before me. A faint *tally ho!* was attempted by my reluctant lips; but I believe the effort was unsuccessful, and I very soon lost, in the straw-room, all that brilliant consciousness of existence, in the possession of which the morning had found me so happy.

Just as I was closing my eyes to a twelve hours' slumber, I distinguished the general roar of '*stole away!*' which rose almost up to the very roof of old Quin's cottage.

At noon, next day, a scene of a different nature was exhibited. I found, on waking, two associates by my side, in as perfect insensibility as that from which I had just aroused. Our piper seemed indubitably dead! but the fiddler, who had the privilege of age and blindness, had taken a hearty nap, and seemed as much alive as ever.

The room of banquet had been re-arranged by the old woman: spitchcocked chickens, fried rashers, and broiled marrowbones appeared struggling for precedence. The clean cloth looked, itself, fresh and exciting: jugs of mulled and buttered claret foamed hot upon the refurnished table, and a better or heartier breakfast I never in my life enjoyed.

A few members of the jovial crew had remained all night at their posts; but I suppose alternately took some rest, as they seemed not at all affected by their repletion. Soap and hot water restored at once their spirits and their persons; and it was determined that the rooms should be ventilated and cleared out for a cock-fight, to pass time till the approach of dinner.

In this battle-royal, every man backed his own bird; twelve of which courageous animals were set down together to fight it out—the survivor to gain all. In point of principle, the battle of the Horatii and Curiatii was re-acted; and in about an hour, one cock crowed out his triumph over the mangled body of his last opponent;—being himself, strange to say, but little wounded. The other eleven lay dead; and to the victor was unanimously voted a writ of ease, with sole monarchy over the hen-roost for the remainder of his days; and I remember him, for many years, the proud commandant of his poultry-yard and seraglio.—Fresh visitors were introduced each successive day, and the seventh morning had arisen before the feast broke up. As that day advanced, the cow was proclaimed to have furnished her full quantum of good dishes; the claret was upon its stoop; and the last gallon, mulled with a pound of spices, was drunk in tumblers to the next merry meeting! All now returned to their *natural* rest, until the evening announced a different scene.

An early supper, to be partaken of by all the young folks, of both sexes, in the neighbourhood, was provided in the dwelling-house, to terminate the festivities. A dance, as usual, wound up the entertainment; and what was then termed a 'raking pot of tea', put a finishing stroke, in jollity and good-humour, to such a revel as I never saw before, and, I am sure, shall never see again.

Poitín

Illicit Distillation

These excerpts are from Kenneth Connell's masterly essay in Irish Peasant Society *which appeared in 1968.*

In 1661, with the re-introduction of an excise duty on Irish spirit, the struggle between 'parliament' whiskey and poteen was resumed, a struggle in which the rout of the illicit distiller took a couple of centuries, and which, even still, he survives. In this essay an attempt is made to survey the history of poteen-making since its heyday in the late eighteenth and early nineteenth centuries. Much in these years fostered the industry. Between the establishment of Grattan's parliament and the ending of the wars with France there was probably some mitigation of the lot of the peasantry: they had, it may be, rather more money to spend; and inclination, like the scarcity of alternative opportunities, persuaded them to spend it on drink. The demand for spirit was further increased by the growth of population; and as grain was more widely grown in Ireland the distiller's raw material was more readily available. These factors, however, encouraged the licensed, no less than the unlicensed, distiller: it was, it seems, ill-conceived excise regulations that specially favoured the poteen-maker. The original duty on Irish spirit was 4*d.* a gallon; it had reached 1*s.* 2*d.* by 1785 and climbed steeply during the wars to 6*s.* 1½*d.* in 1815—when parliament whiskey was selling for nine or ten shillings a gallon. The exchequer, of course, was hard-pressed; but it was questionably wise to increase so substantially the price an impoverished people was asked to pay for parliament whiskey; a people, moreover, whose social life was hinged to cheap drink; who knew how to make poteen, and were not notably law-abiding.

* * *

Early in the nineteenth century most poteen seems to have been made from malt. But malt, while producing an excellent liquor, was a treacherous material to the illicit distiller; he grudged the time and the space needed for its proper preparation; it was risky for him, too, to get it dried or ground by a miller. Continuously, then, malt has been supplemented, and sometimes supplanted, by raw grain. And by the end of the century, grain, whether malted or not, was being displaced: less was grown in the areas of illicit distillation, and if the materials of poteen had to be bought, there were alternatives, making a less palatable liquor, but doing so more cheaply, and with less trouble and risk to the distiller. Molasses was widely used by the 1880s, and then, or soon afterwards, sugar, treacle, and porter: more recently 'almost anything' is said to be distilled—including potatoes, rhubarb, apples, blackberries, and currants.

* * *

The way in which poteen was carried from producer to consumer was determined, very largely, by the risk of detection. In Derry, around 1800, this was not over-rated; for spirit, it is said, was brought to the city in open tubs. Much was carried on men's backs, in casks, or 'tin cases'; or a couple of kegs might be put in a large bag and slung over a horse's back. In Donegal, in the 1820s, there were women ingeniously equipped for the poteen-trade: 'they have pockets made of tin, exactly in the shape of a woman's pocket; and a breast, and a half-moon, that goes before them; and with a cloak round them, they will walk with six gallons, and it shall not be perceived.' Similarly in Joyce's country: a local distiller, it is said, ordered from a tinker 'a tin vessel with head and body the shape of a woman'; he dressed it to resemble his wife, and rode to market, his poteen on the pillion behind him.

* * *

Who was served by this extensive and clandestine traffic? Who were the buyers of poteen? 'There is a sort of fancy gentlemen have, viz., a sort of pride, in saying, "I will give you a drop of the mountain dew."'

Gentlemen esteemed poteen for its flavour and price as well as for its illegality: they paid well, and there was probably relatively little risk in serving them. Well-to-do gentlemen, however, were not numerous in Ireland; and we may presume that their custom, a tiny proportion of the whole, fell to the more accomplished distiller. His colleagues sold to the less discriminating private customer, and to the retailers of spirits, licensed and unlicensed.

* * *

Primarily, then, the wretchedness and precariousness of living conditions explain the extent and persistence of poteen-making: it was the poverty of the peasantry more than their love of mischief that made them try their hand at distilling; and poverty, if it did not add to the consumption of spirits, made parliament whiskey an impossibly expensive substitute for poteen. The industry, favoured by poverty, was fostered, of course, by the natural features of much of the country; and also by the sympathy widely felt for the illicit distiller.

Poteen-making provides a striking example of the proverbial reluctance of the Irish to accept the law's definition of an offence. Continuously the illicit distiller has enjoyed something of the respect and sympathy due to an important and much-tried functionary: the excise officials lament that he bore none of the malefactor's stigma; and in fiction it is the gauger who is outwitted, the distiller who has the last laugh. It is not surprising that the general public connived at, and encouraged, illicit distillation. In the heyday of the industry, and where it was most prevalent, almost all of the local population had a pecuniary interest in its well-being, the interest of distiller or distributor, or grower of grain; and in, and beyond, these districts, the poteen-maker was cherished for the sparkle he brought to social life. He benefited, too, from the widespread distrust of the government— and from its obverse, sympathy for its intended victim: at best of times the State in Ireland was vouchsafed a grudging co-operation, but when it played the spoil-sport it could count on full-blooded opposition.

* * *

The critics of illicit distillation blamed it for more than excessive drinking: it saddled the country, they believed, with unnecessary taxes; it brought the law and the government into disrepute; 'this baneful practice', a Donegal rector maintained, tended 'to promote dissipation, perjury, rebellion, revenge and murder.' The exchequer, certainly, was a substantial loser: in the early 'fifties more than a quarter of the Irish revenue was drawn from the duties on malt and spirit; yet these duties may have been evaded as often as they were paid—in spite of the expenditure of some £45,000 a year on the revenue police. Nor is there any doubt that other malefactors profited by the poteen-maker's popularity. 'A bottle for the sergeant' and a crown for the revenue officer led on to grosser venality. Warmth, drink, and company, all drew men to the private distilleries: they were the meeting-places 'for all the loose and disorderly characters in the neighbourhood, where half-intoxicated they discuss politics, and regulate rents, tithes and taxes'. Illicit distillation, says a member for Clare, 'is the fertile source of half the crime committed in this unfortunate country'. But criticism might have been more fruitful if some of it were deflected from the poteen-maker to the folly of passing excise legislation that was unenforceable as well as unpopular.

The Real Old Mountain Dew

This is a street ballad unconstrained in its praise of poitín.

Let grasses grow and waters flow
In a free and easy way
But give me enough of the rare old stuff
That's made near Galway Bay,
The gaugers all from Donegal
Sligo and Leitrim too,
Oh, we'll give them the slip and we'll take a sip
Of the real old mountain dew.

Chorus (quickly):

Hi the dithery al the dal, dal the dal dithery al,
  Al the dal dal dithery dee—
Hi the dithery al the dal, dal the dal the dithery al
  Dal the dal dal dithery al the dee.

At the foot of the hill there's a neat little still
  Where the smoke curls up to the sky;
By a whiff of the smell you can plainly tell
  That there's poitín, boys, close by.
For it fills the air with a perfume rare,
  And betwixt both me and you,
As home we roll, we can drink a bowl,
  Or a bucketful of mountain dew.

Now learned men who use the pen,
  Have wrote the praises high
Of the sweet poitín from Ireland green
  Distilled from wheat and rye.
Away with pills, it will cure all ills,
  Of the Pagan, Christian or Jew;
So take off your coat and grease your throat
  With the real old mountain dew.

The Hackler from Grouse Hall

*Another ballad concerned with poitín and the vicissitudes suffered by
those making it or consuming it. A hackler, incidentally, assists in the
preparation of linen for spinning.*

I am a rovin' hackler lad that loves the shamrock shore,
My name is Pat McDonnell and my age is eighty-four.
Belov'd and well respected by my neighbours one and all,
On Saint Patrick's Day I loved to stray round Lavey and Grouse
   Hall.

When I was young I danced and sung and drank good whiskey,
   too,
Each shebeen shop that sold a drop of the real old mountain dew
With the poteen still on every hill the Peelers had no call
Round sweet Stradone I am well known, round Lavey and
   Grouse Hall.

I rambled round from town to town for hackling was my trade
None can deny I think that I an honest living made
Where'er I'd stay by night or day the youth would always call
To have some crack with Paddy Jack the Hackler from Grouse
   Hall.

I think it strange how times have changed so very much of late
Coercion now is all the row and Peelers on their bate
To take a glass is now alas the greatest crime of all
Since Balfour placed that hungry beast the Sergeant of Grouse
   Hall.

The busy tool of Castle rule he travels night and day
He'll seize a goat just by the throat for want of better prey
The nasty skunk he'll swear you're drunk tho' you took none at
   all
There is no peace about the place since he came to Grouse Hall.

'Twas on pretence of this offence he dragged me off to jail
Alone to dwell in a cold cell my fate for to bewail;
My hoary head on a plank bed such wrongs for vengeance call
He'll rue the day he dragged away the Hackler from Grouse
    Hall.

He haunts the League, just like a plague, and shame for to relate
The Priest can't be on Sunday free the Mass to celebrate;
It's there he'll kneel encased in steel prepared on duty's call
For to assail and drag to jail our clergy from Grouse Hall.

Down into hell he'd run pelmell to hunt for poteen there
And won't be loth to swear an oath 'twas found in Killinkere.
He'll search your bed from foot to head, sheets, blankets, tick
    and all
Your wife undressed must leave the nest for Jemmy of Grouse
    Hall.

He fixed a plan for that poor man who had a handsome wife
To take away without delay her liberty and life
He'd swear quite plain that he's insane and got no sense at all
As he has done of late with one convenient to Grouse Hall.

His raid on dogs I'm sure it flogs it's shocking to behold
How he'll pull up a six-month's pup and swear it's a two-year-
    old;
Outside of hell a parallel can't be found for him at all
For that vile pimp and devil's imp the ruler of Grouse Hall.

Thank God the day isn't far away when Home Rule will be seen
And brave Parnell at home will dwell and shine in College
    Green;
Our Policemen will all be then our nation's choice and all
Old Balfour's pack will get the sack and banished from Grouse
    Hall.

Let old and young clear up their lungs and sing this little song
Come join with me and let him see you all resent the wrong;
And while I live I'll always give a prayer for his downfall
And when I die I don't deny I'll haunt him from Grouse Hall.

The Poteen Maker

This part of a short story by Michael McLaverty from his
Collected Short Stories *of 1978 describes, in a most educational*
manner, precisely what its title claims.

'I'll show you how to purify the dirtiest of water,' he had told us. 'Even the filthiest water from the old river could be made fit for drinking purposes.' In a glass trough he had a dark brown liquid and when I got his back turned I dipped my finger in it and it tasted like treacle or burnt candy, and then I remembered about packets of brown sugar and tins of treacle I had seen in his press.

He placed some of the brown liquid in a glass retort and held it aloft to the class: 'In the retort I have water which I have discoloured and made impure. In a few minutes I'll produce from it the clearest of spring water.' And his weary eyes twinkled and although we could see nothing funny in that, we smiled because he smiled.

The glass retort was set up with the flaming bunsen underneath, and as the liquid was boiling, the steam was trapped in a long-necked flask on which I sponged cold water. With our eyes we followed the bubbling mixture and the steam turning into drops and dripping rapidly into the flask. The air was filled with a biscuity smell, and the only sound was the snore of the bunsen. Outside was the cold air and the falling snow. Presently the master turned out the gas and held up the flask containing the clear water.

'As pure as crystal!' he said, and we watched him pour some of it into a tumbler, hold it in his delicate fingers, and put it to his lips. With wonder we watched him drink it and then our eyes travelled to the dirty, cakey scum that had congealed on the glass sides of the retort. He pointed at this with his ruler: 'The impurities are sifted out and the purest of pure water remains.' And for some reason he gave his roguish smile. He filled up the retort again with the dirty brown liquid and repeated the experiment until he had a large bottle filled with the purest of pure water.

The following day it was still snowing and very cold. The master filled up the retort with the clear liquid which he had stored in the bottle: 'I'll boil this again to show you that there are no impurities left.' So once again we watched the water bubbling, turning to steam, and then to shining drops. Mr Craig filled up his tumbler: 'As pure as crystal,' he said, and then the door opened and in walked the Inspector. He was muffled to the ears and snow covered his hat and his attaché case. We all stared at him—he was the old, kind man we had seen before. He glanced at the bare firegrate and at the closed windows with their sashes edged with snow. The water continued to bubble in the retort, giving out its pleasant smell.

The Inspector shook hands with Mr Craig and they talked and smiled together, the Inspector now and again looking towards the empty grate and shaking his head. He unrolled his scarf and flicked the snow from off his shoulders and from his attaché case. He sniffed the air, rubbed his frozen hands together, and took a black notebook from his case. The snow ploofed against the windows, the wind hummed under the door.

'Now, boys,' Mr Craig continued, holding up the tumbler of water from which a thread of steam wriggled in the air. He talked to us in a strange voice and told us about the experiment as if we were seeing it for the first time. Then the Inspector took the warm tumbler and questioned us on our lesson. 'It should be perfectly pure water,' he said, and he sipped at it. He tasted its flavour. He sipped at it again. He turned to Mr Craig. They whispered together, the Inspector looking towards the retort which was still bubbling and sending out its twirls of steam to be condensed to water of purest crystal. He laughed loudly, and we smiled when he again put the tumbler to his lips and this time drank it all. Then he asked us more questions and told us how, if we were shipwrecked, we could make pure water from the salt sea water.

Mr Craig turned off the bunsen and the Inspector spoke to him. The master filled up the Inspector's tumbler and poured out some for himself in a cup. Then the Inspector made jokes with us, listened to us singing, and told us we were the best class in Ireland. Then he gave us a few sums to do in our books. He put his hands in his pockets and jingled his money, rubbed a little peep-hole in the breath-covered window, and peered out at the loveliest sight in Ireland. He spoke to

Mr Craig again and Mr Craig shook hands with him and they both laughed. The Inspector looked at his watch. Our class was let out early, and while I remained behind to tidy up the Science apparatus the master gave me an empty treacle tin to throw in the bin and told me to carry the Inspector's case up to the station. I remember that day well as I walked behind them through the snow, carrying the attaché case, and how loudly they talked and laughed as the snow whirled cold from the river. I remember how they crouched together to light their cigarettes, how match after match was thrown on the road, and how they walked off with the unlighted cigarettes still in their mouths. At the station Mr Craig took a penny from his waistcoat pocket and as he handed it to me it dropped on the snow. I lifted it and he told me I was the best boy in Ireland...

The Majesty of the Law

This story by Frank O'Connor deals lightly with the relationship between a poitín-maker and the local sergeant.

'What hurry is on you?' asked Dan. 'Look, your foot was only on the path when I made up the fire.'

'Arrah, Dan, you're not making tea for me?'

'I am not making it for you, indeed; I'm making it for myself, and I'll take it very bad of you if you won't have a cup.'

'Dan, Dan, that I mightn't stir, but 'tisn't an hour since I had it at the barracks!'

'Ah, whisht, now, whisht! Whisht, will you! I have something here to give you an appetite.'

The old man swung the heavy kettle on to the chain over the open fire, and the dog sat up, shaking his ears with an expression of deepest interest. The policeman unbuttoned his tunic, opened his belt, took a pipe and a plug of tobacco from his breast pocket, and, crossing his legs in an easy posture, began to cut the tobacco slowly and carefully with his pocket knife. The old man went to the dresser and took down two handsomely decorated cups, the only cups he had, which, though chipped and handleless, were used at all only on very rare occasions, for himself he preferred his tea from a basin. Happening to glance into them, he noticed that they bore signs of disuse and had collected a lot of the fine white dust-turf that always circulated in the little smoky cottage. Again he thought of the shirt, and, rolling up his sleeves with a stately gesture, he wiped them inside and out till they shone. Then he bent and opened the cupboard. Inside was a quart bottle of pale liquid, obviously untouched. He removed the cork and smelt the contents, pausing for a moment in the act as though to recollect where exactly he had noticed that particular smoky smell before. Then, reassured, he stood up and poured out with a liberal hand.

'Try that now, sergeant,' he said with quiet pride.

The sergeant, concealing whatever qualms he might have felt at the idea of drinking illegal whiskey, looked carefully into the cup, sniffed, and glanced up at old Dan.

'It looks good,' he commented.

'It should be good,' replied Dan with no mock modesty.

'It tastes good too,' said the sergeant.

'Ah, sha,' said Dan, not wishing to praise his own hospitality in his own house, ''tis of no great excellence.'

'You'd be a good judge, I'd say,' said the sergeant without irony.

'Ever since things became what they are,' said Dan, carefully guarding himself against a too-direct reference to the peculiarities of the law administered by his guest, 'liquor isn't what it used to be.'

'I've heard that remark made before now, Dan,' said the sergeant thoughtfully. 'I've heard it said by men of wide experience that it used to be better in the old days.'

'Liquor,' said the old man, 'is a thing that takes time. There was never a good job done in a hurry.'

''Tis an art in itself.'

'Just so.'

'And an art takes time.'

'And knowledge,' added Dan with emphasis. 'Every art has its secrets, and the secrets of distilling are being lost the way the old songs were lost. When I was a boy there wasn't a man in the barony but had a hundred songs in his head, but with people running here, there, and everywhere, the songs were lost…Ever since things became what they are,' he repeated on the same guarded note, 'there's so much running about the secrets are lost.'

'There must have been a power of them.'

'There was. Ask any man today that makes whiskey do he know how to make it out of heather.'

'And was it made of heather?' asked the policeman.

'It was.'

'You never drank it yourself?'

'I didn't, but I knew old men that did, and they told me that no whiskey that's made nowadays could compare with it.'

'Musha, Dan, I think sometimes 'twas a great mistake of the law to set its hand against it.'

Dan shook his head. His eyes answered for him, but it was not in nature for a man to criticise the occupation of a guest in his own home.

'Maybe so, maybe not,' he said non-committally.

'But sure, what else have the poor people?'

'Them that makes the laws have their own good reasons.'

'All the same, Dan, all the same, 'tis a hard law.'

The sergeant would not be outdone in generosity. Politeness required him not to yield to the old man's defence of his superiors and their mysterious ways.

'It is the secrets I'd be sorry for,' said Dan, summing up. 'Men die and men are born, and where one man drained another will plough, but a secret lost is lost forever.'

'True,' said the sergeant mournfully. 'Lost forever.'

Dan took his cup, rinsed it in a bucket of clear water by the door and cleaned it again with the shirt. Then he placed it carefully at the sergeant's elbow. From the dresser he took a jug of milk and a blue bag containing sugar; this he followed up with a slab of country butter and—a sure sign that he had been expecting a visitor—a round cake of home-made bread, fresh and uncut. The kettle sang and spat and the dog, shaking his ears, barked at it angrily.

'Go away, you brute!' growled Dan, kicking him out of his way. He made the tea and filled the two cups. The sergeant cut himself a large slice of bread and buttered it thickly.

'It is just like medicines,' said the old man, resuming his theme with the imperturbability of age. 'Every secret there was is lost. And leave no one tell me that a doctor is as good a man as one that had the secrets of old times.'

'How could he be?' asked the sergeant with his mouth full.

'The proof of that was seen when there were doctors and wise people there together.'

'It wasn't to the doctors the people went, I'll engage?'

'It was not. And why?' With a sweeping gesture the old man took in the whole world outside his cabin. 'Out there on the hillsides is the sure cure for every disease. Because it is written'—he tapped the table with his thumb—'it is written by the poets "wherever you find the disease you will find the cure". But people walk up the hills and down the hills and all they see is flowers. Flowers! As if God Almighty— honour and praise to Him!—had nothing better to do with His time than to be making old flowers!'

'Things no doctor could cure the wise people cured,' agreed the sergeant.

'Ah, musha, 'tis I know it,' said Dan bitterly. 'I know it, not in my mind but in my own four bones.'

'Have you the rheumatics at you still?' the sergeant asked in a shocked tone.

'I have. Ah, if you were alive, Kitty O'Hara, or you, Nora Malley of the Glen, 'tisn't I'd be dreading the mountain wind or the sea wind; 'tisn't I'd be creeping down with my misfortunate red ticket for the blue and pink and yellow dribble-drabble of their ignorant dispensary.'

'Why then indeed,' said the sergeant, 'I'll get you a bottle for that.'

'Ah, there's no bottle ever made will cure it.'

'That's where you're wrong, Dan. Don't talk now till you try it. It cured my own uncle when he was that bad he was shouting for the carpenter to cut the two legs off him with a handsaw.'

'I'd give fifty pounds to get rid of it,' said Dan magniloquently. 'I would and five hundred.'

The sergeant finished his tea in a gulp, blessed himself, and struck a match which he then allowed to go out as he answered some question of the old man. He did the same with a second and third, as though titillating his appetite with delay. Finally he succeeded in getting his pipe alight and the two men pulled round their chairs, placed their toes side by side in the ashes, and in deep puffs, lively bursts of conversation, and long, long silences enjoyed their smoke.

'I hope I'm not keeping you?' said the sergeant, as though struck by the length of his visit.

'Ah, what would you keep me from?'

'Tell me if I am. The last thing I'd like to do is waste another man's time.'

'Begor, you wouldn't waste my time if you stopped all night.'

'I like a little chat myself,' confessed the policeman.

And again they became lost in conversation. The light grew thick and coloured and, wheeling about the kitchen before it disappeared, became tinged with gold; the kitchen itself sank into cool greyness with cold light on the cups and basins and plates of the dresser. From the ash tree a thrush began to sing. The open hearth gathered brightness till its light was a warm, even splash of crimson in the twilight.

Twilight was also descending outside when the sergeant rose to go. He fastened his belt and tunic and carefully brushed his clothes. Then he put on his cap, tilted a little to side and back.

'Well, that was a great talk,' he said.

''Tis a pleasure,' said Dan, 'a real pleasure.'

'And I won't forget the bottle for you.'

'Heavy handling from God to you!'

'Good-bye now, Dan.'

'Good-bye, sergeant, and good luck.'

Poteen

Lusty drinking songs in praise of poitín are only to be expected;
poems like this from Michael Longley's An Exploded View *of 1973*
are more surprising.

Enough running water
To cool the copper worm,
The veins at the wrist,
Vitriol to scorch the throat—

And the brimming hogshead,
Reduced by one noggin-full
Sprinkled on the ground,
Becomes an affair of

Remembered souterrains,
Sunk workshops, out-backs,
The back of the mind—
The whole bog an outhouse

Where, alongside cudgels,
Guns, the informer's ear
We have buried it—
Blood-money, treasure-trove.

For the Record

This brief insight into the life of a poitín-maker is from Eddie Stack's
The West *of 1990.*

Tommo and Dommo Moore were in their late fifties and their spinster sister Megga was a little older. A younger sister called Dodo was forced to emigrate to America many years previously when cheated in love by a neighbour's son. Like the generations before them, the Moores had little stock, a few sinewy geese, three bantam hens, a cross cock and a couple of bedraggled goats who provided more company than sustenance. Once they kept a wild, white cow but hunger forced her to stray down the mountain and across the hazardous bog, honeycombed with deep dank pools. Her saunter came to grief when she tried to wade through a bottomless drain.

This was the first bit of commotion in the region since the gold rush and the loss brought the Moores closer together in the same way a family death sometimes might. Megga said the mishap was a sign to forsake agriculture and return to the old family trade of poteen making. The brothers agreed and since that fateful day, they used the climate, isolation and crystal clear streams to their advantage and developed a thriving distilling business. Their poteen was noted for its punch and purity, a reputation which guaranteed its popularity and an ever-growing market.

Tommo made the moonshine and took enormous pride in his craft. He was considered a master distiller by many authorities and fussed and cared, tested and tasted the wash regularly, to ensure its high quality. After each run he thanked and praised God for sending the rain.

''Tis all in the water,' he used say humbly.

Whatever the weather or season, Tommo never ceased to be happy and when not distilling, he fished the streams and drains for eels and small speckled trout. Unlike his brother, he wore neither cap nor hat but bared his bald, bulb-shaped head to the elements. Tommo always dressed in black—clerical clothes which Father Gill (a customer and holyman from a distant parish) consigned to him every Christmas. Like his sister, he was tall and overweight but they had little else in common.

Megga was the outrider. Every month she lumbered down the narrow, steep and slippery mountain track and carefully picked her way through the treacherous bog, travelling for days on a shaky bicycle, burdened with bags of clinking bottles. She called on the buyers here and there and returned with the money, provisions and the mail from Dodo, which she collected at the post office.

Megga was a stern woman who never displayed signs of emotion—though once she told Father Gill that thoughts of company keeping seldom let her be. He told her to trust in God and ever after gave her religious magazines which Dommo would read aloud at night-time, he was the brainy brother. On Dommo rested the responsibilities of maintaining the still, the bicycle and the wooden churn, as well as all forms of reading and writing.

Sometimes Dodo mailed him back issues of 'Popular Mechanics' and other technical journals which he delighted in reading. He would study the magazines for days before relating articles and inventions to the others while they sat around the smouldering fire at night-time, drinking unwracked poteen. Dommo considered himself smarter than the others but kept his feelings private.

One evening Megga chuckled homewards with a large well-wrapped parcel and a letter—both from Dodo, as well as the usual provisions. She laid two heavy canvas shopping bags on the table, gave Dommo the letter and retreated to her bedroom with the parcel. Tommo rooted through the provisions and described the items to his brother who nodded while he read Dodo's long letter.

'Twelve bottles of stout...what's this?...Jam, two crocks of red jam. A piece of green bacon...tay and sugar...snuff and tabaccy...and Great God Almighty...three new clay pipes. The poor cratur has a heart of gold. Flour, a stone of brown flour...and a new enamel mug...'

Megga emerged from her room and coughed loudly, the brothers turned and stared at her in deadpan disbelief. She walked around the kitchen once or twice before soliciting their opinions on her new clothes. Tommo was first to find words—

'Oh but they are beautiful, beautiful…only pure beautiful. And the lovely colours, beautiful blue, a colour that suits you Megga. And so unusual, very unusual cut…what is it called?'

'Dommo, what does she call it in the letter?' she asked.

'Hold on…hold on 'till I see…"I'm sendin' Megga a Sailor's Suit I bought at a sale in Macy's." A sailor's suit, that's what she called it…'

Megga beamed and purred as she stroked the striped sleeve of her tunic. She took a seat by the fire and related the news from beyond the bogs. Her brothers were quiet but she was full of life.

'An' that's all the news I have for ye now,' she said eventually. 'Tommo open a few bottles a porter like a good lad. Had Dodo any news Dommo?'

The candle was lit, the snuff and porter was passed around and Dommo read aloud the letter from Dodo.

* * *

'God love her, the cratur, and she thinks there's still neighbours here.'

They stared at the fire and silently thought about poor Dodo. She was a gentle soul and Tommo remembered her as a slight young girl with a pale face and wiry curling red hair, a pious girl. Dommo recalled how she made butter for the market and saved her money for a dowry from an early age. Megga remembered how she was jilted in love by a neighbour's son and left home disillusioned and broken-hearted. She hung a black iron pot over the fire and broke the silence.

'How long is she gone, 'tis never thirty years.'

'Oh God, 'tis, and a lot more,' confirmed Tommo, opening three more bottles of porter.

'I remember it well,' reminisced Dommo. ''Twas out in the year. Shure she wrote after landin'. I remember it well. It took her twelve days to get to Queenstown and twenty more to reach America.'

''Tis awful far,' sighed Megga, thinking about the dance bands and the dancers, 'awful far entirely.'

Again they drank in silence, and when the pot began to bubble,

Tommo fetched three enamel mugs and made large portions of sweet, hot poteen. He said to Megga, with a tremor of nostalgia in his voice,

'Do you know, we didn't hear you singin' for ages.'

'Well now, that's right,' agreed Dommo, 'an awful long time indeed. How well Dodo remembers your voice, and of course, you had great songs too.'

* * *

Megga tarried in the low lands longer than usual but this did not alarm the brothers. Though neither of them said it, they relished the lull. Dommo took pen and paper to crags higher up the hill and wrote some poetry—odes to the snipe, curlew and lapwing. Tommo strolled across the marshy ground and thought about the bygone days, when nine families eked a living from Clontom's unfruitful soil.

They were grading poteen one evening when Megga returned. Immediately Dommo observed that she had a lot of drink taken and knew her moods were fickle. As usual he received the letter, Tommo scrutinised the provisions and Megga related the news from the lowlands while warming her weather-beaten legs to the fire. When the candle was lit, Dommo read the letter. Dodo informed them that she was changing her employment and asked as usual for their prayers. Then she described her future boss in a fashion that smacked of romance.

'He is a very nice man and his mother came from Swinford in Mayo. Two autos he owns and a great apartment in the better part of Manhattan. He smiles often when I tell him about Clontom but he is happy here...'

* * *

Dommo talked for hours and Tommo made too many mugs of punch. Megga attempted to sing on a number of occasions but drink had taken its toll. The brothers carried her to bed and she wept her way to sleep, haunted by nice men in the Bronx who bowed and saluted, while they danced on her greasy goose-feathered pillow.

Her night was restless and agitated. Early in the morning the cold breeze from the bog chilled her back to reality when it whistled through the broken bedroom window. Sluggishly she arose and retrieved from a jug in the kitchen dresser the small leather purse which contained her long-collected dowry. She pinned the purse to her underclothes, sprinkled holy water on herself and headed downhill towards the tar road.

Her sudden departure worried the men, especially when they found her empty dowry jug on the table. For days they conjectured and pondered on their plight. Dommo promised to flatter her singing if she ever returned and Tommo pledged to serve her less potent punch.

'But what'll we do if she comes home with a husband?' he wondered.

'What can we do but hope he's someone we know,' said his brother.

Pub Conversations

Ulysses

These extracts from Ulysses *by James Joyce relate what is probably the most celebrated pub conversation to be found in Irish literature— the so-called Cyclops episode. In Homer's* The Odyssey *the Cyclops was a one-eyed mythical giant; in Joyce's book, whose organisational structure parallels that of* The Odyssey, *the Cyclops is represented by the character called 'the citizen', a fanatical, bigoted (one-eyed) nationalist. He holds court in Barney Kiernan's pub in Little Britain Street, living on former glories and gladly accepting free drinks from anyone who offers. His dog Garryowen lies at his feet. Joyce's great gift is his ability to convey, with startling fidelity, the random, disconnected and often confused nature of much Irish pub talk. The episode is narrated by an anonymous third party who arrives in the pub accompanied by a journalist called Joe Hynes.*

So we turned into Barney Kiernan's and there sure enough was the citizen up in the corner having a great confab with himself and that bloody mangy mongrel, Garryowen, and he waiting for what the sky would drop in the way of drink.

—There he is, says I, in his gloryhole, with his cruiskeen lawn and his load of papers, working for the cause.

The bloody mongrel let a grouse out of him would give you the creeps. Be a corporal work of mercy if someone would take the life of that bloody dog. I'm told for a fact he ate a good part of the breeches off a constabulary man in Santry that came round one time with a blue paper about a licence.

—Stand and deliver, says he.

—That's all right, citizen, says Joe. Friends here.

—Pass, friends, says he.

Then he rubs his hand in his eye and says he:

—What's your opinion of the times?

Doing the rapparee and Rory of the hill. But, begob, Joe was equal to the occasion.

—I think the markets are on a rise, says he, sliding his hand down his fork.

So begob the citizen claps his paw on his knee and he says:

—Foreign wars is the cause of it.

And says Joe, sticking his thumb in his pocket:

—It's the Russians wish to tyrannise.

—Arrah, give over your bloody codding, Joe, says I, I've a thirst on me I wouldn't sell for half a crown.

—Give it a name, citizen, says Joe.

—Wine of the country, says he.

—What's yours? says Joe

—Ditto MacAnaspey, says I.

—Three pints, Terry, says Joe. And how's the old heart, citizen? says he.

—Never better, *a chara*, says he. What Garry? Are we going to win? Eh?

And with that he took the bloody old towser by the scruff of the neck and, by Jesus, he near throttled him.

By now, the company has been augmented by the arrival of Alf Bergan and the discovery that Bob Doran, a wastrel, is drunk in another corner of the pub. Earlier in the day, Joe Hynes had attended the funeral of one Paddy Dignam, whom Bergan mistakenly believes he has just seen. This passage opens with the citizen—who combines anti-semitism with his various other phobias—making a contemptuous reference about Leopold Bloom ('that bloody freemason'). Bloom is hanging around the front of the pub in the hope of meeting Martin Cunningham, a Dublin Castle official whose help he wants to clear up a confusion relating to Paddy Dignam's estate. He is, in effect, doing a kindness for Dignam's widow.

—What's the bloody freemason doing, says the citizen, prowling up and down outside?

—What's that? says Joe.

—Here you are, says Alf, chucking out the rhino. Talking about hanging. I'll show you something you never saw. Hangmen's letters. Look at here.

So he took a bundle of wisps of letters and envelopes out of his pocket.

—Are you codding? says I.

—Honest injun, says Alf. Read them.

So Joe took up the letters.

—Who are you laughing at? says Bob Doran.

So I saw there was going to be bit of a dust. Bob's a queer chap when the porter's up in him so says I just to make talk:

—How's Willy Murray those times, Alf?

—I don't know, says Alf. I saw him just now in Capel Street with Paddy Dignam. Only I was running after that...

—You what? says Joe, throwing down the letters. With who?

—With Dignam, says Alf.

—Is it Paddy? says Joe.

—Yes, says Alf. Why?

—Don't you know he's dead? says Joe.

—Paddy Dignam dead? says Alf.

—Ay, says Joe.

—Sure I'm after seeing him not five minutes ago, says Alf, as plain as a pikestaff.

—Who's dead? says Bob Doran.

—You saw his ghost then, says Joe, God between us and harm.

—What? says Alf. Good Christ, only five...What?...and Willy Murray with him, the two of them there near whatdoyoucallhim's...What? Dignam dead?

—What about Dignam? says Bob Doran. Who's talking about...?

—Dead! says Alf. He is no more dead than you are.

—Maybe so, says Joe. They took the liberty of burying him this morning anyhow.

—Paddy? says Alf.

—Ay, says Joe. He paid the debt of nature, God be merciful to him.

—Good Christ! says Alf.

Begob he was what you might call flabbergasted.

*In this passage, the citizen is in full anglophobic flow. Further
drinkers have arrived by now: John Wyse Nolan, J. J. O'Molloy, Ned
Lambert and Lenehan. The citizen's rant is prompted by a reference
which Bloom makes to Britain's colonies and civilisation.
Meanwhile, Lenehan brings the news that Sceptre, the favourite to
win that afternoon's Ascot Gold Cup, has lost to a 20–1 outsider
called Throwaway. Most of the company had backed the favourite.
The Boylan to whom Lenehan refers is Blazes Boylan, Molly Bloom's
lover. The narrator's remark to Lenehan about losing a bob and
finding a tanner is based on slang expressions for pre-decimal
coinage. A bob was a shilling, which was equal to two tanners
(sixpences).*

—Their syphilisation, you mean, says the citizen. To hell with them!
The curse of a goodfornothing God light sideways on the bloody
thicklugged sons of whores' gets! No music and no art and no
literature worthy of the name. Any civilisation they have they stole
from us. Tonguetied sons of bastards' ghosts.

—The European family, says J. J....

—They're not European, says the citizen. I was in Europe with Kevin
Egan of Paris. You wouldn't see a trace of them or their language
anywhere in Europe except in a *cabinet d'aisance.*

And says John Wyse:

—Full many a flower is born to blush unseen.

And says Lenehan that knows a bit of the lingo:

—*Conspuez les Anglais! Perfide Albion!*

* * *

—What's up with you, says I to Lenehan. You look like a fellow that
had lost a bob and found a tanner.

—Gold cup, says he.

—Who won, Mr Lenehan? says Terry.

—*Throwaway*, says he, at twenty to one. A rank outsider. And the rest
nowhere.

—And Bass's mare? says Terry.

—Still running, says he. We're all in a cart. Boylan plunged two quid
on my tip *Sceptre* for himself and a lady friend.

182

—I had half a crown myself, says Terry, on *Zinfandel* that Mr Flynn gave me. Lord Howard de Walden's.

—Twenty to one, says Lenehan. Such is life in an outhouse. *Throwaway*, says he. Takes the biscuit and talking about bunions. Frailty, thy name is *Sceptre*.

So he went over to the biscuit tin Bob Doran left to see if there was anything he could lift on the nod, the old cur after him backing his luck with his mangy snout up. Old mother Hubbard went to the cupboard.

—Not there, my child, says he.

—Keep your pecker up, says Joe. She'd have won the money only for the other dog.

And J. J. and the citizen arguing about law and history with Bloom sticking in an odd word.

—Some people, says Bloom, can see the mote in others' eyes but they can't see the beam in their own.

—*Raimeis*, says the citizen. There's no-one as blind as the fellow that won't see, if you know what that means. Where are our missing twenty millions of Irish should be here today instead of four, our lost tribes? And our potteries and textiles, the finest in the whole world! And our wool that was sold in Rome in the time of Juvenal and our flax and our damask from the looms of Antrim and our Limerick lace, our tanneries and our white flint glass down there by Ballybough and our Huguenot poplin that we have since Jacquard de Lyon and our woven silk and our Foxford tweeds and ivory raised point from the Carmelite convent in New Ross, nothing like it in the whole wide world! Where are the Greek merchants that came through the pillars of Hercules, the Gibraltar now grabbed by the foe of mankind, with gold and Tyrian purple to sell in Wexford at the fair of Carmen? Read Tacitus and Ptolemy, even Giraldus Cambrensis. Wine, peltries, Connemara marble, silver from Tipperary, second to none, our far-famed horses even today, the Irish hobbies, with king Philip of Spain offering to pay customs duties for the right to fish in our waters. What do the yellowjohns of Anglia owe us for our ruined trade and our ruined hearths? And the beds of the Barrow and Shannon they won't deepen with millions of acres of marsh and bog to make us all die of consumption.

—As treeless as Portugal we'll be soon, says John Wyse, or Heligoland with its one tree if something is not done to reafforest the land. Larches, firs, all the trees of the conifer family are going fast. I was reading a report of lord Castletown's…

—Save them, says the citizen, the giant ash of Galway and the chieftain elm of Kildare with a fortyfoot bole and an acre of foliage. Save the trees of Ireland for the future men of Ireland on the fair hills of Eire, O.

—Europe has its eyes on you, says Lenehan.

To Convert Stout into Water

This excerpt from Flann O'Brien's At Swim-Two-Birds *explores some of life's greater mysteries.*

One afternoon I saw the form of Brinsley bent in converse with a small fair-haired man who was fast acquiring a reputation in the Leinster Square district on account of the beauty of his poems and their affinity with the high-class work of another writer, Mr Pound, an American gentleman. The small man had an off-hand way with him and talked with jerks. I advanced without diffidence and learnt that his name was Donaghy. We talked together in a polished manner, utilising with frequency words from the French language, discussing the primacy of America and Ireland in contemporary letters and commenting on the inferior work produced by writers of the English nationality. The Holy Name was often taken, I do not recollect with what advertence. Brinsley, whose education and maintenance was a charge on the rates of his native county—the product of a farthing in the pound applied for the purpose of enabling necessitous boys of promising intellect to enjoy the benefits of University learning— Brinsley said that he was prepared to give myself and Donaghy a pint of stout apiece, explaining that he had recently been paid. I rejoined that if his finances warranted such generosity, I would raise no objection, but that I (for my part) was no Rockefeller, thus utilising a figure of speech to convey the poverty of my circumstances.

Name of figure of speech: Synecdoche (or Autonomasia).

The three of us walked slowly down to Grogan's, our three voices interplaying in scholarly disputations, our faded overcoats finely open in the glint of the winter sun.

Isn't there a queer smell off this fellow? said Brinsley, directing his inquiring face to that of Donaghy.

I sniffed at my person in mock appraisement.

You're in bad odour, said Donaghy.

Well it's not the smell of drink, I answered. What class of a smell is it?

Did you ever go into a room early in the morning, asked Brinsley, where there had been a hooley the night before, with cigars and whiskey and food and crackers and women's scent? Well that's the smell. A stale spent smell.

There's a hum off yourself, I said.

We entered the tavern and ordered our dark drinks.

To convert stout into water, I said, there is a simple process. Even a child can do it, though I would not stand for giving stout to children. Is it not a pity that the art of man has not attained the secret of converting water into stout?

Donaghy gave a laugh but Brinsley restrained me from drinking by the weight of his hand upon my arm and named a proprietary brand of ale.

Did you ever taste it? he asked.

I did not, I said.

Well that crowd have the secret if you like, he said. By God I never tasted anything like it. Did *you* ever try it?

No, said Donaghy.

Keep away from it if you value your life.

Here there was a pause as we savoured the dull syrup.

We had a great feed of wine at the Inns the other night, observed Donaghy, a swell time. Wine is better than stout. Stout sticks. Wine is more grateful to the intestines, the digestive viscera, you know. Stout sticks and leaves a scum on the interior of the paunch.

185

Raising my glass idly to my head, I said:

If that conclusion is the result of a mental syllogism, it is fallacious, being based on licensed premises.

Two laughs in unison, these were my rewards. I frowned and drank unheedingly, savouring the dull oaten after-taste of the stout as it lingered against my palate. Brinsley tapped me sharply on the belly.

Gob you're getting a paunch, he said.

Leave my bag alone, I answered. I protected it with my hand.

We had three drinks in all in respect of each of which Brinsley paid a sixpence without regret.

The ultimate emptors: Meath County Council, rural rating authority.

Reprisal

Taken from the end of Hugh Fitzgerald Ryan's Reprisal *of 1989, this extract, relating to the period after the sack of Balbriggan in 1920, is a finely written example of the kind of political post-mortem often to be overheard in Irish pubs.*

'All the same, if that's all we have to complain about,' said one man, thoughtfully regarding the collar on his pint, 'it wasn't too bad a day.' Understated as usual: it had been a great day altogether. The band had been in powerful form.

'That's a grand tune, "St Patrick's Day", and right for the day that was in it, our own national saint,' said another, 'and our own parish saint too.' Homegrown saints, like most other things, are always better than the foreign variety, Italians, bleeding all over the place, with their eyes rolling in their heads, young ones that never got a hoult of a man in their lives being martyred as virgins. There was something blasphemous, maybe, in his point of view, but worth thinking about. A decent saint that would let the odd roar out of him, or maybe a few curses, was worth ten of the other kind.

'But he wasn't an Irishman at all,' interpolated another, more for the hell of it than in the interests of historical accuracy, 'he was an Englishman.'

A pause. The theologian took a long and disparaging pull at his drink. He replaced it on the counter, wiped his sleeve across his upper lip and regarded his interlocutor. 'He was no such thing,' he explained, with long-suffering patience. 'He was an ancient Briton, a Celt like ourselves. Do ye never read books? More important, he was a fuckin' Catholic.'

'Well then,' conceded the other, 'I suppose he was all right, but wouldn't ye think he'd allow us a jar on his own feast day?' It was a serious flaw in any saint's reputation, particularly an adopted Skerryman, a flaw that might yet come to the attention of the Devil's Advocate in any serious re-examination of Patrick's cause. 'I mean, slidin' in the back door. It's a bit undignified.'

'Jaysus,' snorted the theologian, 'you lose none of your nimbility over the years when it comes to slidin' into pubs. By the way, Skinner,' he continued, noticing Ned for the first time, 'I remember you was barred from this place.'

'Barred, how are ye?' expostulated Skinner in outrage.

'Barred! Kit Donovan isn't the man to bar his old comrades. You can take that back for a start.' He made as if to rise from his stool and the theologian backed away. Skinner subsided again.

'I often meant to ask,' said another, 'what brought yourself into the Movement anyway, Skinner?'

Skinner drank slowly from his glass, then wiped his mouth. He furrowed his brow and spoke deliberately. 'Well,' he began, 'when the Donovan lads went into it, I figured I'd better go along, just to keep well in. I mean, if the boss ever married into the Donovan family like, it would do no harm.' He laughed, gargling his porter and the others laughed too. Skinner had mellowed with age. His eyes misted over with a kind of wonder. 'She still gets the sweetbreads. True love is a marvellous thing.'

There was a reverent silence. They could not divine whether he was serious or not.

'Did I ever tell yiz about the time we burned the soldiers out of the Wireless Field?'

'Aye. Wasn't there an enquiry or somethin' about that?'

'Sweeney wanted to know how the soldiers got away, seein' as how we burned the huts and took the rifles off them. It was level peggin', three against three, but we got the rifles.'

'Aye, but how did they get away?'

'Well there y'are,' said Skinner. 'That's just it. Out comes a white flag and Kit just walks up to the door and tells them to throw out their weapons. "Hold your fire," he says to us.' He sighted along an imaginary gun-barrel. 'I had one of them in me sights. Had him dead to rights.'

'And what did Sweeney say to all this?'

'"Well," says Kit, lookin' him in the eye, "I was the officer on the spot. We achieved our objectives, didn't we?" and he throws the rifles on the table. Sweeney never said another word about it. Aw, we was a team, I'm tellin' yiz.'

'But why did you join, really?' asked the original questioner.

Skinner scratched his head. 'I dunno,' he said half-apologetically, 'I suppose—the lads, like, y'know.' He shrugged and addressed himself to his drink.

The door opened a fraction and Mr Drew entered, with a practised glissade, closing it behind him so quickly that one could not have been entirely sure that it had ever opened. It was a movement of which any matador might have been proud, less flamboyant than the *veronica* perhaps, but with the economy of effort that is the mark of the true artist.

'A black an' tan,' he said to the man behind the bar, and turned to survey the company, old comrades together, enjoying the day of reminiscence.

'A great day Mr Drew, considerin',' the theologian greeted him.

'Considerin'?' inquired Mr Drew and waited.

They thought they had him at last. 'Well considerin' the fact that the memorial to Tom Bennett was damaged before it was even unveiled.' Let him wriggle out of that one.

Mr Drew gazed into vacancy. His voice was heavy with solemnity, hushed with awe. 'God moves in mysterious ways,' he said.

There was obviously more to come. Silence settled on the room.

'A Greater Hand than mine was at work today.' He spoke in capital letters, holding his gnarled and calloused hand aloft for their inspection. 'The harp of Erin, and one of her strings broken. What more fitting symbol for a dead patriot? It's symbolic don't ye see?' There was a tremor in his voice.

The men looked at each other uncertain as to whether he was pulling their legs or not, but reluctant to be the first to laugh. He had done it again.

'That was a damn fine speech Mr Sweeney made though,' said the theologian, acknowledging defeat. Not Master Sweeney anymore, now that he was an elected representative of the people and a man of some weight in the community.

'A fine speech,' they agreed. Mr Sweeney could put the words together.

'A nice touch, the few words in Irish at the start,' said another man, savouring a phrase: '"…proud to number Tomás Bennett among my friends and proud to have worked with him in our common cause." Them's the words that'll stick in the mind for many a long year.' He nodded appreciatively.

They were silent for a time, remembering. Captain McNaughten drew out his knife and pared pensively at a finger nail. Idly he regarded the heathen symbols on the ivory handle. A Lascar or a Chinaman; it was all the one now.

'Funny when ye look back,' mused Mr Drew, 'but weren't we the unlikeliest crew to take on the greatest empire in the world. Look at yiz.' He encompassed them all with a gesture. 'Fishermen, tradesmen like meself, men that looked at the back end of a horse all their life. Do yiz ever think about the significance of it all?'

'I don't know about significance, but we bet them. That's all I care about.'

'Aye,' volunteered another, 'I carried that banner up the street this afternoon with *Fingal Brigade* on it, and I'll tell yiz one thing, I held the oul' head up high. I was a proud man today.'

They murmured assent.

'That's what it was all about, holdin' your head up in your own town,' Mr Drew stabbed his stubby finger dogmatically on the counter.

The talk drifted to other matters until one of them mentioned Duffy.

'I needn't tell ye I was surprised to see him standin' there in the crowd today.'

'Who? Duffy?'

'Where did he go after he left here?'

'Aw, down the country somewhere, where he belonged. He had a terrible down on poor Tom Bennett. Tried everything to catch him out. He never managed it though. Tom was always a jump ahead. Nearly drove the sergeant mad.'

'You know,' said one of the men, 'they wouldn't take him into the Civic Guards.'

'Is that a fact?'

'That's true,' nodded Mr Drew. 'I remember now. He wrote a long report after Balbriggan was burned and there was a big enquiry into what he was doin' there at all. It seems his coat was found with blood on it. The enquiry wasn't finished when they handed over, so the matter was dropped, but the Civic Guards wouldn't have him.'

'Proper order,' said a voice. 'Damn lucky he wasn't shot.'

Off the Record

Pubs, sometimes incongruously chosen, are often the scene of important encounters, as in this short scene from Off the Record *(1989) by Joe Joyce. As author of* The Boss, *his experience and expertise could not be more authentic.*

Darkness was falling as Seamus Ryle hurried along Molesworth Street, late. Ahead of him the large iron gates of Leinster House stood open and the building itself was a series of lighted windows stacked upon each other. He turned into Buswell's Hotel and stood at the door of the bar. It was packed with politicians and their friends, big countrymen who watched everyone and everything with undisguised interest. There was no sign of Jim Whelan.

Two women left a corner table and Ryle took their places and settled down to wait, hoping that Whelan hadn't been and gone. He had his back to the bar but he could see everything in the wall of mirrors before him.

He could never understand why politicians preferred to meet journalists in Buswell's when they weren't sure they should be talking to them. They were as likely to be seen there by their colleagues as in the Leinster House bar. He must ask Whelan. But Whelan had other things on his mind when he arrived, flustered.

'That place is a mad house.' He sat down and quickly scanned the other occupants of the bar. 'You forget what it's like when you get away from it even for a few weeks.'

'What's up?'

'Crazy stories. Mostly your fault, of course. You've set off all sorts of mad rumours about Maurice. Election fever. You name it.'

'Is there any chance of an election?'

'Are you mad? Who wants an election in the dead of winter? No, that's only Opposition play-acting. They'd get the fright of their lives if one was sprung on them.'

'What are they saying about Maurice?'

'Utter nonsense, head-banger stuff.' Whelan looked around again. 'Let me get you a drink.' He shot off to the bar as though his re-election depended on it. Another hour in the members' bar after leaving Lyster had exposed him to the full extent of the gossip and to a barrage of questions. He had left in a state of confused agitation.

'Tell me about the rumours,' Ryle persisted when Whelan returned, balancing two glasses of whiskey and a jug of water.

'It's all bullshit,' Whelan said impatiently.

'I know. I'm only curious.'

Whelan sighed heavily and poured some water into his whiskey. 'The usual. An irate husband did it after he caught him on the job. He really died in a minister's car driven by a drunken minister which may or may not have killed someone else as well in a hit-and-run accident. He was shot by a drugs dealer in a row over money. Think up one yourself.'

'Might it have been an irate husband?'

'Ah Jesus, Ryle.' Whelan moaned and threw his hands in the air. 'There you go. That's the trouble with these rumours: people start speculating and adding two and two and making forty. I told you it's all bullshit.'

'Did the Taoiseach tell the party meeting anything about it?'

'There was no discussion. Just a minute's silence and then the meeting was adjourned. No one said anything. You're the only one who seems to know anything,' he added pointedly.

'Well, he wasn't shot, but he was armed,' Ryle said. 'That's about all I know.'

'But what was he doing there? Shooting a dog?' Whelan gave him a bewildered look.

Ryle shrugged. 'I haven't a clue. Did you know he had a gun?' Whelan shook his head. 'Any reason why he might have had one?'

'No. Of course not.'

'Any threats to his life?'

'No. Listen.' Whelan leaned forward and tapped the edge of a cardboard beer mat on the mottled marble table. 'I know you think we're all gangsters and shysters, but even if we were Maurice wouldn't have been like that. You know what I mean?'

'Sure.' Ryle grinned. 'He wasn't a gangster like the rest of you.'

Whelan ignored the taunt. There were dark rings under his eyes and he had the grey pallor of somebody who spent too much time indoors. 'He was the straightest person I've ever known, in or out of politics. I used to say to him in fact that he had to be prepared to bend things a little if he wanted to get on.'

'How do you mean?'

'Small things.' Whelan gestured impatiently. 'Constituents asking him to do something about social welfare payments or whatever. He would look into their cases in detail and then tell them they weren't entitled to anything.'

'What's wrong with that?'

'Nothing.' Whelan threw the beer mat onto the table and sat back. A skelp of loud laughter broke from a group of men at the bar. 'Nothing at all. But there's ways of doing these things. You can't just tell people bluntly they're not entitled to something and thank you very much for calling. They probably know that already if they're calling on you. But they want to hear you say you'll do what you can, see you go through the motions. Voters are like God—they love a trier.'

'How was he so successful as a politician then?'

'He was one of the lucky ones, above the mundane stuff to a certain extent. To the extent that anyone can be in this system. And you guys liked him so the party bosses liked him because it's nice to have a bit of integrity to show off.'

'Jesus,' Ryle muttered in surprise. He had never heard Whelan talk like this before. 'You're becoming more cynical than me. Has this got something to do with your constituency problem?'

Whelan shook his head. 'I thought you wanted to talk about Maurice.' He sighed and went on: 'He should never have been in politics. He should have stayed an academic and I always told him so.' He let out a short laugh. 'He used to say I was displaying my ignorance about academic politics.'

Pound in the Pub

This poem by Eithne Strong from her 1993 collection Spatial Nosing *is viciously effective.*

The son of a famous image
recites the poetry of Pound;
his father's son indeed,
in love with self-projection:
reflexes in fine variance
of voice, as much display
of him as Pound.

This beautiful phraser,
indubitably agile,
wears a cardinal bland hat,
his indispensable crown
on the plastic pub throne
above the beer:
he rouses me stone cold.

Pubs and Publicans

A Roadside Inn this Summer Saturday

This charming description of a roadside inn is from Four Sonnets *by Thomas Caulfield Irwin, a little-known poet who died in 1892.*

A roadside inn this summer Saturday:
The doors are open to the wide warm air,
The parlour, whose old window views the bay,
Garnished with cracked delph full of flowers fair
From the fields round, and whence you see the glare
Fall heavy on the hot slate roofs and o'er
The wall's tree shadows drooping in the sun.
Now rumbles slowly down the dusty street
The lazy drover's clattering cart; and crows
Fainter through afternoon the cock; with hoes
Tan-faced harvest folk trudge in the heat:
The neighbours at their shady doors swept clean,
Gossip, and with cool eve fresh scents of wheat,
Grasses and leaves, come from the meadows green.

The People of the Glens

This short extract from J. M. Synge's In Wicklow, West Kerry and Connemara *of 1919 shows a nice distinction between town pubs and country pubs.*

One night I had to go down late in the evening from a mountain village to the town of Wicklow, and come back again into the hills. As soon as I came near Rathnew I passed many bands of girls and men making rather ruffianly flirtation on the pathway, and women who surged up to stare at me, as I passed in the middle of the road. The thick line of trees that are near Rathnew makes the way intensely dark, even on clear nights, and when one is riding quickly, the contrast, when one reaches the lights of Wicklow, is singularly abrupt. The town itself after nightfall is gloomy and squalid. Half-drunken men and women stand about, wrangling and disputing in the dull light from the windows, which is only strong enough to show the wretchedness of the figures which pass continually across them. I did my business quickly and turned back to the hills, passing for the first few miles the same noisy groups and couples on the roadway. After a while I stopped at a lonely public-house to get a drink and rest for a moment before I came to the hills. Six or seven men were talking drearily at one end of the room, and a woman I knew, who had been marketing in Wicklow, was resting nearer the door. When I had been given a glass of beer, I sat down on a barrel near her, and we began to talk.

The Bailey

*This description of a well-known Dublin hostelry is from Oliver
St John Gogarty's* As I Was Going Down Sackville Street *of 1937.*

'Gentlemen?' large-nosed, red-haired Lewis inquired.

'Two tankards and a small one.'

The Bailey is the only tavern where there still are tankards of pure
silver. A few now, but one time one hundred and sixty. Trophy collecting
and other forms of theft have reduced their number to seven or eight.

The fire in the corner fireplace was smouldering. The north light
fell on the mirror which closed what had once been the folding-door
to the smoke-room where Arthur Griffith held his sway, and before
him, Charles Stewart Parnell. Joe sat sideways across the little room,
George in the corner at his left, and I faced the fireplace and the
mirror. Doors to the left and right of us.

'It's very quiet here,' said Joe.

'If we're not interrupted by the famous bores, we'll be right
enough,' George remarked.

'We can ascend,' said Joe.

In Arthur Griffith's day Mr Hogan gave us the use of a reserved
room one storey higher. In it, some of Griffith's messages to the Irish
people were composed. Solemnly, when invaded by the town's
tiresome ones, we were wont to bid ourselves good-evening publicly
and to go up privately and unobtrusively to the privileged room. There
we could sit *laudatores temporis acti*: living in the imagined
successes of our past.

Now no Whelan holds the gate against intruders on Arthur. Griffith
was dead and we, his disciples, meet but rarely in the upper chamber.
We can let our talk range freely in the smoking-room until we are
driven out by some insufferable but respectful bore, who calls us 'Sir'.

'We met Thwackhurst on our way here. That delayed us.'

'He is one of those who cannot be accused of being *cupidus rerum
novarum*,' Joe said quietly.

'Nor quite satisfied with their results.'

'He prefers poverty and freedom to observance and respectability. I like him well. Seumas brought me to his digs high up in a gable, where he lives with his cat. It was the morning of Christ's nativity. He got out of bed, put on a short reefer jacket over his naked form, stepped into his boots and, nether naked, squatted before his fireless grate with: "It was the winter wild...God blast my old huer of a landlady. Which of yez has a match?"'

'Has she forgotten the mistletoe?'

'She has forgotten the bloody fire.'

'I saw him looking out of his window in Oxo after his cat this morning,' said I.

'Another character, Maturnin, the best authority the *Encylopaedia Britannica* could enlist, used to do his work at the bar downstairs.'

'It's a great tavern right enough.'

'What amazes me,' said George, 'is that the Germans are sending over professors of English to trace out the imaginary itinerary of Joyce's imaginary Mr Bloom through the different pubs he is supposed to have visited. They all miss the one that Joyce liked.'

'The Bloom that never was on sea or land! He is quite unconvincing. A mere chorus to Joyce.'

'Was he Elwood?'

'Lord, no!' said I.

'I should hate to have my pubs stalked by German professors who took pub-crawling seriously. The moment our pubs become the subject of literature, that is the moment they are undone. Even we who patronise them would become self-conscious. The last thing drink should do is to make one self-conscious. We would become actors, as it were, in a play, and not simply patrons of our pub.'

'Even in our ashes live their Reuter's wires.'

'Talking of ashes, we saw that wonderful doctor who thinks that he is the cigar. He passed us in Dawson Street in a hurry, in his Ford.'

'Probably he was going to lay another wreath on the grave of the "Unknown Soldier".'

'To whom he was related.'

'In that he was more or less unknown.'

'Just the same again, Lewis,' said I.

'Right you are, sir. Fawcus rode another winner to-day, sir.'

The unnecessary boy who makes a noise with the grate lingered to overhear, but left the fire slacked.

The Fanatic

This is the beginning of a story, from The Pedlar's Revenge and Other Stories, *by Liam O'Flaherty, who died in 1984. The description of the 'gloomy tavern' and its proprietor is horrendous.*

Everything in the gloomy tavern, which also served as a general store, was literally covered with dirt. The old wooden counter was dappled like a leopard's hide with dried daubs of porter froth and a labyrinthine pattern of rings left by the bottoms of pint measures. The floor was pocked with holes, some of which were large enough to let a child fall through into the cellar. Rats made a great tumult down below, as they scurried to and fro. The light of day was barely able to penetrate the foul mass of dust and garbage on the window panes. There were thousands of flies roaming about the place, feeding and making love and gambolling at their leisure. The air was laden with a nauseating stench. The sound of normal healthy life, that came through the open street door from the little country town outside, seemed to be unreal and even plaintive.

Good Lord! It really was like a place invented by Father Mathew, the famous apostle of temperance, while preaching a sermon about the horrors of indulgence in alcohol.

'God save all here,' I said in a loud voice.

Nobody answered and it was hardly reasonable to expect that anybody should; for it seemed that there was nothing alive in the place above ground except flies and the spiders that were trying to catch them in their webs up among the rafters.

'Anybody here?' I called out once more.

'Yes,' said a voice.

I looked to my left and saw a man's face framed between the two posts of the open door that led to the kitchen in the rear. Owing to the poor light, I could see nothing attached to the face. It was like an apparition, that yellow countenance hanging without attachment on the dark air. I got somewhat frightened.

'Good Heavens!' I said to myself, while a tremor of apprehension passed slowly down my spine. 'What place is this? The tavern of the dead? Or has the unaccustomed heat unhinged my reason?'

Then a polite little cough issued from the face and I saw a tall lean man come towards me very slowly behind the counter. He walked with downcast head and he was rubbing the palms of his blue-veined hands together, back and forth continually, in front of his navel. He went past me without glancing in my direction, walking silently on the tips of his toes. After he had passed, he shrugged his narrow drooping shoulders three times in quick succession, a gesture that usually denotes a habitual drunkard.

'Thanks be to God,' he said in a gentle low voice, after he had come to a halt in front of the window, 'it's a lovely fine day.'

'Praised be God,' I replied, 'it would be difficult to find fault with it, right enough.'

'It may keep fine like this now for a good spell,' the man said. 'A good spell of it would come in handy.'

'It would,' I agreed. 'It would come in very handy.'

'Oh! Indeed, it would,' he said. 'There's no doubt at all but that a good long spell of it would suit the country down to the ground, in God's holy name.'

Then he clasped his hands behind the small of his back and let the upper part of his body come slanting gently towards me; exactly like a person on a ship's deck in breezy weather striving to keep his balance against the anarchy of the sea's movement.

'Where was your hurry taking you?' he asked politely.

'It was how I dropped in for a bottle,' I replied.

'Ha! Then,' said he, 'it was a wish for a bottle that brought you.'

'Yes indeed,' said I. 'It was a wish for a bottle of porter.'

He straightened himself suddenly, raised his shoulders and shook his head violently, like a man suffering from cold.

'Upon my soul,' he said, 'you have no reason at all for feeling ashamed of such a wish on a day as boiling hot as this.'

'True enough,' I said, 'it was the heat made me thirsty.'

'Oh! Indeed,' he said with deep feeling, 'it's proud of your thirst you should be on a day like this, instead of feeling the least little bit ashamed.'

Then he looked at me, back over his shoulder.

'Don't be afraid, good man,' he added in a very friendly tone. 'I have a nice fresh bottle for you here, full of porter that is just as sweet and wholesome as the milk of any cow you ever saw in all your natural life. It is, 'faith and no doubt about it.'

He was stiff-necked. He had to turn his whole body right up from his knees before he was able to look me in the face from that position. Good Lord! His eyes were of an extraordinary beauty. They were like a woman's eyes soft and gentle and amorous. It was quite impossible to identify their colour in that dark room. They seemed to be a mixture of brown and grey and green; like the little smooth multi-coloured stones that lie at the bottom of a swiftly-running mountain torrent on whose surface the bright rays of the sun are dancing.

'Come now,' said I. 'Oblige me, in God's name, by handing me that fine bottle. Will you have one yourself, good man?'

He shook his head sadly.

'Thank you, treasure,' he said, 'but I haven't tasted a drop, either good or bad, for the past two years.'

Then he started and began to turn his body ever so slowly, with his head poised in ludicrous immobility on his stiff neck. When he had finally put about, he gave his shoulders a nervous twitch, coughed in his throat, and walked towards me on tip-toe. He kept his face turned from me as he went past and his hands were clasped before his navel like a person at prayer. Judging by the movement of his jaw muscles, his lips were framing words. Yet I heard no sound of uttered speech issue from them.

'Oh! Yes,' I said to myself. 'The poor fellow is deranged.'

He picked up a bottle, pulled the cork and filled a glass, which he placed before me on the counter. I gave him a half-crown.

'You are like a man,' he said, while looking for my change in the till, 'that has travelled a fair share of the world.'

'I've been here and there,' I said.

'That's what I thought,' he said. 'You have the cut of a traveller about your wise face.'

'Thank you,' I said.

'You're welcome,' said he.

He approached me once more behind the counter with downcast head. As he was going past, he handed me the change without glancing in my direction. Then he kept moving along slowly on tip-toe, until he reached a tiny wooden cubicle that lay between the end of the counter and the open door that led out into the street. The business accounts of the shop were kept in the cubicle. He thrust his head into it and then stood stock still, with his hands clasped behind his back and his legs spread out wide away behind him; exactly like a frightened sheep hiding its head in a hole and exposing its big tremulous rump to the oncoming danger.

'He's deranged without a doubt,' I said to myself once more.

Then I drank some of the porter and lit a cigarette. In spite of the man's boast, the liquor was sour and almost repulsively tepid. It left a frightful taste on my tongue. Neither of us spoke for some time. The only sound in the shop was the scuffling of the rats down in the cellar. Away out along a country road beyond the town, cart wheels were turning and a man was singing a gay song of love.

The Barmen of Sexford

This wickedly amusing poem by Rita Ann Higgins is from her 1988 collection Witch in the Bushes.

> In March
> Sexford
> can be as cold
> as any
> disappearing relative
> with a toothache
> you may find yourself
> not siding with
> in a hurricane.

The barmen
have no problem
with the cold,
they rip off your tights
with their fast
Indian bread breath,
never stopping
for traffic or history.

The people here
are warm
but black tights
means only one thing
to the men
of Sexford
the barmen of Sexford.

When you
clear your throat
here
the barmen
think
you are addressing them
they say,
'Were you
calling us just then
Black Legs,
can we
do anything for ya,
can we
shine yer knees
please, please?'

The comfort
here
tumbled out
in hot whiskies
and a backbiting fire.

In Sexford
the fire was always there
but the barmen
didn't really exist
only
in their mother's prayers
and in
Communion photos
on the dusty mantle
beside the dead president
who was leaning against
the Sacred Bleeding Heart
and of course
in some kind old headmaster's
estimation.

The Eagles and the Trumpets

This is the beginning of a story from James Plunkett's The Trusting
and the Maimed. *It illustrates what the author describes as 'the easy
familiarity of the country town'.*

When the girl crossed from the library, the square was bathed in August
sunshine. The folk from the outlying areas who had left their horses and
carts tethered about the patriotic monument in the centre were still in
the shops, and the old trees which lined either side emphasised the
stillness of the morning. She went down a corridor in the Commercial
Hotel and turned left into the bar. She hardly noticed its quaintness, the
odd layout of the table, its leather chairs in angles and corners, the long
low window which looked out on the dairy yard at the back. After six
years in the town she was only aware of its limitations. But the
commercial traveller startled her. She had not expected to find anyone
there so early. He raised his eyes and when he had stared at her
gloomily for a moment, he asked, 'Looking for Cissy?'

One of the things she had never got used to was this easy familiarity of the country town. But she accepted it. One either accepted or became a crank.

'No,' she answered, 'Miss O'Halloran.'

'You won't see her,' he said. 'It's the first Friday. She goes to the altar and has her breakfast late.' He had a glass of whiskey in front of him and a bottle of Bass. He gulped half the whiskey and then added, 'I'll ring the bell for you.'

'Thank you.'

His greyish face with its protruding upper lip was vaguely familiar. Probably she had passed him many times in her six years without paying much attention. Now she merely wondered about his black tie. She heard the bell ringing remotely and after a moment Cissy appeared. The girl said:

'I really wanted Miss O'Halloran. It's a room for a gentleman tonight.' She hesitated. Then reluctantly she added, 'Mr Sweeney.' As she had expected, Cissy betrayed immediate curiosity.

'Not Mr Sweeney that stayed here last autumn?'

'Yes. He hopes to get in on the afternoon bus.'

Cissy said she would ask Miss O'Halloran. When she had gone to inquire, the girl turned her back on the traveller and pretended interest in an advertisement for whiskey which featured two dogs, one with a pheasant in its mouth. The voice from behind her asked:

'Boy-friend?'

She had expected something like that. Without turning she said, 'You're very curious.'

'Sorry. I didn't mean that. I don't give a damn. Do you drink?'

'No, thank you.'

'I was going to offer you something better than a drink. Good advice.' The girl stiffened. She was the town librarian, not a chambermaid. Then she relaxed and almost smiled.

'If you ever do,' the voice added sadly, 'don't mix the grain with the grape. That's what happened to me last night.'

Cissy returned and said Mr Sweeney could have room seven. Miss O'Halloran was delighted. Mr Sweeney had been such a nice young man. Her eye caught the traveller and she frowned.

'Mr Cassidy,' she said pertly, 'Miss O'Halloran says your breakfast's ready.'

The traveller looked at her with distaste. He finished his whiskey and indicated with a nod of his head the glass of Bass which he had taken in his hand.

'Tell Miss O'Halloran I'm having my breakfast,' he said. But Cissy was admiring the new dress.

'You certainly look pretty,' she said enviously.

'Prettiest girl in town,' the traveller added for emphasis.

The girl flushed. Cissy winked and said, 'Last night he told me I was.'

'Did I?' the traveller said, finishing his Bass with a grimace of disgust. 'I must have been drunk.'

O'Farrell's Snug

Snugs are a very precious feature of Irish pubs and a loving encomium on O'Farrell's is contained in John Broderick's The Flood *of 1990.*

The snug in O'Farrell's was very much like all the other compartments set up in bars to provide wordahs for the women who never, *of course*, drank with the men in the public area. These tiny cloisters were usually situated at the end of the bar counter, so that a hatch could be opened conveniently, and the ladies given their drinks, uncontaminated by the lustful eyes of the men, who would also, so the theory went, not know how much the womenfolk were spending on fire-water. In reality everyone knew exactly what any particular lady drank at any particular time, and how often she drank it; but at least she was spared the embarrassment of being seen to do so. Young women were not served in respectable bars, even in snugs, and O'Farrell's dimbo had never been occupied by any female less than fifty.

But O'Farrell's snug had a distinction which made it unique among the cloisters of Bridgeford. Like all the others it had a bench running along the wall, a table and two or three chairs. But Fenny's mother had an aunt, who claimed to have been taken by her husband to the Cafe Royal in London, long before Oscar Wilde made it notorious. Her description of this famous and exclusive place had fired old Mrs O'Farrell's imagination. She had her snug bench covered with red plush, and had a fake pillar of rounded wood put in at the end of the bar and painted with gold leaf. Over the bench she hung a coloured photograph of Piccadilly Circus as it was in 1900, and obviously taken from the first floor of Swan and Edgars. The old lady would point to this scene with some pride, for it had been given to her by her rich English-based aunt, and run her finger along the picture until she came to the frame. Then she would indicate a spot on the wall about two inches from the photograph. 'There,' she would say proudly, 'just about there, in Regent Street, you know, is the Cafe Royal, where my aunt used to dine, oh long before it got a bad name.' On this spot Fenny in his youth had painted a large, gold leaf X to mark the site of the celebrated cafe, and of course the snug was known locally, especially to older women as The Cafe Royal. And many a story of a slightly bawdy nature was told about it.

Refined Drinking and Parties

Colloquy of the Ancients

This brief extract from Standish O'Grady's translation of The Colloquy *sketches altogether too innocent a party to be called a carousal!*

They reached *carn na finghaile* or 'the cairn of fratricide', now called *dumha na con* or 'the mound of wolf-dogs', where as they stepped up the *tulach* they saw nine lovely women that with a queen of excellent form in their midst awaited them. A smock of royal silk she had next to her skin; over that an outer tunic of soft silk, and around her a hooded mantle of crimson fastened on her breast with a golden brooch. Upon seeing Caeilte the lady rose and gave him three kisses; then he asked: 'maiden, who art thou?' She replied: 'I am Echna daughter of Muiredach mac Finnachta, the king of Connacht's daughter that is to say.' Now the bevy of them had a chess-board, on which they played; a can of delicious mead too, which they drank, and in which floated a fair polished horn. Every time that a game was won and ended they took a draught: they caroused in fact and made merry. The manner of the lady was this: she had three perfections; for of the whole world's wise women she was one, and he whom she should have counselled had as the result both affluence and consideration.

A Hooley

*While a British gunboat came up the Liffey and poured shells into
Liberty Hall, Maisie Collins gave a hooley—while the sky was
crimson with funeral pyres. This extract from* Come Trailing Blood
(1959) *by Paul Smith illustrates neatly how for the Irish it is as
natural to give a hooley, whatever the circumstances, as it is for a
cat to wash.*

In a crimson dress, a deep crimson, inseparable from the lines of her
flanks, her thighs, her breasts, and wearing every scrap of jewellery she
owned and some she didn't, Maisie stood at one end of the room and
surveyed the fruits of her own and Harriet Reilly's labour. Splendidly
lit by three oil lamps, no crevice of the room was exposed to the
dangers of mystery. The big double bed had been taken down and
stored out in the hall. Along the wall opposite the fireplace, two snowy
covered tables, one of which she had borrowed, stood and proclaimed
that the material world was, after all, the one and only. Among the
sparkle of glass and the glitter of silver, two cold hams, taken from
Smyths on The Green, stood up beside rounds of roast and corned beef,
swiped from Doolins in Wexford Street; loaves of brown and white
bread, slabs of rich cake, jellies and serious blancmanges, apples, figs,
nuts; whiskey, brandy and black-bottled bottled stout; and in the very
centre a huge, ornate, solid silver bowl of punch—made especially by
Ba. In a friction of excitement, of people arriving and people leaving,
Maisie eyed the silver bowl of punch uneasy in her mind, for Ba Fay
could say what he liked about it being a ladies' drink, but she had
distinctly seen two bottles of brandy go into the making of it. To prove
its innocence, he had given her a couple of glasses, and no mistake it
was very nice and was helping her cope with the hazards of a gathering
for which she was responsible, but she'd hate to have to swear to the
priest on the altar that she was cold, cold sober.

Through the orchestration of lights, glass, food, and a mutually
appreciative exchange of opinions going on between those passing

and repassing, Maisie looked at her guests who had arrived early and had risked or were now risking, and they were all looking suspiciously unlike themselves. All except her old friend Judy Madden, who was still her own burnt-to-an-orange-brown-sober little self as she entered the arena picking nervously at the feathers trimming the neck of her dress and peering over them and around for the first sign of treachery. She saw Judy pause to frown black over the loaded tables before moving on to settle beside Harriet Reilly sitting on her own on the only sofa in the whole house.

'I see that certain poor souls around here have decided not to go hungry either,' Judy said to Harriet just as Ba, urged forward by Maisie to attend to the wants of her guests, bent and let his hand rest on her knee.

In his white shirt and blue suit he was looking rakish.

'And Judy the only capitalist among us and not drinking.' He aimed at her his most stunning grin.

'A Vimto, Ba, a Vimto,' she said when she could, and just managed to keep herself erect as his hand shifted and closed tight about her knee.

'Isn't that the right oul' ram,' she said, after him moistening her lips at the prospect, just as 'The Sphinx', who had arrived with some others, drew up a chair and sat down beside her. The glance Harriet and Judy threw the lethargic sombrely black-hatted and black-coated woman was one of criticism and, as with all Dubliners, was and for no reason, hostile. Prepared to carry on as though she wasn't there Judy and Harriet did no more than nod and from the deep folds of her fat, 'The Sphinx' stared stonily back.

'You're like a rose,' Harriet shouted to Maisie going past with Jeremiah Hudson.

'She'd plunder attention from any rose,' Jeremiah replied.

'She's upsetting that man's sober decencies,' Judy said.

'It's just as well you can't see what she's doing to mine,' Ba said, as he returned with Judy's drink, bringing an extra one for 'The Sphinx' without being asked. 'That will put lead in your pencils.'

With rapacious hands, 'The Sphinx' and Judy reached.

'Oh, Ba, you shouldn't!' Judy looked imploringly up from the sparkling amber punch in her glass. She could have been asking him to take on a responsibility, or accept a sacrifice.

'Well, here's to another lovely war,' Harriet said, into the clash of voices growing vigorous as people adjusted themselves and found their tongues, and as 'The Sphinx' slowly raised her glass of stout, the only drink she ever drank, to her lips.

Judy downed her punch and turning on the disbelieving smile, with which she sometimes rewarded those she found herself amongst, cast an eye on Maisie standing now with Ba and laughing at some whispered remark. The woman was no class, she thought, seeing Maisie rest herself against Ba for a second as one of his hands curved round her breasts, but you had to give it to her, she was a beauty, and too good for Ba Fay. Although it was nothing short of a miracle, the change finding him had brought about in her. For even Judy admitted that the truth known had to be recognised, and who better than herself knew what the truth was? But Rose was right! And them tits of hers were having a terrible struggle with that dress. She turned to Harriet.

'It's new isn't it?'

'What is?'

'Maisie's dress.'

'It is.'

'And yours?'

'Thanks to the Famine Queen and the Republicans.'

'You're getting your queens ballsed-up!'

'I know it, but I'm right about the Republicans. Up the Republicans!' Under the liquid action of the purest, subtlest silk Harriet stood up in a moss green flounce and froth to salute, then sat down again.

'That's the advantage of having nothing. You can't lose it.' Judy offered her smile to the room and the blare of the gramophone. 'And if you don't mind my saying so Harriet—you, and the rest of the working class, have *nothing*. But flag-waving, my dear, never filled anybody's belly! And what about commerce? And the little man? Like me for instance? I'll lose the shift off my back if this Rebellion goes on, for it's already causing havoc to my ladies' trade so it is.'

'What about me, Judy Madden?' A big pink woman was shouting big. 'The best hustler in Dublin, and not able to hustle. And now the British have brought in martial law, Jasus only knows when Dawson

Street and the four sides of The Green will see me again.'

'Ah, be spartan, Martha, for Christ's sake. Pretend it's Lent and give your poor oul' chassis a rest. After all, men seven nights a week for the past ten years must be having some effect.'

'It is, Ma'am. It is.' Martha Liller laughed raucous and drew back from the young fella she was dancing with, to bounce her breasts with both hands. 'It's oiling the wheels and keeping the engine purring. But look and long, Judy, look and long.'

Judy watched Martha dance away and beside her 'The Sphinx', whom she knew slightly and disliked, said to no one in particular, 'Mary Pickford for President!' Judy turned back to Harriet.

'It's the exodus that's fretting me,' she said. 'Because all my ladies, like the rest of the gentry and moneyed classes, are packing up and going back to England...'

'And taking with them everything they can leave their thieving hands on!' Harriet said, and turned a bland smile up at a black stranger. She heard a woman say, 'If I'd known what the world was going to be like, I never would've bothered me arse about growing up.' And beside her, in an anxiety she could no longer disguise even had she wanted to, Judy asked, 'What class are they at all, at all?'

'Who? Your ladies? Or the brave bastards that sent the British gunboat up the Liffey this morning to bomb the town and leave us all corpses?'

'Neither!' Judy clamped disapproving lips over small pointed teeth. 'The wans doing the looting.'

'Oh, now there I leave you,' Harriet said. 'But I'll tell you something for nothing, Judy Madden; the groans you hear coming from them tables is the direct result of two days' hard work. And so is me own and Maisie's finery.'

'Youse took all youse could and forgot to thank God. I thought so! The figs from Tunis and the oranges from Spain.'

'Whiskey from Scotland, and brandy from France.'

'Jasus, youse will die roaring!'

'And Luther's at peace with God and himself!' Jeremiah Hudson had come to join them, bringing with him handfuls of fresh drinks.

'And as for that dizened, double-dyed hoor of Babylon!' Judy said up to Martha Liller dancing by.

211

'She's like some old Divinity disguised, aren't you, Martha?' Jeremiah raised his glass.

'What's coming between me and me rest is what'll happen to this kip of a country if the English do clear out,' Judy said. 'For fifteen years now, and in the midst of breeze and blast, I've been going round the best Protestant houses in this city, buying and selling the grandest of second-hand clothes. Now what I want the Republicans to tell me is this: who, and what, am I to replace them with? For with all due respects, our own crowd of penny pinching craw-thumping muck-grubbers—God help us—will never be up to them.'

There was a raucous bray of male laughter and the more impudent thin reeds of girlish giggles at one end of the room, and on the chair beside Judy 'The Sphinx' stuck her nose into the glass of stout in her hands and downed it in one loud gulp. She sat back, 'All right then,' she said, 'Charlie Chaplin for President, and fuck the lot of youse!'

As a business woman who was on speaking terms with the great and near great, Judy could not allow herself to approve of any kind of eccentricity. She glanced at Harriet whose laugh at 'The Sphinx' had burst from her and said, 'The Republicans are turning this country into a randy-voo for rowdyism.'

'Ah, drink up for Jasus sake, Judy,' Harriet said finishing off hers and looking after Jeremiah going to get her another.

'I don't see Chrissy Swords, or the Gosses?' Judy said, and asked, 'Did Maisie not give them an invite?'

'She did,' Harriet wiped the laugh from her face. 'But Chrissy's out and about her business in the dark, and surely you heard about the Gosses!'

'Heard what?'

'The Republicans took John out yesterday and eyes haven't been clapped on him since.'

'I didn't know John Goss was a Republican.'

'You would if you'd been listening. But then your hearing isn't what it was.'

'Is anything?' Judy asked wryly.

'You heard about the shooting of the British officers in the Park this morning?'

'Who hasn't? And it was only *one* officer!' Judy corrected Harriet. '*One* officer and three soldiers.' For the details of the ambush had taken precedence over the news of the proclamation posted on the walls all over the city announcing martial law, and even over the fairy tales published in one newspaper that the country was at peace again, and even over the sight and sound of the British gunboat bombarding from the Liffey the very heart of the city.

'The Republicans didn't give those poor bastards a chance,' Ba Fay came with Martha Liller to a halt beside them.

'The bastards manning the British gunboat didn't give us much of a chance either,' Harriet's smile was feline but friendly.

'Ambushed an officer and three soldiers, and after blowing the head off the officer, they bundled the three soldiers still alive into the car and set fire to it.'

'Oh, Christ!'

Ba watched the shock on Martha's face.

'You must be the only one in the city who didn't know,' he said, forgetting—if he ever knew—that Martha seldom, if ever, saw the light of day.

'Jesus, aren't they the right heathens?' she said. 'Have they been caught?'

Ba tossed back his drink. 'No, but they will be. And Jasus help them when they are. The English have been going through every house and yard with a fine comb since morning.'

'I hope they catch them!' Martha spoke with quiet vehemence.

'You would, you vicious hoor!' one woman remarked.

Some of those gathered in the room audibly agreed with Martha, while others hushed mouths in full or half-emptied glasses.

'The room is humming with accusations,' Jeremiah said.

'Well, it's only natural a thing like this would cast a gloom over the proceedings,' Judy replied.

'Perhaps! But I was just thinking: how people who, up to now, haven't cared one way or the other, and who've maintained a singular reticence about their own particular sympathies, have suddenly sprung into voice and violent protest at the death of these four men in the Park, and loudly demanding—like you, Martha—retribution upon the guilty.'

Kate's Party

This description of a rather sedate Christmas party is from The Big
Sycamore *(1958) by Joseph Brady.*

About Christmas time Kate gave a party for old friends. The parlour
was scrubbed out with Monkey-Brand soap. Aunt Hannah's painting
of the Mill Wheel and Kate's own crayon drawing of Kilkenny Castle,
done at the Loreto Convent, were taken down from the wall and
freshened up. The old stuffed cockatoo (or was it a Bird of Paradise?)
had his feathers preened. The photographs in the family album were
dusted and re-arranged. On the sideboard shone the big silver teapot
that did the rounds of the parish. Bottles of whiskey and stout were
laid in, and lemonade for the total abstainers. Maurice did not like to
see drink in circulation. In his later years he had a fanatical hatred of
it. He could not stand the sight of a man 'under the influence'. He had
seen many homes left in poverty by over-indulgence in liquor. He was
afraid lest any of his children would ever get fond of it.

The parlour could not contain the full gathering of friends, so the
overflow was catered for in the kitchen. The children were darting in
and out from parlour to kitchen. High jinks were going on in the yard
and in the shop. From the kitchen could be heard the popping of
corks. Mick Stack was having a royal time. To celebrate the occasion
he danced 'cover the bucket'. This was Mick's own speciality. An
empty bucket was placed on the floor. The dancer's art was in
alternating his feet with such speed that the bucket seemed to be
constantly covered with one foot, while the other twinkled with
lightning speed on the floor. The bucket must not be touched. For this
dance Matt Cooney played on his melodeon the lively tune *I buried
my wife and danced on top of her*. Mick never created the illusion of
covering the bucket, but his performance was greeted with a great
burst of cheering.

Mick loved to bask in the *aura popularis*. He never failed to find
an audience that played up to him, whether it was applause for a
dancing exhibition, or a suitable expression of admiration when he

214

told of his own exploits or those of his deceased mother. He said that she was 'the best man that ever filled a load of furze'. When he was asked by Maurice how many loads of top dressing had he taken during the week from the manure heap to the tillage field, Mick gave the innocent reply: 'Some days more loads, more days some loads.' The poor honest man could not count, but he faithfully chalked up on the side of the dray the figure one for each load which he had carted.

The party in the parlour was more sedate, almost formal. Father Phil opened the entertainment with the song, *Let each man learn to know himself*. The priests of Mullenaglock were all beloved by the people, but none of them evoked such affection as Father Philip Dooley, affectionately known by all as Father Phil. He was a huge man, powerfully built. His laughter was gargantuan and contagious. He wore heavy-lensed glasses that gave one the impression of beholding a great friendly seal. He had heavy chops and a jowl. When he walked he rested sideways on a big stout stick which he always carried. He blew out his cheeks as he progressed. In his big pockets he carried bags of sweets which he doled out to children whom he met on his way. He spent many hours in his attendance at the bedside of invalids. Once when he was terminating his visit to an old bed-ridden man in Garryduff, he said, 'Goodbye now, Michael. I've brought you to the Gate of Heaven.'

'Ah, Father Phil,' pleaded Michael, 'don't leave me at the Gate.'

One summer's day when he entered a bathing box at Tramore, some wag told the bystanders that 'the big man' was a famous swimmer and that he was about to swim to Dunmore Head, thence to the Metal Man, and back again to the jetty. Father Phil emerged in his bathing togs, smoking a pipe. The crowd clapped. As he wasn't wearing his glasses he wasn't recognised. Father Phil was not aware that the applause was for himself. He sat splashing himself in a shallow pool of water close to the diving board. Then he moved into deep water and floated on his back, still smoking. He laughed heartily when he heard that he was mistaken for a steamer.

An encore to Father Phil's first song was always called for. Then Father Phil would sing in deepest *basso profundo* the famous German drinking song, *In Cellar Cool*. His voice sounded as if it really came from a barrel. The windows rattled. The glasses on the sideboard tinkled. Even the empty buckets in the shop reverberated. When the applause died down, Father Phil said the magic words, 'Knockshaydoushay lathshay, Knockshaydoushay lumpshay; you can all go to pot, as Billy Richardson used to say.' Then he laughed, his whole body, stomach, head, legs, and hands vibrating. Everyone joined in the laughing until tears streamed down cheeks.

The people were at first mystified by the allusion to Billy Richardson. Some friend gave the key to the mystery. Father Phil once went to a circus in Liverpool, where he was a missionary priest for some years after his ordination. The proprietor of the circus was Billy Richardson. Father Phil went into convulsions at some joke which misfired on the other spectators. Father Phil's laugh was so contagious that it set the whole crowd into roars of laughter. Billy Richardson was so pleased that he gave Father Phil a free pass for every season.

When the applause for Father Phil's performance had subsided, Maurice's song was called for. Half closing his eyes and slightly swaying his body to the rhythm, he sang in a beautiful baritone voice *Shule Agrá*. All his songs were in a minor key, as indeed are most of the favourite Irish airs. Has not G. K. Chesterton said of the Irish: 'For all their wars are merry, and all their songs are sad.' Maurice put his whole being into a song, with the result, as they said in Letterlee, that 'he could put a song through you'. He ended the last line, 'Iss go dhe' thoo mavourneen slaun' in a recitative, as was the custom in the parish.

Social Drinking

The Dark Cave

This short extract is from Bird Alone *(1936) by Seán Ó Faoláin.*

'He was a vain man,' somebody who knew him once said to me, 'and ambitious; but very weak in the carnalities.'

I must say all the 'carnalities' I ever saw in him at *that* time was when he would be with his friend Arty Tinsley, and I after him with young Christy Tinsley, in and out of every pub in the city of Cork, and rain, hail or snow, every third Sunday of the month galloping out the country in wagonettes, decorating the graves of the Fenian dead. Then we would be, the four of us with his friends, over a pub fire in Kilcrea or Ovens or Kilcroney, the talk floating up the chimney with the steam of our legs, while the rain hissed into the misty grass and the pokers hissed in the mulled stout, surrounded by a procession of names, hour by hour, corner to corner, Rossa and O'Neill-Crowley, Land and Labour, Davitt and the Tory 'hoors'; a drink to Lomasney who was found in his own clots of gore on the mud of the Isle of Dogs after floating down from London Bridge that he had tried to blow up— nothing less would appease his wild imagination, I suppose: and a drink to the men who swung for the agent they sunk in a bog near Tipperary: and a drink to His Lordship of Cashel who talked up to the Pope when he went to Rome *ad audiendum verbum*…all ending with the road thick with night and a singing born of liquor, and Christy Tinsley and myself wrapped into one another with cold and sleep.

The Ritual

This picture of ritualistic supping featuring two elderly ladies is from
John Broderick's The Fugitives *of 1962.*

It was a ritual. Every Monday and Friday Mrs Lagan stopped outside
the shop-door and paused with her black-gloved hand on the latch for
one last look up and down the street. Then, quickly, almost as if she
were afraid of being seen, she slipped into the shop and announced
her arrival with a light, affected cough: a little strangulated sound, like
a kitten that has not yet learned to mew. Carefully, she put down her
umbrella, grasped her purple toque with both hands and settled it
firmly on her white curls, while her handbag slid down her arm and
settled in the crook of her elbow. Then she wriggled her shoulders,
shook herself inside her long black coat, took up her umbrella and
tapped on the floor.

'Mrs Fallon,' she called. 'It's me.'

Hetty was already waiting for her inside the 'snug', a small
enclosure behind one of the windows, closed off from the rest of the
shop by a wooden partition.

'Come in,' called Hetty, pushing open the door of the 'snug'.

'Oh, there you are, Mrs Fallon. I was just passing. I thought I'd
drop in for a moment.'

'Come in here and sit down,' said Hetty, reciting her part of the
antiphon. 'I've just finished my rosary.'

'The Sorrowful Mysteries to-day,' said Mrs Lagan, edging her way
into the 'snug'. This part of the ritual varied with the day. On
Mondays and during Advent the Joyful Mysteries, on Fridays and
during Lent the Sorrowful Mysteries.

The mulled port was already waiting on the table with one
Digestive biscuit beside each glass. Since it was Friday Mrs Lagan
took off her gloves and sniffed her fingers delicately.

'Do I smell of fish?' she asked.

'I hate the smell of fish,' said Hetty in her oblique way.

'I don't really smell of it at all,' retorted Mrs Lagan, as she had
every Friday for the last twenty years when Hetty made her remark.

'It's just that I think I do. You know I have a very delicate nose. The least odour and I think I'm contaminated. I can't bear anything offensive. It's a terrible way to be, considering the dirt of other people.'

During this speech Hetty always closed her eyes and turned down the corners of her mouth. Slowly, carefully, her short fingers reached for the glass of port and closed about the stem.

'Ah, well,' she said, 'in the honour of God.'

They raised their glasses.

'In the honour of God.'

'A lovely drop of port, thank God,' said Mrs Lagan, wiping her mouth delicately with the corner of a lace handkerchief. 'Just the way I like it.'

'It will do you good,' said Hetty, shifting heavily in her seat and looking at Mrs Lagan with half-closed eyes. 'You look a bit pale.'

Mrs Lagan closed her eyes and slumped in her chair, letting her hands fall by her side in a gesture of complete exhaustion. 'I don't know what way I am,' she said in a weak voice. 'I feel completely washed out. Not a wink of sleep last night, sitting up every ten minutes sprinkling holy water over the poor souls in Purgatory, and then dragging myself out for eight o'clock Mass. I feel I could just drop down and die.'

'Terrible sudden times,' said Hetty, shaking her head. 'Nothing but people dropping dead all over the place. I'd go to bed for a few days if I were you, your lips are very blue. Mrs Sheridan was the very same. In here getting her groceries one minute and stone dead on the bridge ten minutes later. But I noticed her lips. Blue.' She sipped her port contentedly.

'There's nothing the matter with me,' said Mrs Lagan firmly, drawing herself up. 'Old age runs in our family. It's just that I'm too conscientious, always worrying about the way the world is going, always working myself to the bone when I have no need to.' She grasped her glass firmly and raised it to her lips.

'I don't know what way the world is going,' said Hetty. 'Mad, if you ask me.'

'Business is quiet is it?' Mrs Lagan sighed. 'This end of the town is a back-water.'

'I'm doing all I'm able to do,' said Hetty with a black look. 'My customers don't desert me.'

Mrs Lagan smiled pityingly.

'All the same,' she said, 'it's not the same as it was in the old days. I remember well when you were behind the counter here the shop used to be packed.'

There was nothing in the world that Hetty liked being reminded of less than the years she had spent working in Fallons before her marriage.

'Have you heard from Peter lately?' she asked gruffly.

Mrs Lagan stirred uneasily in her chair. Her only son had gone to Australia years before, and everybody knew that he had never written to her since.

'Oh, yes,' she said brightly, tapping her glass angrily with her nail, 'the usual letter, you know. Going on well.'

'It's a wonder he never comes home,' said Hetty inexorably.

'Business, you know. He has such a terrible lot to do. Of course he's always writing for me to go out, but I'm too old to settle down in a new country. Besides, Ireland is the best place. Thanks be to God for one place where God and his Blessed Mother are given Their due. Not like England.'

'Or Australia.' Hetty sipped her port contentedly.

'I see you have Lily home,' countered Mrs Lagan. 'Poor girl, she looks washed out. Is she sick?'

'No,' replied Hetty shortly. 'Is that a new blouse you have on?'

Mrs Lagan was not to be put off. She patted her blouse and crossed her legs, a daring gesture, made only when she felt she was really going to discomfort her old friend.

'I've had this blouse for ages. A really good thing never wears out, or goes out of fashion. Did Lily bring you home any clothes from England?'

'I don't need any clothes,' said Hetty angrily.

'I suppose she's on holiday, poor girl,' went on Mrs Lagan with a pitying smile. 'What is she working at now?'

'She's a supervisor.'

'All those supervisors,' hooted Mrs Lagan. 'London is full of them, all Irish.'

'I suppose it's the same in Australia. What does Peter say?'

'Peter has his own business. He employs several supervisors.' There was a pause during which Hetty smiled into her port.

'And Paddy too, home as well,' went on Mrs Lagan hastily. 'You must be worn to a thread cooking and attending them all. I really don't know how you stick it.'

Hetty was about to make a spirited reply when the two old ladies stopped dead. Only their keen ears could have detected the slight rustle of skirts on the stairs beyond the shop. It was Kate, going out for her afternoon walk. She walked quickly through the shop well aware of the presences in the snug. Mrs Lagan stood up and watched her cross the street.

'She's failing,' she said turning back and catching Hetty's eye. They nodded: Kate was the only thing on which they could agree. 'All this year I can notice it. Wouldn't you think it would bring her to her senses?'

Hetty sighed and pursed her heavy lips.

'It's a terrible trial for you,' went on Mrs Lagan. 'How many years is it since she was at Mass?' This too, was a ritual question. Mrs Lagan could never ask it often enough.

'Forty-seven. The priests have given her up for years.'

'It's a disgrace, that's what it is. When the whole world is steeped in paganism and in need of every prayer it can get, we have the like of that right on our doorsteps.'

'Shocking,' muttered Hetty.

'Mad, mad, mad,' exclaimed Mrs Lagan. 'It's the only explanation. And to think that she was going to be a nun once. I remember well the week she went off to the convent. And to leave it after four years!'

'Shocking.'

'I don't know how you can stay in the house with her.' She paused and fingered her glass. 'But of course you have to, haven't you? It was a terrible will for your husband to make, leaving her a room and her keep for life. It was no kindness to you. I feel for you, you poor thing.'

'Paddy was a charitable man,' said Hetty, torn between self-pity and the reflection on her husband's consideration for her.

'Ah, to buggery with charity!' exclaimed Mrs Lagan, hammering on the table, almost upsetting her glass of port. 'What kind of charity is that, will you tell me?' The old lady had picked up her surprising swear word years ago without the faintest idea of its meaning. Her sudden use of it at heated moments regularly stunned the numerous pious societies of which she was a member.

'Of course,' she went on, 'you might have a chance of starving her out if it wasn't for Lily sending her home money.'

'She has the Old Age Pension.'

Mrs Lagan sniffed.

'It wouldn't keep her in cigarettes, not the way she smokes. Isn't it awful that she wouldn't be afraid of damnation? And having you, you poor thing, slaving and cooking for her, especially with business the way it is.'

'Mrs Fagan is very bad to-day,' said Hetty abruptly. 'Vomiting all the time and her sight is gone now.'

Mrs Lagan craned her neck and looked up at the window behind which all night the light burned.

'When I heard they were giving her morphia I knew it was the end,' she said.

'I knew it long before that. Eighteen months ago.'

But Mrs Lagan was not listening to her. She was peering out at the street with her eyes screwed up.

'Who's that man?' she asked. 'That man passing in front of Foleys. The dark-haired man with the big mouth.'

Hetty lumbered to her feet.

'I don't know. Why?'

'I've seen him in town for the past few days. He's staying at the Imperial Hotel. I met him at the bottom of the street near the river as I was coming in.'

Hetty sat down and took up her glass of port. She remembered the stranger quite well; but the idea of sharing the slightest confidence with her old friend would have appalled her.

'Oh, some stranger, a traveller perhaps.' She finished her port quickly. 'I'm persecuted with them night, noon and morning.'

'Are you?' Mrs Lagan's voice was suspicious. 'I don't see many of them any time I'm here. I thought they had given up visiting this part of town.'

She turned back and saw that Hetty's glass was empty. This

signified that the visit was over. To stay any longer would be to lose face. She drained her own glass quickly and stood up. Then she opened her bag and took out a small gilt reliquary in which a tiny fragment of bone was embedded in red velvet. This was a relic of St Hyacinth of Rheims, to whom Mrs Lagan had a particular devotion. She kissed the relic devoutly with closed eyes before offering it to Hetty, who pressed it to her lips with somewhat less enthusiasm. But it was part of the ritual. That and the fact that Mrs Lagan bought a half-pound of tea at the grocery counter, took back the Sunday paper which she lent to Hetty on Mondays, contributed sixpence to the box which her friend kept for the Foreign Missions, and received a sixpence from Hetty for the weekly raffle for the new Parochial House.

Then the two old women bade each other a cold farewell.

Not a Patch on their Fathers

This extract from Christy Brown's Down All the Days *of 1970 explores the musings of a man 'who has drink taken' making his way home from the pub.*

Father moving homeward through narrow corkscrew streets at dusky pub close of evening, the comfortable weight of the half-dozen under his arm, the naggin snug in his hip pocket. The slate as long as a countryman's mile, a blessing and a curse. They knew his strength, knew he always paid up sooner or later. He kept the place alive, pouring out his lungs for them week after week. He had a good voice in his young days. Still could sing the old songs well, remembering Dan Lowery and his famous variety theatre. That wasn't today or yesterday. 'Speak to me Thora, Speak from your heaven to me.' Not much of a pub, to be sure, dwarfed as it was in the sombre shades of the ancient cathedral. That was where your man Swift ended his days. The mad Dean. Founded a hospital for the alcoholics of Dublin town, the decent man. Not much of a pub. Bare wooden floors, thin partition walls of a diarrhoea green, dog-kennel of a front snug. Still, sound people they were, once they knew your strength. Long-jewelled Dublin matrons dipping into deep apron pockets. Wasn't that terrible about poor Liza's babby born all stiff and blue on the steps of the Municipal Gallery and she not a stone's throw away from the Rotunda? Just shows you, the hand of God. Upstairs the wide living-room, reminder of a gentler age, the tall black piano in the corner. Vista of the perfect little park directly opposite through the beaded window-panes. Timeless clock forever tolling, telling you how many more murderous hours you have left. A right bloody mess these streets are and a mile between every lamp-post, a breeding-ground for corruption. The corporation again, never did anything right. No need to go to London. Bombs on the far North Strand not enough. Look at them doing it bare-faced in open tenement hallways, like animals, and the kids looking on. In his day a man couldn't as much as kiss a girl in the street without somebody running for the priest. That whiskey had an extra horsepower to it tonight. A break away from the home wars. The trees in Mount Jerome dripping with rain in the young dark winter. But they would probably bury him out in the wilds of Glasnevin in an unmarked bloody grave. Let the daisies grow undisturbed. Not that it mattered where they buried him. He could never understand why some people were so particular about where they were to be buried. No matter where they dug your hole, the worms got you in the end. Maggots had to live too. Poor under-the-earth creatures, as lost as the over-the-earth ones. And soon we were all lost.

The woman of the house. Alanna was her name. A lively, dark young thing and the quaint Northern brogue of her. Great big brown eyes. There was something about a North of the Border brogue that caught the heart unawares. Pert and pretty in her crisp apron, pulling pints better than any trade-union barman. The dark head of her bent over the taps, cascading the brown creamy stuff into tilted tumblers. The young and old men at the bar not missing the soft valley of her fine high-flung breasts as she bent, waiting for them to pop out over her low-cut dress, all white and dimpled and the nipples fat and dark, maybe. Not long ago he would have fancied her a bit himself, but that kind of thing appeared to be dead entirely inside him now. Good strong legs on her and the wide hips made for carrying babies. Four already and she looking as innocent as a nun professed yesterday. Your man knew his onions even if they were Spanish. A shrewd customer he was, slippery as an eel, foolish as a fox. The round shining bald head of him, the eyes pale blue never straying far from his gay long-legged wife or the monotonous click of the cash register. Not far from the wrong side of the border. You could always tell by their canny little ways, famous for the minding of mice at the cross-roads. A homely little pub, just the same, home away from home for many a man weary like himself from domestic warfare. The cream of the citizenry. Sure a man needed some sort of escape, a trap-door to open suddenly under him, letting him get away for a while. The drink made him forget the terrible headaches that seldom left him now. Made him almost blind, that pain, made him appear half-jarred and him with maybe not a drop taken all the week. It pressed down upon him like an iron fist, squeezing, gripping, never letting go. He felt like tying a bandage around his neck and pulling it tight, tight, until the pain stopped. Never a day sick in his life, not even from the drink. Up with the lark he was, every morning, no matter what hour he put his head down on the pillow. That was something they couldn't take away from him, though the volume of his sins filled the sky itself. The young men of today couldn't say as much. Women was all they ever thought about. The opening between the thighs. Gateway to paradise. Moy-ah. Christ, if they only knew the trouble it led a man into, they would let the poor bloody cock sleep. The hot young stallions of today, keeling over dead-drunk after a couple of pints, the leer and grin fading from their kissers. Not a patch on their fathers, the men of his generation. Pale amber whiskey or the black velvet pints came all as one to him and the men like him. Hard they lived and hard they died. Hard grafters, hard drinkers, hard men in bed with their women, begetting themselves bloody kids who sprang up all of a sudden into men and women and went their own way, disremembering all the backbreaking years of toil and sweat a man went through to put food in their bellies and clothes on their backs and the fear of God in their mean little hearts. Pain they were coming into the world, pain going out of it. And the way they just happened, the bloody thoughtless, casual way they just kept on multiplying until a man found himself in next to no time knee-deep in them. Rabbits. Jesus Christ. Let a man think about that for a while, and he would soon tie a bloody knot in it.

A Late Drink

This extract from Emma Cooke's Eve's Apple *of 1985 is a rather touching description of two ladies 'enjoying' a late drink.*

We decide that in the circumstances the best thing to do is to go somewhere else for a late drink.

And when we do, Edna harps back to Noelle and her father. I tell her that Noelle's father is very ill.

'What's his surname?'

'Martin.' Invention becomes easier with practice—there is a money box on the pub counter topped by the figure of a black saint. An inscription beneath reads, 'Blessed Martin pray for us.'

Edna always reads the death notices in the paper. She'll look out for Martin. I let her flow on—asking questions while I nibble one of the shrivelled olives that look as if they have lain on a saucer for a long time.

'They're left over from the happy hour,' the barmaid says as she takes our order.

Edna is beginning to forget her own troubles. She wants to know more about Mr Martin's case. Medicine is her thing, her bedroom bookshelf is stacked with medical encyclopaedias, plus books about how to enjoy sex and books about how to keep young.

'Mr Martin is eighty-four...I don't know whether they operated or not,' I reply to her questions.

I count the olive stones when I have finished. Lady, baby...gypsy...queen...Soon there are empty glasses to match. I've got an uneasy feeling that I'm going to give birth to an agonised old man instead of a squalling brat. Right now Mr Martin and the child in my womb are concepts of equal value. Well, as far as paternity is concerned they are both figments of the imagination. As far as Edna and Mr Martin, and Robin and 'his' child are concerned anyway. It's a wise child that knows its own father. Not that it matters. It is the basic ingredient that counts. I'm feeling philosophical after all these drinks. 'Here's to life,' I say, lifting my whiskey glass. It occurs to me that I didn't have very much to eat all day. A slice of ham, a few cubes of cheese, an apple—and these olives which seem to have lodged in my chest.

Edna isn't at all interested in my optimistic approach. She stops speaking, stares at me curiously, and then—as tears well up again—says, 'You're priceless, Angel.'

Thanks, but I'm not. And Edna is getting me down. I wish it was Geraldine with her coppery hair who was sitting here beside me, both of us having a good laugh.

We should have gone into the hotel piano-bar after all, cocked a snook at the pianist. This isn't our kind of place. Everything seems dusty. I'm beginning to feel slightly olive green.

Edna launches into a discussion of the dresses in the show—I should have paid more attention. What was that about favourite in the harem? Talking to Edna—or May, or any of the coffee ladies—is like going for a paddle instead of having a good swim. 'You're priceless, Angel,' accompanied by a smirky grin. And they all have those buttoned up titters. Although I must say Edna took me by surprise out in the hotel with her 'fuck off'. That was overheard. That will be held against her. I saw her getting the sort of glances you get when you speak too loudly in the library. Not that Edna goes to the library, all she reads are those medical encyclopaedias and the sex and beauty manuals.

The place has started to empty. The barmaid returns to collect the dirty glasses and the saucer of olive stones.

'They were lovely,' I say, although they have made me full of wind.

Edna is speaking in derogatory terms about her piano-playing rival. It is time we went home. I wish I could catch the barmaid's eye and ask her the way to the bathroom. Or perhaps I should go straight to the hospital...I'd give anything to put my head down on a pillow. I'm the very opposite of the princess and the pea in the fairy-story, I'd even sleep like a top on a mattress stuffed with olive stones...

I don't know what brought us into this place. If you look at it aesthetically, it is a perfect example of lack of taste...

'Can I get you ladies a taxi?' The owner of the bar must think that we're celebrities. He comes over and asks us this without even introducing himself.

We're both quite happy lolling here on his banquette. And I'm feeling much better. That last drink did the trick. The olives are now floating around as comfortably as my baby. 'Jewish girls are the most beautiful girls in the world.' I felt a quiver of pain when Leo said that. Not so much for myself, but because it seemed so unfair to Anne and Jenny...

'You're forcing me to call the guards,' the owner says.

He should be glad of our custom...

The latter part of the evening has flown. Robin will probably be at home when I get there.

'Come on, fatty,' the owner says.

He's a young man with no respect for ladies. That's why he tosses my mink coat at me so roughly. I'm aware that Edna is leaving by the side exit. The front door seems to be locked. There's no one in the place except myself and this barrack-square monster. I'm afraid he's a bit cuckoo. I find it difficult to get into my coat.

'Sorry, missus, you're pickled,' he says. 'You should be at home saying the rosary.'

I don't know why we came into his filthy little bar. As soon as I have my mink safely on I tell him what I think of it. I don't care whether he agrees with me or not.

I say nothing as I climb into the car beside Edna. We don't speak until we get back to my house.

'Next time round we'll go somewhere more pleasant,' Edna says as I get out of the car.

Weddings

Shane Fadh's Wedding

These two extracts from one of the stories in William Carleton's
Traits and Stories of the Irish Peasantry *of 1843 describe the
preparations for, and the aftermath of, an Irish wedding in the mid-
nineteenth century.*

While he was speaking, he stamped his foot two or three times on the
flure, and the housekeeper came in.—'Katty,' says he, 'bring us in a
bottle of whiskey; at all events, I can't let you away,' says he, 'without
tasting something, and drinking luck to the young folks.'

'In troth,' says Jemmy Finigan, 'and begging your Reverence's
pardon, the sorra cow you'll sell this bout, any how, on account of me
or my childhre, bekase I'll lay down on the nail what'll clear you wid
the bishop; and in the name of goodness, as the day *is* fixed and all, let
the crathurs not be disappointed.'

'Jemmy,' says my uncle, 'if you go to that, you'll pay but your
share, for I insist upon laying down one half, at laste.'

At any rate they came down with the cash, and after drinking a
bottle between them, went home in choice spirits entirely at their good
luck in so aisily getting us off. When they had left the house a bit, the
priest sent after them—'Jemmy,' says he to Finigan, 'I forgot a
circumstance, and that is, to tell you that I will go and marry them at
your own house, and bring Father James, my curate, with me.' 'Oh,
wurrah, no,' said both, 'don't mention *that*, your Reverence, except
you wish to break their hearts, out and out! why, that would be a
thousand times worse nor making them stand to do penance: doesn't
your Reverence know, that if they hadn't the pleasure of *running for
the bottle*, the whole wedding wouldn't be worth three half-pence?'
'Indeed, I forgot that, Jemmy.' 'But sure,' says my uncle, 'your
Reverence and Father James must be at it, whether or not—for that we

intended from the first.' 'Tell them, I'll run for the bottle too,' says the priest, laughing, 'and will make some of them look sharp, never fear.'

'Well, by my song, so far all was right; and may be it's we that wern't glad—maning Mary and myself—that there was nothing more in the way to put off the wedding-day. So, as the bridegroom's share of the expense always is to provide the whiskey, I'm sure, for the honour and glory of taking the blooming young crathur from the great lot of bachelors that were all breaking their hearts about her, I couldn't do less nor finish the thing dacently; knowing, besides, the high doings that the Finigans would have of it—for they were always looked upon as a family that never had their heart in a trifle, when it would come to the push. So, you see, I and my brother Mickey, my cousin Tom, and Dom'nick Nulty, went up into the mountains to Tim Cassidy's still-house, where we spent a glorious day, and bought fifteen gallons of stuff, that one drop of it would bring the tear, if possible, to a young widdy's eye that had berrid a bad husband. Indeed, this was at my father's bidding, who wasn't a bit behindhand with any of them in cutting a dash. 'Shane,' says he to me, 'you know the Finigans of ould, that they won't be contint with what would do another, and that, except they go beyant the thing, entirely, they won't be satisfied. They'll have the whole countryside at the wedding, and we must let them see that we have a spirit and a faction of our own,' says he, 'that we needn't be ashamed of. They've got all kinds of ateables in cart-loads, and as we're to get the drinkables, we must see and give as good as they'll bring. I myself, and your mother, will go round and invite all we can think of, and let you and Mickey go up the hills to Tim Cassidy, and get fifteen gallons of whiskey, for I don't think less will do us.'

This we accordingly complied with, as I said, and surely better stuff never went down the *red lane* than the same whiskey; for the people knew nothing about watering it then, at all at all. The next thing I did was to get a fine shop cloth coat, a pair of top-boots, and buck-skin breeches fit for a squire; along with a new Caroline hat that would throw off the wet like a duck. Mat Kavanagh, the schoolmaster from Findramore bridge, lent me his watch for the occasion, after my spending near two days learning from him to know what o'clock it was. At last, somehow, I masthered that point so well, that in a quarter of an hour at least, I could give a dacent guess at the time upon it.

Well, at last the day came. The wedding morning, or the bride's part of it[1], as they say, was beautiful. It was then the month of July. The evening before, my father and my brother went over to Jemmy Finigan's, to make the regulations for the wedding. We, that is my party, were to be at the bride's house about ten o'clock, and we were then to proceed, all on horseback, to the priest's, to be married. We were then, after drinking something at Tom Hance's public-house, to come back as far as the Dumb-hill, where we were to start and run for the bottle. That morning we were all up at the skriek of day. From six o'clock, my own faction, friends and neighbours, began to come, all mounted; and about eight o'clock there was a whole regiment of them, some on horses, some on mules, others on raheries[2] and asses; and, by my word, I believe little Dick Snudaghan, the tailor's apprentice, that had a hand in making my wedding-clothes, was mounted upon a buck goat, with a bridle of salvages tied to his horns. Anything at all, to keep their feet from the ground; for nobody would be allowed to go with the wedding that hadn't some animal between them and the earth.

To make a long story short, so large a bridegroom's party was never seen in that country before, save and except Tim Lannigan's, that I mentioned just now. It would make you split your face laughing to see the figure they cut; some of them had saddles and bridles—others had saddles and halthers: some had back-suggawns of straw, with hay stirrups to them, but good bridles; others had sacks filled up as like saddles as they could make them, girthed with hay-ropes five or six times tied round the horse's body. When one or two of the horses wouldn't carry double, except the hind rider sat strideways, the women had to be put foremost, and the men behind them. Some had dacent pillions enough, but most of them had none at all, and the women were obliged to sit where the pillion ought to be—and a hard card they had to play to keep their seats even when the horses walked asy, so what must it be when they came to a gallop! but that same was nothing at all to a trot.

From the time they began to come that morning, you may be sartain that the glass was no cripple, any how—although, for fear of accidents, we took care not to go too deep. At eight o'clock we sat down to a rousing breakfast, for we thought it best to eat a trifle at home, lest they might think that what we were to get at the bride's breakfast might be thought any novelty. As for my part, I was in such a state, that I couldn't let a morsel cross my throat, nor did I know what end of me was uppermost. After breakfast they all got their cattle, and I my hat and whip, and was ready to mount, when my uncle whispered to me that I must kneel down and ax my father and mother's blessing, and forgiveness for all my disobedience and offinces towards them—and also to requist the blessing of my brothers and sisters. Well, in a short time I was down; and my goodness! such a hullabaloo of crying as was there in a minute's time! 'Oh, Shane Fadh—Shane Fadh, a cushla machree!' says my poor mother in Irish, 'you're going to break up the ring about your father's hearth and mine—going to lave us, avourneen, for ever, and we to hear your light foot and sweet voice, morning, noon, and night, no more! Oh!' says she, 'it's you that was the good son all out; and the good brother, too: kind and cheerful was your voice, and full of love and affection was your heart! Shane, avourneen deelish, if ever I was harsh to you, forgive your poor mother, that will never see you more on her flure as one of her own family.'

Even my father, that wasn't much given to crying, couldn't speak, but went over to a corner and cried till the neighbours stopped him. As for my brothers and sisters, they were all in an uproar; and I myself, cried like a Trojan, merely bekase I *see* them at it. My father and mother both kissed me, and gave me their blessing; and my brothers and sisters did the same, while you'd think all their hearts would break. 'Come, come,' says my uncle, 'I'll have none of this: what a hubbub you make, and your son going to be well married—going to be joined to a girl that your betters would be proud to get into connexion with. You should have more sense, Rose Campbell—you ought to thank God that he had the luck to come acrass such a colleen for a wife; that it's not going to his grave, instead of into the arms of a purty girl—and what's better, a good girl. So quit your blubbering, Rose; and you Jack,' says he to my father, 'that ought to have more sense, stop this instant. Clear off, every one of you, out of this, and let the young boy go to his horse.—Clear out, I say, or by the powers I'll—look at them three stags of huzzies; by the hand of my body they're blubbering bekase it's not their own story this blessed day.

Move—bounce!—and you, Rose Oge, if you're not behind Dudley Fulton in less than no time, by the hole of my coat, I'll marry a wife myself, and then where will the twenty guineas be that I'm to lave you?

God rest his soul, and yet there was a tear in his eye all the while—even in spite of his joking!

* * *

When we got to the Priest's house, there was a hearty welcome for us all. The bride and I, with our next kindred and friends, went into the parlour: along with these, there was a set of young fellows, who had been bachelors of the bride's, that got in with an intention of getting the first kiss[3] and, in coorse, of bateing myself out of it. I got a whisper of this; so by my song, I was determined to cut them all out in that, as well as I did in getting herself; but you know, I couldn't be angry, even if they had got the foreway of me in it, bekase it's an ould custom.—While the priest was going over the business, I kept my eye about me, and, sure enough, there were seven or eight fellows all waiting to snap at her. When the ceremony drew near a close, I got up on one leg, so that I could bounce to my feet like lightning, and when it was finished, I got her in my arm, before you could say Jack Robinson, and swinging her behind the priest, gave her the husband's first kiss. The next minute there was a rush after her; but, as I had got the first, it was but fair that they should come in according as they could, I thought, bekase, you know it was all in the coorse of practice; but, hould, there were two words to be said to that, for what does Father Dollard do, but shoves them off, and a fine stout shoulder he had—shoves them off, like childre, and getting his arms about Mary, gives her half a dozen smacks at least—oh, consuming to the one less—that mine was only a *cracker*[4] to. The rest, then, all kissed her, one after another, according as they could come in to get one. We then went straight to his Reverence's barn, which had been cleared out for us the day before, by his own directions, where we danced for an hour or two, his Reverence and his Curate along with us.

When this was over we mounted again, the fiddler taking his ould situation behind my uncle. You know it is usual, after getting the knot tied, to go to a public-house or *shebeen*, to get some refreshment after the journey; so, accordingly, we went to little lame Larry Spooney's— grandfather to him that was transported the other day for staling Bob Beaty's sheep; he was called Spooney himself, for his sheep-stealing, ever since Paddy Keenan made the song upon him, ending with 'his house never wants a good ram-horn spoon'; so that let people say what they will, these things run in the blood—well, we went to his shebeen house, but the tithe of us couldn't get into it; so we sot on the green before the door, and, by my song, we *took*[5] dacently with *him*, any how; and, only for my uncle, it's odds but we would have been all fuddled.

It was now that I began to notish a kind of coolness between my party and the bride's, and for some time I didn't know what to make of it—I wasn't long so, however; for my uncle, who still had his eye about him, comes over to me, and says, 'Shane, I doubt there will be bad work amongst these people, particularly betwixt the Dorans and the Flanagans—the truth is, that the old business of the law-shoot will break out, and except they're kept from drink, take my word for it, there will be blood spilled. The running for the bottle will be a good excuse,' says he, 'so I think we had better move home before they go too far in the drink.'

Well, any way, there was truth in this; so, accordingly, the reckoning was *ped*, and, as this was the thrate of the weddiners to the bride and bridegroom, every one of the men clubbed his share, but neither I nor the girls, anything. Ha—ha—ha! Am I alive at all? I never—ha—ha— ha—!—I never laughed so much in one day as I did in that, and I can't help laughing at it yet. Well, well! when we all got on the top of our horses, and sich other iligant cattle as we had—the crowning of a king was nothing to it. We were now purty well I thank you, as to liquor; and, as the knot was tied, and all safe, there was no end to our good spirits; so, when we took the road, the men were in high blood, particularly Billy Cormick, the tailor, who had a pair of long cavalary spurs upon him, that he was scarcely able to walk in—and he not more nor four feet high. The women, too, were in blood, having faces upon them, with the hate of the day and the liquor, as full as trumpeters'.

There was now a great jealousy among them that were bint for winning the bottle; and when one horseman would cross another, striving to have the whip hand of him when they'd set off, why you see, his horse would get a cut of the whip itself for his pains. My uncle and I, however, did all we could to pacify them; and their own bad horsemanship, and the screeching of the women, prevented any strokes at that time. Some of them were ripping up ould sores against one another as they went along; others, particularly the youngsters, with their sweethearts behind them, coorting away for the life of them, and some might be heard miles off, singing and laughing; and you may be sure the fiddler behind my uncle wasn't idle, no more nor another. In this way we dashed on gloriously, till we came in sight of the Dumb-hill, where we were to start for the bottle. And now you might see the men fixing themselves on their saddles, sacks and suggans; and the women tying kerchiefs and shawls about their caps and bonnets, to keep them from flying off, and then gripping their fore-riders hard and fast by the bosoms. When we got to the Dumb-hill, there were five or six fellows that didn't come with us to the priest's, but met us with cudgels in their hands, to prevent any of them from starting before the others, and to show fair play.

Well, when they were all in a lump,—horses, mules, raheries, and asses—some, as I said, with saddles, some with none; and all just as I tould you before;—the word was given and off they scoured, myself along with the rest; and divil be off me, if ever I saw such another sight but itself before or since. Off they skelped through thick and thin, in a cloud of dust like a mist about us: but it was a mercy that the life wasn't trampled out of some of us; for before we had gone fifty perches, the one third of them were sprawling a-top of one another on the road. As for the women, they went down right and left—sometimes bringing the horsemen with them; and many of the boys getting black eyes and bloody noses on the stones. Some of them, being half blind with the motion and the whiskey, turned off the wrong way, and gallopped on, thinking they had completely distanced the crowd; and it wasn't until they cooled a bit that they found out their mistake.

But the best sport of all was, when they came to the *Lazy Corner*, just at Jack Gallagher's *flush*[6], where the water came out a good way acrass the road; being in such a flight, they either forgot or didn't know how to turn the angle properly, and plash went above thirty of them, coming down right on the top of one another, souse in the pool.

By this time there was about a dozen of the best horsemen a good distance before the rest, cutting one another up for the bottle: among these were the Dorans and Flanagans; but they, you see, wisely enough, dropped their women at the beginning, and only rode single. I myself didn't mind the bottle, but kept close to Mary, for fraid that among sich a divil's pack of half-mad fellows, anything might happen her. At any rate, I was next the first batch: but where do you think the tailor was all this time? Why away off like lightning, miles before them—flying like a swallow: and how he kept his sate so long has puzzled me from that day to this; but, any how, truth's best—there he was topping the hill ever so far before them. After all, the unlucky crathur nearly missed the bottle; for when he turned to the bride's house, instead of pulling up as he ought to do—why, to show his horsemanship to the crowd that was out looking at them, he should begin to cut up the horse right and left, until he made him take the garden ditch in full flight, landing him among the cabbages. About four yards or five from the spot where the horse lodged himself was a well, and a purty deep one, by my word; but not a sowl present could tell what become of the tailor, until Owen Smith chanced to look into the well, and saw his long spurs just above the water; so he was pulled up in a purty pickle, not worth the washing; but what did he care? although he had a small body, the sorra one of him but had a sowl big enough for Golias or Sampson the Great.

As soon as he got his eyes clear, right or wrong, he insisted on getting the bottle: but he was late, poor fellow, for before he got out of the garden, two of them comes up—Paddy Doran and Peter Flanagan, cutting one another to pieces, and not the length of your nail between them. Well, well, that was a terrible day, sure enough. In the twinkling of an eye they were both off the horses, the blood streaming from their bare heads, struggling to take the bottle from my father, who didn't know which of them to give it to. He knew if he'd hand it to one, the other would take offince, and then he was in a great puzzle, striving to raison with them; but long Paddy Doran caught it while he was spaking to Flanagan, and the next instant Flanagan measured him with a heavy loaded whip, and left him stretched upon the stones.— And now the work began: for by this time the friends of both parties came up and joined them. Such knocking down, such roaring among the men, and screeching and clapping of hands and wiping of heads among the women, when a brother, or a son, or a husband would get his gruel! Indeed, out of a fair, I never saw any thing to come up to it. But during all this work, the busiest man among the whole set was the tailor, and what was worst of all for the poor crathur, he should single himself out against both parties, bekase you see he thought they were cutting him out of his right to the bottle.

They had now broken up the garden gate for weapons, all except one of the posts, and fought into the garden; when nothing should sarve Billy, but to take up the large heavy post, as if he could destroy the whole faction on each side. Accordingly he came up to big Matthew Flanagan, and was rising it just as if he'd fell him, when Matt, catching him by the nape of the neck, and the waistband of the breeches, went over very quietly, and dropped him a second time, heels up, into the well; where he might have been yet, only for my mother-in-law, who dragged him out with a great deal to do: for the well was too narrow to give him room to turn.

As for myself and all my friends, as it happened to be my own wedding, and at our own place, we couldn't take part with either of them; but we endeavoured all in our power to *red* them, and a tough task we had of it, until we saw a pair of whips going hard and fast among them, belonging to Father Corrigan and Father James, his curate. Well, it's wonderful how soon a priest can clear up a quarrel! In five minutes there wasn't a hand up—instead of that they were ready to run into mice-holes.

---

1   The morning, or early part of the day, on which an Irish couple are married, up until noon, is called the bride's part, which, if the fortunes of the pair are to be happy, is expected to be fair—rain or storm being considered indicative of future calamity.

2   A small, shaggy pony, so called from being found in great numbers on the Island of that name.

3   There is always a struggle for this at an Irish wedding, where every man is at liberty— even the priest himself—to anticipate the bridegroom if he can.

4   Cracker is the small, hard cord which is tied to a rustic whip, in order to make it crack. When a man is considered to be inferior to another in anything, the people say, 'he wouldn't make a cracker to his whip.'

5   Drank.

6   Flush is a pool of water that spreads nearly across a road. It is usually fed by a small mountain stream, and in consequence of rising and falling rapidly, it is called 'Flush'.

A Wedding

This extract from Glenanaar *(1918) by the Very Rev. P. A. Canon*
Sheehan gives a hint of the lavish provisions made for country
weddings.

'How is the night?' said the old man, anxious to change the
conversation. 'Do you think ye'll have everythin' in for the weddin',
Bess?' he said to his wife. 'How many gallons of sperrits did ye
ordher?'

'We ordhered thirty,' said the *vanithee*. 'But sure we can get more.'

'An' the rounds of beef?'

'They're all right!'

'An' the hams?'

'They're all right,' said the wife, impatiently. 'Can't you lave thim
things to ourselves; and not be interfaring with our work? Did you
settle wid the priest yourself?'

'I did, God bless him!' said her husband, 'an' 'twas aisy settlin'.
He'll have twinty weddings that day, and more cummin' in; but he'll
be here at three o'clock to the minit, he says; so that we can have nine
hours rale *Keol*, before Ash Winsday breaks upon us!'

And they had,—real, downright, tumultuous, Irish fun and frolic.
From North, South, East, West, the friends came, as heedless of the
snow that lay caked upon the ground, and the drifts that were piled in
the ditches and furrows, as a Canadian with his horses and sleds.
There was the house far off—the objective of all the country that
night—with its small square windows blazing merrily under the fierce
fires upon the hearth; and afar off, clearly outlined against the white
pall on the ground, were the dark figures of the guests who had
gathered to do honour to a family on which no shadow of a shade of
dishonour had ever rested. And they feasted, and drank, and danced;
and, late at night, the old people gathered around the fire in the
kitchen, and told stories, whilst the youngsters, to the sound of
bagpipes and fiddle, danced themselves into a fever in the decorated
and festooned barn. And Donal led out Nodlag, and insisted on

dancing an Irish reel with her, much to the disgust of his intended bride, who watched the child with no friendly eyes, and half determined that the moment she became mistress of Glenanaar farm, out that waif and foundling should go, and seek a home elsewhere. But no shadow crossed the mind of the child, now thoroughly recovered from her illness; but she danced, and danced with Donal, and Owen, and Jerry; and some old people shook their heads, and said 'twas the fairies brought her and left her, and that somehow there was something uncanny about it all.

At last, twelve o'clock rang out from the kitchen timepiece—an old grandfather's clock, an heirloom in the family for generations—and Lent broke solemnly on the festivities of the night. Some of the youngsters, a little heated, insisted on keeping up the fun till morning, and quoted as an excuse for additional revels the old distich:

> Long life and success to the Council of Trint,
> That put fast upon mate, but not upon drink!

Whiskey

Whiskey

This extract from an article that appeared in the Ulster Journal of
Archaeology *for 1858 explores the early use and production of
whiskey in Ireland. It shows no sign of the identity of the author,
being ascribed merely to an enigmatic 'J. B.'*

Usquebaugh is a compound term, from the first part of which our
modern word, *whiskey*, has its origin. The public, not always correct in
its judgments, has given Ireland the credit, or the discredit, as the case
may be, of being at present, and of having been from time immemorial,
a country famous for the production and consumption of this subtle
fluid. The social questions connected with the latter point, as bearing
upon the condition of the people, occupy the pages of publications of a
special class, and exercise the lungs of orators of note; and it only
proves how wide is the range of Archaeology, that a subject so
apparently unpromising—a subject however, certainly, not of so dry a
nature as persons who know no better declare Archaeology in all its
details and ramifications to be—should in any form find admission into
this *Journal*. Yet it is quite in our way. We would wish to know
something of the drinks of the ancient Irish, but more particularly of
that for which we have obtained so great a reputation. We would wish
to inquire into the antiquity of the art of distillation in Ireland, how it
affected the progress of the people, its extent in early times, whether
Ireland was really more noted for skill in the practice of it than other
nations, its domestic influence, its connection with the labour and
productions of the country, from what materials this famous old Irish
usquebaugh was extracted, and many other questions: the only matter
for regret is that to none of them can any very precise or satisfactory
solution be obtained. There seems in truth to be a sort of blank in our
ancient records and among our early historians, in connection with this

subject; either because it was considered to be one altogether of minor importance, or was so well known that no one thought it necessary to make a note about it. On the other hand, some persons seem to deny that any proof could possibly exist in the places alluded to, for the very sufficient reason that the knowledge of distillation among the native Irish population is in reality not ancient, but comparatively modern; and maintain that the general opinion regarding its antiquity among us is a mere popular error. Thus, a learned inquirer, whose researches into documentary evidence have been most extensive, has expressed to us an opinion, as resulting from that source of proof, that the 'mere Irish' (will our readers pardon the not very respectful appellation), previously to the seventeenth century, were entirely destitute both of the chemical and mechanical knowledge necessary to practise distillation, which was, in reality, carried on by foreign traders only, in early times, in the large towns. In this opinion, however, we cannot concur. The distillatory art is, from every evidence, of the highest antiquity, and, when carried on in a rude way, requires a very small amount of either mechanical or chemical knowledge. Its introduction into Europe, in anything approaching to a perfect form, is generally attributed to those pioneers of civilisation, the Arabs, when possessed of dominion in Spain; and that it might reach this island from that quarter, if not before known in it, is a circumstance every way probable. Besides, we must give our remote ancestors credit for some ingenuity; nor do we mean to disparage them when we say that they probably exhibited an inclination, which clings to a few of their descendants to the present day, rather for those occupations in which there is some novelty, which require aptitude, and, at the same time, irregularity of labour, than for more severe and sustained employment,—a disposition to which the art of distillation would present attractions not easily resisted. Besides, has not the Irish native been a joyous temperament in every age, and is it not at least likely that any bewitching stimulant which would enable him to leave dull earth still farther behind, if the slightest knowledge of it had once gained admittance into the land, would take root and spread? All this, no doubt, in the absence of direct evidence, is mere conjecture; but such notices as we have been enabled to glean, both of early and more recent date, we shall proceed to lay before our readers, being well aware, at the same time, how few and imperfect they are,

241

and how entirely the subject of the antiquity and extent of the art of distillation in Ireland still remains an open question.

Carolan's Receipt

The 'receipt' is to be construed as a 'prescription'—a prescription, issued by Dr John Stafford, for whiskey in abundance.

Má's tinn nó slán do thárlaidheas féin,
Ghluaiseas tráth 's dob fhearrde mé
   Ar cuairt chum Seóin chum sócamhail d'fhagháil,
An Stafardach breágh sásta, nach gnáth gan chéill.
Is i dtaca an mheódhain oidhche do bhíodh sinn ag ól,
   Agus ar maidin arís an córdial:
'Sé mheas sé ó mhéinn mhaith gurb é súd an gléas
   Le Cearbhallán caoch do bheódhughadh!

Chorus:
   Seal ar misge, seal ar buile,
   Réabadh téad 's ag dul ar mire,
An faisiun sin do chleachtamar ní sgarfam leis go deó!
   Deirim arís é,
   Is innsim don dtír é,
Má's maith libh do bheith saoighlach bídhidh choidhche ag ól!

* * *

If sick or strong I chanced to be,
I went along—'twas well for me!—
   To Doctor John to find relief,
Brave Stafford, skilful leech is he!
About the witching hour we would start our carouse,
   By morn our zest for whiskey was the sharper:
Sensible man! for such was his plan
   To put life in the poor blind harper!

Chorus:

 Sometimes tipsy, sometimes raking,

 Wild in frenzy, harpstrings breaking,

The custom that we followed, we will never let it die!

 I tell you once again, Sirs,

 I always will maintain, Sirs,

For a long and merry life of it, be drinking for aye!

Conversation with Whiskey

This song speaks for itself—both on the part of the bard and on the part of the whiskey.

An bard ag ceasacht

Go sloigtear thú, a Uisce!

 Is tú d'fhág scallta mo scóig;

Is minic d'fhág tú folamh mé,

 Gan airgead nó ór;

Ba tú an millteoir, a mhic na mallacht,

 'Gus shlad tú mé as mo stór;

Nuair bhíos mo phóca craite,

 Téann tú 'dtaisce i dtigh an óil.

An fuisce ag freagairt

Ná habair dadamh as bealach liom

 Is mé crann-seasta gach spóirt;

Níl áit ar bith dhá mheasúla

 Nach mé an chré deamhain (?) ar an mbord;

Is mé ceann siamsa ar fud na mbailteacha

 Ag an mbeag is ag an mór;

'S go dtabharfainn croí fairsing, carthanach,

 Don té bhíos cruaidh go leor.

An bard

Is buachaill mé chomh measúil
  Agus bhí insan tír seo fós
Nó go bhfuil mé anois fáil tarcaisne
  Mar gheall ar bheith dod' ól;
Is minic a chaill mé an tAifreann leat,
  Mo dhinnéar is mo 'breac fasta';
'Sé mo léan gan mise scartha leat
  Is tú lom (?) an mhí-á-mhóir.

An fuisce

Tá ceannfortacha Shacsana
  Go mór mo dhiaidh sa tóir,
Níl áit ar bith dá dtaitním leo
  Nach ndéanaim leo an chóir;
Tá an sean 's an t-óg i ngean orm
  Is an rí tá faoi an gcoróin
Is na sagairt féin dob ait leo
  Mo bholadh fháil faoina sróin.

An bard

Níl bealach ar bith dá ngabhaim
  Nach tú an chrostacht bhíos romham
Go salaíonn tú mo bhalcaisí
  'S go ngearrann tú mo shrón;
Buaileann tú faoin talamh mé
  Agus fágann tú gan spreacadh mé
Ach leigheasann tú ar maidin mé
  Agus maithim duit níos mó.

An fuisce

Níl locht ar bith ar m'fhaisiún
  Is ní scarfaidh sé liom go deo,
Is mé údar méadaithe an charthanais
  Is cóir smachtaithe ar gach gleo,
Saol fada ag an té bhíos blaiseadh liom
  Is go maire sé i bhfad beo,
Is dá bhrí sin líontar thart
  Is ná bíodh tart ort níos mó.

* * *

The bard complains

That you may be swallowed, oh, whiskey!
  It's you've left my windpipe scalded;
It's often you left me empty
  Without silver or gold.
'Twas you were the destroyer, you son of curses;
  Sure you robbed me out of my store.
When my pocket does be shaken out
  You go and are put by in the house of drink.

The whiskey answers

Speak nothing out of the way with me,
  I am the sustaining-prop of every sport.
There is no place, however respectable,
  That I am not the credit on the table.
I am the head of merriment throughout the towns
  With the great and with the small,
And sure I would give a generous, friendly heart
  To him who does be very hard.

The bard

I am a person as respectable
  As ever was in this country yet
Until I am now getting reproach
  On account of being drinking you.
It's often I lost the Mass with you,
  My dinner and my breakfast, too,
My grief I am not parted from you,
  You are the bareness (?) of the great ill-luck.

The whiskey

The captains of Sesanie (England)
  Are greatly after me in pursuit.
There is no place in which I please them
  That I do not do the right with them.
The old and the young have affection for me,
  And the king who is under the crown,
And the priests themselves they would like
  To have the smell of me under their nose.

The bard

There is no place to which I go
    That you are not the wickedness that is before me.
Sure you dirty my clothes,
    And sure you cut my nose.
You knock me on to the ground,
    And you leave me without energy;
But you cure me in the morning,
    And I forgive you for the future.

The whiskey

There is no fault (to be found) with my fashion (ways),
    And it will never part from me.
I am the author of the increase of friendliness,
    And the means that checks every quarrel.
Long life to him who does be tasting me,
    And that he may live long;
And therefore let (the glasses) be filled round,
    And let you have no more thirst.

Acknowledgments

For permission to reproduce copyright material, grateful acknowledgment is made to the following:

A. M. Heath & Co., and © the Estate of the late Flann O'Brien for extracts from *At Swim-Two-Birds* and *Irish Writing* 1946.

Anvil Books *The Clanking of Chains* by Brinsley MacNamara.

A. P. Watt Ltd for 'Burns in Ulster' from *An Ulster Childhood* and 'St Patrick and Lager Beer' from *A Bowl of Broth* by Lynn C. Doyle.

Bloomsbury Publishing for 'For the Record' from *The West* by Eddie Stack.

The Blackstaff Press for 'Rathard' from *December Bride* by Sam Hanna Bell.

Constable & Co. Ltd for an extract from *Bird Alone* by Seán Ó Faoláin.

Curtis Brown for an extract from *Off the Record* by Joe Joyce.

Dedalus Press for an extract 'Mixed Drinks' from *Collected Poems* by Denis Devlin.

Emperor Publishing for an extract from *The Red Telephone* entitled 'Peggy O'Grady's Disappearance' by Kathleen O'Connor.

Mattie Fox Management for *Delirium Tremens* by Christy Moore.

Faber and Faber Ltd for an extract 'Sloe Gin' from *Station Island* by Seamus Heaney.

The Author and The Gallery Press for 'Bulmer' from *Poaching Rights* by Bernard O'Donoghue.

The trustees of the Estate of Patrick Kavanagh, c/o Peter Fallon, Literary Agent, Loughcrew, Oldcastle, Co. Meath, for 'Drunkard' from *Complete Poems* by Patrick Kavanagh.

The Harvill Press for extracts from *A Goat's Song*, by Dermot Healy, first published in Great Britain 1994 by Harvill. © Dermot Healy.

John Johnson (Authors' Agent) Ltd, and the Estate of John Broderick for 'The Fugitives' (published 1962) by John Broderick.

Index of Authors